PC
QuickSteps

GUY HART-DAVIS

McGraw-Hill/Osborne

New York Chicago San Francisco
Lisbon London Madrid Mexico City
Milan New Delhi San Juan
Seoul Singapore Sydney Toronto

McGraw-Hill/Osborne
2100 Powell Street, 10th Floor
Emeryville, California 94608
U.S.A.

To arrange bulk purchase discounts for sales promotions, premiums, or fund-raisers, please contact **McGraw-Hill**/Osborne at the above address. For information on translations or book distributors outside the U.S.A., please see the International Contact Information page immediately following the index of this book.

PC QUICKSTEPS

1234567890 WCK WCK 01987654

ISBN 0-07-225872-1

PUBLISHER / Brandon A. Nordin

VICE PRESIDENT & ASSOCIATE PUBLISHER / Scott Rogers

ACQUISITIONS EDITOR / Roger Stewart

ACQUISITIONS COORDINATOR / Agatha Kim

TECHNICAL EDITOR / Marty Matthews

COPY EDITOR / Lisa McCoy

PROOFREADERS / Chara Curtis, Kellen Diamanti

INDEXER / Kellen Diamanti

LAYOUT ARTIST / Bailey Cunningham, Keith Eyer

ILLUSTRATORS / Kathleen Edwards, Pattie Lee, Bruce Hopkins

SERIES DESIGN / Bailey Cunningham

COVER DESIGN / Pattie Lee

Contents at a Glance

1
2
3
4
5
6
7
8
9
10

To Rhonda and Teddy

Contents

Chapter 7   Securing Your PC 133

Chapter 8   Setting Up a Home Network 157

Chapter 9   Getting Maximum Use out of Your Laptop PC........... 185   9

Chapter 10   Troubleshooting Hardware 207   10

Acknowledgments

My thanks go to the following people, who put in a huge amount of work on this book:

Marty Matthews, series editor and technical editor, developed the book, checked it for technical accuracy, and made countless suggestions for improvements throughout.

Lisa McCoy, editor, edited the book skilfully and with good humor.

Bailey Cunningham, series designer and layout artist, laid out the book with great skill, turning the raw manuscript and graphics into a highly polished book.

Chara Curtis, proof reader, caught widely varied inconsistencies and suggested improvements to the text.

Kellen Diamanti, indexer, not only created the index for the book but also proofread much of it, making many helpful suggestions.

Roger Stewart, Editorial Director at Osborne, helped create the series and pulled strings in the background throughout the process.

Introduction

QuickSteps books are recipe books for computer users. They answer the question "how do I…" by providing a quick set of steps to accomplish the most common tasks with a particular operating system or application.

The sets of steps are the central focus of the book. QuickSteps sidebars show how to quickly perform many small functions or tasks that support the primary functions. QuickFacts sidebars supply information that you need to know about a subject. Notes, Tips, and Cautions augment the steps, presented in a separate column to not interrupt the flow of the steps. The introductions are minimal rather than narrative, and numerous illustrations and figures, many with callouts, support the steps.

QuickSteps books are organized by function and the tasks needed to perform that function. Each function is a chapter. Each task, or "How To," contains the steps needed for accomplishing the function along with the relevant Notes, Tips, Cautions, and screenshots. You can easily find the tasks you need through:

- The Table of Contents, which lists the functional areas (chapters) and tasks in the order they are presented

- A How To list of tasks on the opening page of each chapter

- The index, which provides an alphabetical list of the terms that are used to describe the functions and tasks

- Color-coded tabs for each chapter or functional area with an index to the tabs in the Contents at a Glance (just before the Table of Contents)

Conventions Used in this Book

PC QuickSteps uses several conventions designed to make the book easier for you to follow. Among these are

- A ⊛ in the table of contents and in the How To list in each chapter references a QuickSteps sidebar in a chapter, and a ⬤ references a QuickFacts sidebar.

- The ⊞ represents the **WINDOWS KEY** on the keyboard. (Some keyboards don't have this key.)

- **Bold type** is used for words or objects on the screen that you are to do something with—for example, click the **Start** menu, and then click **My Computer**.

- *Italic type* is used for a word or phrase that is being defined or otherwise deserves special emphasis.

- <u>Underlined type</u> is used for text that you are to type from the keyboard.

- SMALL CAPITAL LETTERS are used for keys on the keyboard such as **ENTER** and **SHIFT**.

- When you are expected to enter a command, you are told to press the key(s). If you are to enter text or numbers, you are told to type them.

How to...

Chapter 1

Getting to Know Your PC

PCs are indispensable to many people, are a source of daily frustration to other people, and are both to many people. This book shows you how to get a PC that suits you and make it do the things you need it to do.

This chapter explains what a PC is and what it does, advises you on how to choose a PC and operating system that meet your needs, shows you how to set up the PC, and tells you how to start the PC and shut it down.

Understand What a PC Is and Does

PC is the abbreviation for *personal computer*, a computer designed to be used by an individual rather than by a department or a company as a whole. PCs come in various sizes, formats, and capabilities (Figure 1-1 shows examples), but the term is generally used to mean an IBM-compatible personal computer that can run the Windows operating system. By contrast, the computers made by Apple Computer, Inc. are generally referred to as Macintoshes, or Macs, after the name Apple uses on its predominant line of computers.

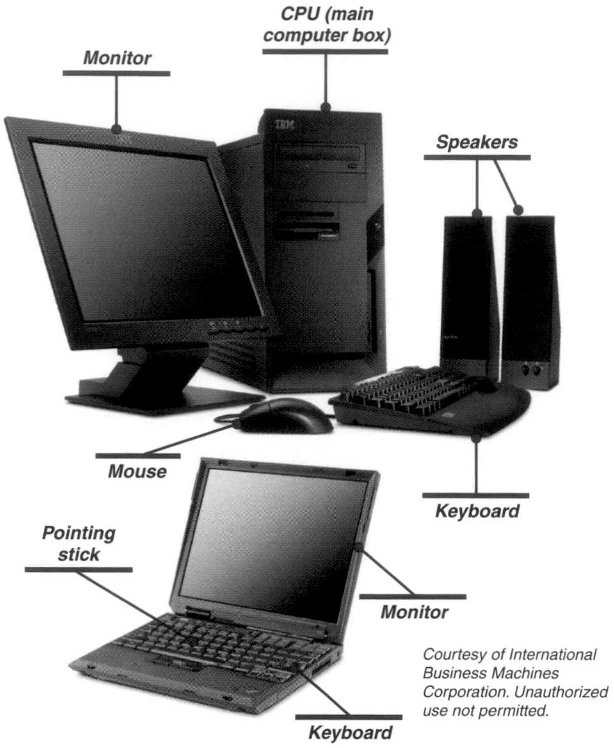

A PC's purpose is to manipulate information in the ways you tell it to, but most people find it easier to think of a PC's purpose in terms of what they can do with it. For example, with the right software, you can:

- Create a memo, letter, or spreadsheet
- Edit a digital picture
- Send and receive e-mail
- Record and play back digital audio files
- Edit video files and burn CDs and DVDs

You can use a PC by itself if you choose, but you can gain access to vast amounts of information (or data) by connecting your PC to the Internet, the worldwide computer network. At home or at work, you can connect your PC to other PCs using a local area network (LAN) so that it can share data, services, and hardware resources with other computers.

Understand Desktops and Laptops

The two main types of PCs are desktops and laptops (see Figure 1-1).

- A *desktop* is a PC designed for use in a static location, typically a desk. Most desktop PCs consist of several separate parts: the CPU, or main computer box; the monitor; and a separate mouse and keyboard. (Some desktop PCs are built as all-in-one units—a monitor with all the CPU components built into it.)
- A *laptop* is an all-in-one PC with an integrated keyboard, pointing device (such as a touchpad or a pointing stick), and monitor (in a lid that folds shut for protection).

Identify the Components of a PC

Most PCs consist of a number of standard components, although these components may look different or be physically different in different PCs. This section explains those components. You don't need to understand the components of a PC in order to use it, but having a basic understanding of the components usually helps when you're planning to buy a PC and when you need to troubleshoot problems (see Chapter 10).

Courtesy of International Business Machines Corporation. Unauthorized use not permitted.

Figure 1-1: A desktop PC typically has a separate monitor, keyboard, and mouse. A laptop PC has all its components integrated into a single unit for portability.

Labels: Monitor, CPU (main computer box), Speakers, Mouse, Keyboard, Pointing stick, Monitor, Keyboard

QUICKFACTS

UNDERSTANDING HARDWARE AND SOFTWARE

Hardware is the general term used for the physical components of your PC: the monitor; keyboard; mouse; CPU, or main computer box, and its innards; and other components (speakers, printers, and other items) you attach to your PC.

Software is the general term for the operating system you install on your PC and the programs you run on it. Software needs hardware to run on, and hardware needs software to make it useful. When you buy a new PC, the manufacturer usually installs the operating system and some basic programs for you. After that, you can install additional software to meet your needs.

NOTE

Almost all desktop PCs use 32-bit processors. 32-bit means that there are 32 data wires running in parallel, allowing the PC to manipulate 32 bits of data at once. Standard versions of Microsoft Windows XP and Windows programs are designed for 32-bit processors and won't run on processors with fewer bits or more bits. Intel and AMD (two processor manufacturers) have now introduced 64-bit processors—processors with 64 wires running in parallel. 64-bit processors can handle far more data at once than 32-bit processors, but they require 64-bit operating systems and programs for best performance. Some 64-bit processors, such as AMD's Athlon 64, can also run 32-bit programs at nearly full speed.

CPU

The *central processing unit*, or *CPU*, technically refers to the PC's processor, but also tends to be used as a general term for the main box of a desktop computer—the box that contains the PC's motherboard (or main circuit board), processor, memory, hard drive, and other components. You can see a CPU box in Figure 1-1.

The CPU contains most of the components of a desktop PC: the processor and memory; the hard drive, optical drive, and floppy drive; the graphics, sound, and network cards; the power supply; and all the cables that connect these components together. On a typical desktop PC, the CPU is usually a rectangular box designed to lie flat on your desk or stand on end, either on your desk or on the floor; a mini-tower or larger tower box designed to stand upright on the floor; or a miniature unit designed to fit unobtrusively where there's space. In a laptop PC, the CPU lies under the keyboard and the other surface of the lower part of the PC, together with most of the components of the PC apart from the monitor.

PROCESSOR

The processor, or microprocessor, is the main chip in the PC. This is where the bulk of the computing gets done. Your PC runs Windows courtesy of the microprocessor performing millions of calculations per second. XP requires a 233-MHz Pentium or faster processor, which is ancient and slow by today's standards. (At this writing, processors are nearing 4 GHz, more than 15 times faster than 233 MHz.)

Courtesy of Intel Corporation.

The processor is one of the main influences on the speed at which the PC performs tasks. You can upgrade the processor on most desktop PCs and some laptop PCs, but as such an upgrade typically requires a certain level of technical expertise, it's important to choose a suitable processor when you buy a PC.

TIP

Processor speeds, or *clock speeds*, are confusing because different processor designs perform different numbers of actions per processor cycle. For example, Intel's Pentium M processors, which are designed for laptop PCs, perform more actions per cycle than Intel's Pentium IV processors. So a 2-GHz Pentium M processor can outperform a 3.2-GHz Pentium IV processor. Similarly, a processor that has a 64-bit data path can perform many more actions, even at a lower clock speed, than a processor with a 32-bit data path.

CAUTION

If your hard drive fails, you can lose some or all of your data, so it's important to back up (store outside your computer) any data that you can't easily recover from other sources. See Chapter 7 for instructions on backing up your data.

CAUTION

Note the words "temporarily store" in the definition of RAM. When power is removed from a PC, the contents of RAM are lost. When you shut down Windows using its normal procedure, it will prompt you to save any unsaved data in your documents that are in RAM before the power is shut off and the contents of RAM are lost. To prevent a power failure from causing a loss of RAM contents and other problems, you may need an uninterruptible power supply (UPS), which is described in Chapter 7.

Historically, processor speeds have been measured in megahertz (MHz; millions of cycles per second) and gigahertz (GHz; billions of cycles per second). Faster processor speeds, or *clock speeds*, have typically meant faster performance. All other things being equal, a 3-GHz processor performs ten times more calculations per second than a 300-MHz processor and will deliver better performance.

HARD DRIVE

The *hard drive*, or *hard disk*, is the device on which your PC stores most of your information. For example, in almost all PCs, the operating system is stored on the hard drive. If you create a file in a word processor (such as Microsoft Word), you usually store it on your hard drive so that you can access it again later. (In a business situation, you will often store your files on a network drive rather than on your PC's hard drive.)

Courtesy of Seagate Technology LLC

Most PCs have one hard drive, but many desktop PCs and a few laptop PCs have space for additional internal hard drives. You can also attach external hard drives to a desktop or a laptop PC using a Universal Serial Bus (USB) or FireWire connection.

MEMORY (RAM)

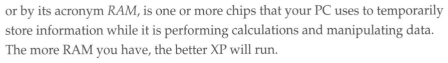

Random access memory, generally referred to simply as "memory" or by its acronym *RAM*, is one or more chips that your PC uses to temporarily store information while it is performing calculations and manipulating data. The more RAM you have, the better XP will run.

XP requires a theoretical minimum of 128 MB of RAM to run at all; 256 MB is a practical minimum for light use of XP; 512 MB is a good idea for standard use; and 1 GB (1024 MB) or more is recommended for heavy use. If XP runs too slowly on your PC, adding memory is likely to be the most effective way of boosting performance.

CHOOSING A PROCESSOR

Most desktop PCs use processors made by either Intel Corporation or AMD (Advanced Micro Devices, Inc.).

All current desktop processors are more than fast enough to run XP.

- **Pentium IV** is Intel's flagship line of desktop processors.
- **Celeron** is Intel's less expensive and less capable version of Pentium IV.
- **Athlon** is AMD's answer to Pentium IV. Athlon 64 is a 64-bit version of Athlon that can also run 32-bit applications.
- **Duron** is AMD's less expensive and less capable version of Athlon.

Laptop PCs can use either desktop processors or processors designed for laptop PCs. All current laptop processors are fast enough to run XP. Choose a processor to meet your needs and your budget.

- **Desktop-replacement laptops** use processors designed for desktop PCs or modified processors, such as Mobile Pentium, Mobile Athlon, and Mobile Athlon 64. These processors provide impressive speed at an affordable price, but may overheat if used for a long period of time. You may need to use a fan under the PC to prevent it from becoming too hot. Battery life in these laptops varies from short to disappointing.
- **Economy laptops** use lower-specification desktop processors (such as Intel Celeron processors or AMD Mobile Duron processors). These processors provide adequate speed at a low price, produce a fair amount of heat (but less than high-specification desktop processors), and deliver modest battery life.
- **High-performance laptops** use processors designed for laptop PCs. These processors deliver impressive performance along with modest heat and long battery life but are expensive. Intel's Centrino and Centrino 2 processor packages include built-in wireless network capabilities.

How much RAM you can put in your PC depends on the number of memory sockets on the motherboard and the capacity of the memory chips you buy. Many PC motherboards have two memory sockets, each of which can hold a 128-MB, 256-MB, 512-MB, or 1-GB memory chip, giving up to 2 GB total. Motherboards for heavier-duty computers, such as video workstations and servers, have more memory slots and so can take more RAM. 256-MB chips and 512-MB chips offer the best value for the money at this writing; 1-GB chips are proportionally much more expensive.

FLOPPY DRIVE

The floppy drive is used for reading data from a 3½-inch floppy disk. Push the floppy disk into the drive so that the mechanism accepts it. To eject the disk after you've finished using it, press the eject button on the drive.

Floppy disks have a maximum capacity of 1.44 MB—a miniscule amount of data by modern standards—and would have been eliminated from general use several years ago except that millions of people have valuable documents stored on floppy disks and still need to be able to access them at will. For this reason, many PCs still include floppy drives. (By contrast, Apple eliminated floppy drives from Macs more than five years ago.)

OPTICAL DRIVES

An optical drive is a drive that works with an optical disc, such as a CD or DVD, as opposed to a magnetic disk. Most PCs have a CD drive, a DVD drive (which can also read CDs), or both.

Some optical drives can only read data, while others can write to CDs, DVDs, or both. CD and DVD writers are commonly called *burners*. Some burners can write data to a CD or DVD only once, but others (rewriters) can write data, erase it, and write again. To rewrite data, you must use rewritable optical discs.

QUICK**FACTS**

CHOOSING A HARD DRIVE

Hard drives for PCs come with different rotation speeds (measured in revolutions per minute, or rpm), buffers (measured in megabytes, or MB), seek times (measured in milliseconds, or ms), and capacities (measured in gigabytes, or GB).

- A faster rotational speed usually gives better performance, but the drive may be noisier and will definitely be more expensive. For a desktop computer, get a 7200-rpm drive, or even a 10,000-rpm drive, rather than a 5400-rpm drive. Most laptop drives run at 5400 rpm or 4200 rpm.

- A bigger buffer improves performance.

- A lower seek time (smaller number)—the average time to access data—is better than a higher seek time.

- Buy as large a drive as you can reasonably afford. Multimedia data (such as audio and video files) take up a huge amount of space. For a desktop PC, you may be able to get more space for your buck, and maybe increased reliability, by buying two or more medium-sized drives than one colossal drive.

- Commodity hard drives—those not intended for professional use—typically last for several years, but you should always back up your data (see Chapter 7) in case of trouble. Any hard drive can fail at any time without warning.

TIP

If you're still storing your files on floppy disks, give serious consideration to a better medium. Recordable CDs can hold 700 MB and cost around a quarter each when bought in bulk. Perhaps the most convenient medium for carrying data with you is the USB memory key, which comes in capacities from 32 MB up to 1 GB or more and is quite inexpensive.

Speeds for burning DVDs and CDs are denoted with 1X, 2X, and so on. 1X for CDs is 150 KBps, while 1X for DVDs is 1.32 MBps—about nine times as fast. This is why a DVD drive can burn DVDs at "only" 6X, but burn CDs at 40X or more—the measurements are of different speeds. At 1X, burning a DVD takes about 55 minutes; at 4X, 15 minutes; and at 10X, 6 minutes. Burning a CD at any speed over 32X takes only a couple of minutes, so higher-speed CD burning is largely irrelevant—you're not likely to notice the difference.

SOUND CARD

The *sound card* enables your PC to output sound to your speakers, headphones, or receiver and receive sound input from a line input or microphone. With a sound card, you can use your PC to play music and record audio. On many desktop PCs and almost all laptop PCs, the sound card, is built into the motherboard, so you don't get a choice of sound card. If, however, that sound card doesn't produce the quality of sound you need, you can replace it with an internal sound card (on a desktop PC) or an external USB sound card (on either a desktop or a laptop PC) and bypass the built-in sound card.

Standard sound cards typically produce good enough sound for listening to music or general audio. If you plan to use your PC to produce music, canvass your musician friends for recommendations for a high-quality sound card.

GRAPHICS CARD

In order to display images on your monitor, your PC needs a *graphics card* (also called a *graphics adapter*, *video card*, or *video adapter*). A laptop's graphics card routes its output directly to the laptop's monitor, but you usually can also connect a supplementary external monitor via the graphics connector. A desktop PC's graphics card has a connector to which you connect the monitor's cable.

The graphics card is built into many desktop PCs and almost all laptop PCs. On a desktop PC, you can install another graphics card and use it either in tandem with or instead of the built-in graphics card. On a laptop PC, you can seldom change the built-in graphics card.

CHOOSING MEMORY

Memory comes in a bewildering variety of types that use different memory technologies, different speeds, and different physical formats. These days, most memory comes in pieces called dual inline memory modules, or DIMMs. Older PCs used single inline memory modules, or SIMMs. When choosing memory, you must get not only exactly the right type of chip for your PC, but also the right kind of chip to complement your existing chips. If you don't know what type that is, visit an automatic memory configuration utility, such as that found at Crucial Technology (www.crucial.com) or Kingston Technology (www.kingston.com), talk to an expert at an online store, or have your local computer store examine your computer and tell you what you need.

Courtesy of International Business
Machines Corporation. Unauthorized
use not permitted.

Figure 1-2: CRT monitors (left) can display multiple resolutions and are less expensive than LCD monitors (right), which can display only one resolution sharply.

NETWORK CARD

The *network card* enables your PC to connect to a network so that it can share data with or receive data from other PCs. There are two main types of network cards: wired network cards that you use with a cabled network, and wireless network cards that create a network across the airwaves. Chapter 8 discusses how to choose hardware for wired and wireless networks, including network cards.

MONITOR

The *monitor*, sometimes called the *display* or *screen*, is the device on which your PC displays information for you to see. The amount of data that the monitor displays at any one time is called the *resolution* and is described by the number of *pixels* (picture elements, or dots) used across the screen and the number used down the screen. For example, the resolution 1024 × 768 means the monitor uses 1024 pixels across the screen and 768 pixels down it. Monitors come in two main types:

- *CRT* (cathode-ray tube) monitors are the larger type of monitor, like a standard TV set. CRTs can display a variety of resolutions, but none of them is perfectly sharp. Also, CRTs take a lot of desk or table space and are heavy.

- *LCD* (liquid crystal display) monitors are the slimmer type of monitor. Most LCDs can display only one resolution sharply; this is called the LCD's *native resolution* and matches the pixel count of the screen. Other resolutions require the LCD to split display information across pixels, which makes for a blocky and hard-to-read effect.

Figure 1-2 shows a CRT monitor and an LCD monitor.

Both CRTs and LCDs come in a variety of sizes and resolutions. Laptop PCs have a built-in LCD display that you can't change without major surgery. In almost all desktop PCs, the monitor connects via a cable to the CPU, so you can use various types of monitors.

When choosing a monitor, choose one that provides the resolution you need and a picture you like. LCDs deliver a sharper, more stable picture and take up less room on the desktop, while CRTs are less expensive and can usually display a wide variety of resolutions.

QUICKFACTS

CHOOSING AN OPTICAL DRIVE

DVDs are great for backing up large amounts of data. The DVD–R standard is 4.7 GB, while a CD holds only 700 MB (0.7 GB). When choosing an optical drive, first consider a DVD rewriter—a DVD drive that can write and erase and rewrite to both DVDs and CDs, and can play both DVDs and CDs.

There are six different recordable DVD standards: DVD+RW, DVD-RW, DVD+R, DVD-RAM, DVD-R for General, and DVD-R for Authoring. The two you should focus on are DVD+RW and DVD-RW.

- DVD+RW can write data to a disc multiple times and looks like it is becoming the dominant format for rewritable DVDs.
- DVD-RW can write data to a disc multiple times, but is now less widely used than DVD+RW. DVD-RW and DVD+RW use different technologies to perform the same tasks, much as VHS and Betamax VCRs used different technologies.

For greatest flexibility, get a combination drive that can handle DVD+RW and DVD-RW. These drives are sometimes described as DVD±RW drives. If such combination drives are too expensive, your best bet is a DVD+RW drive that can read multiple DVD formats. If you don't need to burn DVDs, get a combination DVD/CD-RW drive—a drive that can play DVDs and write and rewrite CDs.

MOUSE

Mouse is the generic term for the pointing device used with the PC. The mouse is a small, usually curved box that you put your hand on and move on a flat surface, such as a mouse pad, to indicate where you want the mouse pointer on the screen to move.

Mice (some people say *mouses*) are widely used, but you can also use many other pointing devices, such as the following:

- A *trackball* is a stationary device in which you roll a ball with your fingers or hand to move the mouse pointer. Because you don't move the whole trackball, you can use it in a smaller space than a mouse, which is good for small or crowded desks, and some people find them easier for moving the pointer precisely.

- A *touchpad* is a touch-sensitive surface on which you drag your finger to move the mouse pointer. Touchpads are widely used on laptop PCs, but you can get them for desktop PCs as well. (You can also get desktop keyboards that have a touchpad built in.)

- A *pointing stick* is a pressure-sensitive button embedded between the G, H, and B keys. You move the mouse pointer by pressing the pointing stick. (Pointing sticks are normally used on laptops, but you can get desktop keyboards with a pointing stick built in.)

A laptop PC typically has a touchpad, a pointing stick, or a trackball built in. Some laptop PCs have both a touchpad and a pointing stick built in.

QUICK**FACTS**

CHOOSING A GRAPHICS CARD

In the old days of computing (say, before the turn of the millennium), graphics memory was so expensive that you had to consider carefully how much you were prepared to pay for a graphics card. These days, graphics memory is affordable, and even modest PCs come with adequate graphics cards for most normal use. You may need to upgrade your graphics card if:

- You play action games on your PC
- You want to watch or record TV on your PC
- You work extensively with video

NOTE

See *Windows XP and Office 2003 Keyboard Shortcuts*, published by McGraw-Hill/Osborne, for a detailed discussion of the different types of keyboards available and advice on how to choose a suitable keyboard.

KEYBOARD

Almost every PC comes with a keyboard, but most manufacturers supply inexpensive, basic keyboards with their desktop PCs unless you choose to pay for a more expensive model. A basic keyboard works fine for light PC usage, but if you use your PC extensively, consider buying a custom keyboard. A wide variety of models are available, from standard models featuring different keyboard "feels" to ergonomic one-handed and two-handed keyboards featuring exotic key layouts.

On a laptop PC, the keyboard is important. For desktop use, you can plug in any standard desktop keyboard instead of using the built-in keyboard. If you take your laptop PC traveling, however, lugging an extra keyboard is usually not practical, so you'll want to get the best laptop keyboard you can.

TECHNOLOGIES FOR CONNECTING PERIPHERALS

PCs use several types of technologies for connecting peripheral devices. Which technologies you need depends on which types of devices you plan to attach to your PC.

Serial Ports

Serial ports are used for connecting devices such as older mice, some organizers, external modems, and some uninterruptible power supplies (UPSs). All PCs except "legacy-free" PCs (PCs built without older technologies) have one or two serial ports built in.

Parallel Ports

Parallel ports are used primarily for connecting older printers. All PCs except "legacy-free" PCs have one parallel port built in.

CHOOSING A MONITOR, MOUSE, AND KEYBOARD

The monitor, mouse, and keyboard—and to a lesser extent the sound card and speakers—form the user interface of your PC. Having a good, easily visible monitor that displays enough data and a mouse and keyboard that you find comfortable and easy to use, make more difference to your computing experience than having a fast processor, colossal hard drive, or high-end graphics card.

When buying a PC, pay the most attention to these interface components because they'll make or break your enjoyment of using the PC. It's like buying a car: having comfortable seats and easy steering are almost always preferable to being able to go from 0 to 60 in four seconds in searing discomfort.

Most manufacturers supply moderate monitors and basic keyboards, mice, and speakers with their desktop PCs. Consider upgrading the monitor when you purchase your PC and replacing the other components with your preferred input and output devices.

In a laptop PC, the monitor, keyboard, and pointing device are built-in and are almost impossible to replace, so be sure to test each laptop PC you're thinking of buying. While you can supplement these devices with external devices easily at your desk (for example, you can plug in a different pointing device to replace the built-in pointing device), you'll probably need to use the built-in devices when working with the laptop PC on the move.

When evaluating PCs, consider also how much noise they make. Many PCs have fans and hard drives loud enough to be distracting. If peace is important to you, consider buying a specially quietened PC.

USB

Universal Serial Bus, or USB, is a technology for connecting external drives and peripheral devices to your PC. USB can be used for connecting anything from a keyboard, mouse, or other input device to connecting external hard drives or optical drives.

All recent and current PCs have USB, but it's important to get USB 2.0 rather than USB 1.1 (or USB 1.0) connections. This is because USB 2.0 is quite fast (up to 480 megabits per second, Mbps), while USB 1.1 is quite slow (12 Mbps). USB 1.1 works well for devices such as keyboards and mice, which need to transfer only a small amount of data, but for devices such as hard disks and optical discs (CDs and DVDs), which need to transfer large amounts of data quickly, USB 2.0 is essential.

FireWire

FireWire is a high-speed connection technology for connecting external drives and peripheral devices to your PC. Usually, only high-end PCs have FireWire built in. If you need to import video footage from a digital video camera, you'll need FireWire on your PC. You can add FireWire to a desktop PC by installing a PCI card, and to a laptop PC by inserting a PC Card.

SCSI

SCSI (Small Computer Systems Interface, pronounced "scuzzy") is a long-standing connection technology. SCSI has largely been superseded by USB 2.0 and FireWire, but if you have a SCSI device (for example, a professional-quality scanner or large, fast hard drive) that you need to connect to your PC, you'll need SCSI. You can add SCSI to a desktop PC by installing a PCI card, and to a laptop PC by inserting a PC Card.

Get Started with Your PC

To get started with your PC, you may need to choose and install an operating system, set up your PC, and then be able to turn it on and shut it down.

Choose Your Operating System

To make your hardware do anything useful, you need software. The first essential is an operating system, or OS. The OS is the software that makes the PC operate and enables programs to communicate with hardware components as necessary. Programs, or *applications*, are the software that run on the operating system and that you use to get most of your work done. For example, a word processor (such as Microsoft Word) is a program, as is an e-mail program (such as Microsoft Outlook Express).

The vast majority of PCs in the world run a version of Microsoft Windows, either Windows XP (the latest version of Windows) or an earlier version, such as Windows 2000, Windows Me, or Windows 98. If you're choosing an operating system for your PC, Windows XP is probably the best choice.

XP PROFESSIONAL OR XP HOME EDITION

There are two primary versions of Windows XP: XP Home Edition and XP Professional. XP Home Edition is intended for consumer use, and XP Professional for use by professionals in companies of any size, from home businesses up to international corporations. XP Professional has all the capabilities of XP Home Edition plus features designed for business and professional users. If XP Professional comes bundled with your PC instead of XP Home Edition, you can use it at home with no problems.

There are many differences between XP Professional and XP Home Edition, but most of them are fairly subtle. The main differences likely to affect your choice between the two are:

CHOOSING BETWEEN A DESKTOP AND A LAPTOP PC

(Continued)

the prices are much closer, and it's worth considering a laptop PC even if you plan to use it mostly in a single location.

With the same capabilities, laptop PCs still cost more than desktop PCs for a couple of reasons. First, most laptop PCs use custom parts, from the case to many of the innards. Second, almost all laptop PCs these days have LCD panels, which are more expensive than the cathode-ray tube (CRT) monitors supplied with many desktop PCs.

CAPABILITY

Until about 2001, laptop PCs lagged behind desktop PCs in speed and capability to such an extent that buying a laptop PC was a severe trade-off. Since then, laptop PCs have improved so substantially that they offer nearly the same performance as desktop PCs. Even better, PC hardware has improved faster than PC software's demands have grown, so even more modestly configured desktop PCs and laptop PCs can easily run all widely used programs.

ERGONOMICS

Because laptop PCs are less configurable than desktop PCs, they tend to be less ergonomic (comfortably and safely usable by a human). If you're choosing a laptop PC, make sure that its ergonomics are at least adequate for the uses you're planning.

When you're at your desk, you can attach an external keyboard, mouse, and monitor to make your laptop PC easier to use. When you're on the road, you're not likely to want to carry extras beyond an external mouse.

- XP Professional can connect effectively to larger networks using domains, while XP Home Edition cannot. (A *domain* provides a way to administer a larger network.)
- XP Professional lets you access your computer remotely using the Remote Desktop feature, share your fax modem with other computers, and run a small-scale web server.
- XP Professional can be managed centrally on a network.
- XP Professional includes enhanced security features, including encrypting and securing files.

LINUX

Windows is not the only OS you can run on a PC, but it's by far the most popular. The next most widely used OS for PCs is Linux. (Macs—computers made by Apple Corporation—run Mac OS, which doesn't run on PCs. Macs can't run Windows.) Figure 1-3 shows Xandros, a version of Linux aimed at consumers (rather than at businesses).

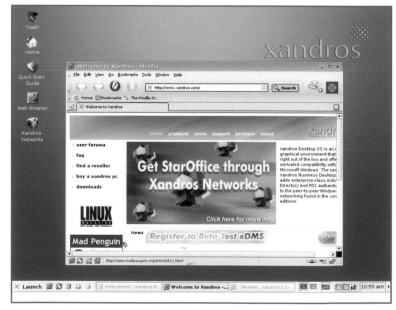

Figure 1-3: Linux is a low-cost alternative to Windows, but it's not as easy to use and can't run most Windows programs.

The main motivation for choosing Linux is to reduce the total cost of your PC. If you already have a PC with an Internet connection, you can download several versions of Linux for free. Others cost a few dollars on CD. Full-packaged versions of Linux typically cost between $30 and $100, but many include a wide selection of programs, so you're less likely to need to spend additional money on programs. Many packaged versions of Linux are licensed for installation on multiple PCs, so if you're equipping a home or an office with several PCs, this can save you a lot of money on software.

Generally speaking, Linux is not as easy to use as XP and is better suited to advanced computer users who need the additional features and security that Linux offers. Out of the box, most versions of Linux cannot run Windows programs, so if you're used to Windows programs, you'll need to learn new ones. Some versions of Linux, however, include Crossover Office, which enables you to run Microsoft Office and some other widely used Windows programs on Linux.

Another drawback to Linux is that, despite the coding efforts of the Linux community, Linux supports only some of the most widely used hardware devices.

Set Up Your PC

If you've just bought a PC, unpack it from its box, and follow the instructions that came with it to put it together.

- For a desktop PC, you'll need to plug several cables into the CPU—at a minimum, cables for the keyboard, mouse, monitor, and power supply. Figure 1-4 shows a typical desktop PC with the connections labeled.

- For a laptop PC, you'll need to connect the power supply, any cables required for your network or Internet connections, and external devices (for example, speakers). You may need to charge your laptop's battery fully before switching it on.

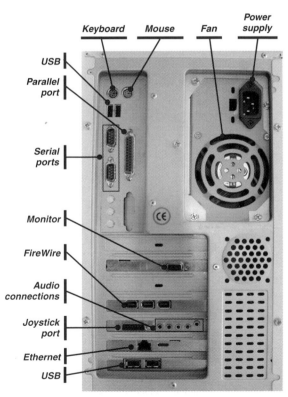

Keyboard Mouse Fan Power supply

USB
Parallel port
Serial ports
Monitor
FireWire
Audio connections
Joystick port
Ethernet
USB

Figure 1-4: Connections available on the back of the CPU of a recent desktop PC.

2

3

4

5

6

7

8

9

10

Start Your PC

To start a desktop PC, press the power button on the CPU and the power button on the monitor. To start a laptop PC, press the power button or slide the power switch, depending on the model. If you have a printer connected to your PC, switch that on, too.

Your PC displays startup information as it starts (as shown here). Most of this is just information about the hardware it discovers, but you'll also see a message telling you which key (usually **DELETE** or **F2**) to press to enter the Setup routine. Assuming your PC was set up correctly by whomever assembled it, you shouldn't need to use this Setup routine unless you change your PC's hardware configuration—or unless something goes wrong with your PC.

```
AMIBIOS(C)2001 American Megatrends, Inc.
BIOS Date: 07/17/02 11:21:09  Ver: 08.00.02

Press DEL to run Setup
Checking NVRAM..

228MB OK
Auto-Detecting Pri Master..IDE Hard Disk
Auto-Detecting Pri Slave...Not Detected
Auto-Detecting Sec Master..CDROM
Auto-Detecting Sec Slave...Not Detected
```

You'll then see the Windows XP logo as Windows loads, until the logon screen is displayed.

If your PC is set up for multiple people to use, XP displays the logon screen shown in Figure 1-5. Click your user name to log on. If XP prompts you to enter your password, type it and press **ENTER**. XP displays the desktop.

If your PC is set up for just you to use, XP logs you on automatically and displays the desktop.

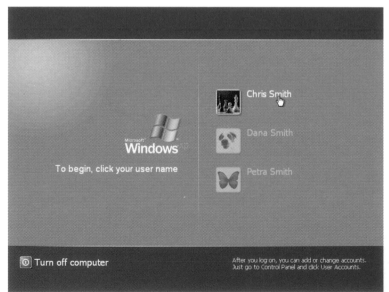

Figure 1-5: On the logon screen, click your user account and, if necessary, enter your password.

SUPPLYING POWER TO A DESKTOP PC

The main points for supplying power to a desktop PC are:

- Most desktop PCs have separate power cables for the CPU and the monitor. If you have a printer or other external component, it will probably have its own power supply.

- Most laser printers draw a lot of electricity and need to be plugged into a wall socket rather than into a power strip.

- Unless your house or office is well supplied with electrical sockets, use a power strip to provide enough sockets to power all your hardware at once. Any power strip with adequate capacity will do, but power strips designed for PC use tend to offer more space for each socket. This makes it easier to plug large power adapters into the sockets without blocking other sockets. Also, power strips designed for PCs often provide protection from power surges.

- To keep your PC running through brownouts (dips in the power supply, so-called because they make electric lights look brown) and outages, use an uninterruptible power supply (UPS). See Chapter 8 for more details.

NAVIGATE THE DESKTOP

The XP desktop (see Figure 1-6) normally displays a picture as wallpaper in the background, which can change its look completely.

The mouse is the primary means of navigating the Windows desktop.

- Move the mouse or other pointing device so that the mouse pointer is over the object you want to affect.

- Click an object to select it.

- Double-click an object (click twice in quick succession) to open it.

- Right-click an object to display a context menu, or shortcut menu, of commands related to the object.

Start menu; used to start programs and access control functions, folders, and other menus

Desktop; holds windows, dialog boxes, and icons

Mouse pointer; used to indicate and select objects

ScreenTip; shows information about the object to which the mouse pointer is pointing

Chris Smith

Internet
Internet Explorer

E-mail
Outlook Express

Windows Movie Maker

FreeCell

WordPad

MSN Explorer

Notepad

Tour Windows XP

All Programs

My Documents

My Pictures

My Music

My Computer

Control Panel

Set Program Access and Defaults

Help and Support

Search

Run...

Gives access to, and information about, the disk drives, cameras, scanners, and other hardware connected to your computer.

Log Off   Turn Off Computer

start   Untitled - Notepad   Calculator   12:59 PM

Recycle Bin

Figure 1-6: The XP desktop is highly customizable, but this is its basic look.

Recycle Bin; opens a folder of deleted items

Start button; opens the Start menu

Taskbar; shows a button for each running program or open document

Notification area; holds the system clock and icons for frequently used programs

QUICKFACTS

BUYING A NEW PC OR UPGRADING AN OLDER ONE

If you have an older PC (for example, a hand-me-down), you may need to decide between upgrading your clunker to run XP or buying a new PC. XP requires at least a 233-MHz processor, 128 MB of RAM, and 2 to 3 GB of hard drive space. If your older PC comfortably exceeds these requirements, you may choose to try running XP on it. With computer prices continuing to drop as faster and more capable hardware is released, however, it makes less and less sense to spend money upgrading an older PC unless you have a compelling reason to do so. (At this writing, July 2004, capable desktop computers with monitors and Windows XP Home Edition are available for under $600, while laptops are available for under $1,000.)

USE THE START MENU

Click the **Start** button to display the Start menu (see Figure 1-7), which provides access to most of the programs on your PC and to essential commands (such as turning off your PC). The six icons on the middle-left area of the Start menu are programs Windows thinks you might want to use (at first). After you've used Windows for a while, these icons change to reflect the programs you've used most frequently.

To access other programs on the Start menu, click **All Programs**, click the menu that contains the program you want, and then click the program.

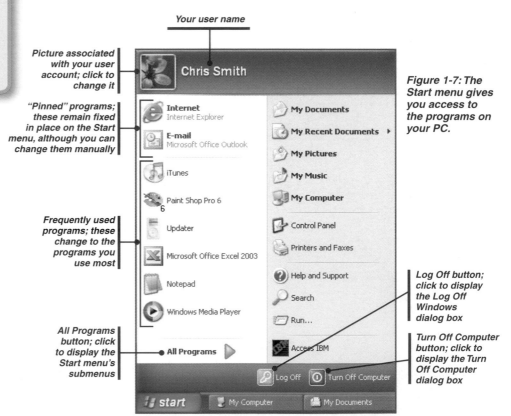

Figure 1-7: The Start menu gives you access to the programs on your PC.

Install XP

Three normal ways to install XP are:

- Have your computer manufacturer install XP for you.
- Upgrade a supported version of Windows to XP.
- Install XP on a computer that doesn't have a supported version of Windows installed, or install XP alongside your existing version of Windows.

GET XP PREINSTALLED

If you decide to get XP as the operating system for your new PC, your best bet is to have XP preinstalled by the PC manufacturer. Buying XP preinstalled is much less expensive than buying a boxed copy of XP, but be sure that the manufacturer includes an XP CD with the PC so that you can reinstall the OS if necessary. (Some manufacturers include the XP installation files on the PC's hard drive. From here, you can burn them to a CD manually, but it's easy to forget to do so. If your PC suffers severe problems and you haven't yet burned an XP CD, it may be too late to do so.)

UPGRADE TO XP

If your PC has an earlier version of Windows installed, you can upgrade to XP. Upgrading preserves your applications and settings, so you don't need to reinstall them or reconfigure Windows after the upgrade.

To begin the upgrade, start your current operating system. When the current version of Windows has completed loading, insert the XP CD. The Welcome To Microsoft Windows XP window should open automatically; if not, double-click **My Computer** to open the My Computer window, right-click the icon for your CD drive, and click **AutoPlay**. The Welcome To Microsoft Windows XP window opens. Click the **Install Windows XP** link. In the Welcome To Windows Setup dialog box (shown here), make sure that **Upgrade (Recommended)** is selected in the Installation Type drop-down list box. Click **Next**, accept the license agreement, enter the product key (the 25-character number on the Windows CD packaging), click **Next** again, and the upgrade process begins.

> **NOTE**
>
> Upgrade versions of XP are less expensive than full, new versions but work only if you have a supported version of Windows: Windows 98 or Windows Me for XP Home Edition; and Windows 98, Windows Me, Windows NT 4 Workstation, or Windows 2000 Professional for XP Professional.

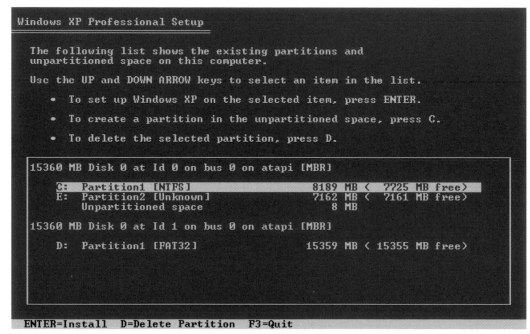

NOTE

You may need to configure your PC's BIOS (Basic Input/Output System) to start from the CD. To do so, press the key mentioned in the startup message (usually **DELETE** or **F2**) to access the BIOS. The names of boot options vary depending on the BIOS and version, but look for an option such as Boot Sequence or Boot Device Priority. Use the options to make your CD a boot device before the hard drive, and then exit the BIOS configuration screen, saving your changes. When your PC restarts, it will offer to boot from the CD.

INSTALL XP YOURSELF

Perhaps the least likely scenario is that you need to install a full version of XP on a PC that has no operating system installed. In this case, you need to pay for a full version of XP, either Home Edition or Professional.

Put the CD in the optical drive, and restart your PC. Press **SPACEBAR** to boot from the CD when your PC prompts you to do so.

The XP installation process is as straightforward as Microsoft was able to make it, and takes around an hour, depending on the speed of your PC. The first point at which you must really pay attention is choosing the physical disk and partition on which to install XP. Figure 1-8 shows an example of the partitioning screen, from which you can delete existing partitions and create new partitions.

- Deleting a disk partition deletes all the data it contains. Delete a partition only if it contains no data you want to keep.

- XP requires a partition of between 2 GB and 3 GB for a comfortable installation; a much bigger partition is better.

- XP's efficient NTFS file system makes it reasonable to partition each hard drive as a single partition.

```
Windows XP Professional Setup

    The following list shows the existing partitions and
    unpartitioned space on this computer.

    Use the UP and DOWN ARROW keys to select an item in the list.

      • To set up Windows XP on the selected item, press ENTER.
      • To create a partition in the unpartitioned space, press C.
      • To delete the selected partition, press D.

  15360 MB Disk 0 at Id 0 on bus 0 on atapi [MBR]
    C:    Partition1 [NTFS]               8189 MB (   7725 MB free)
    E:    Partition2 [Unknown]           7162 MB (   7161 MB free)
          Unpartitioned space               8 MB
  15360 MB Disk 0 at Id 1 on bus 0 on atapi [MBR]

    D:    Partition1 [FAT32]            15359 MB ( 15355 MB free)




  ENTER=Install  D=Delete Partition   F3=Quit
```

Figure 1-8: On the partitioning screen, use the ARROW keys to select the disk and partition on which to install XP.

CAUTION

Always close Windows by clicking the **Start** button and clicking **Turn Off Computer** rather than pressing the power button on your PC. Pressing the power button when Windows is running can lose information in RAM, corrupt vital files on the hard drive, and cause Windows problems when you try to restart it.

TIP

You can configure the actions Windows takes when you press the power button or sleep button on your PC. See Chapter 9 for more information.

NOTE

Most desktop PCs are happy to keep running for as long as you care to keep paying for the electricity. Provided that the PC has adequate ventilation and the ambient temperature hasn't reached Death Valley levels, the PC won't get too hot, and it will be ready for you to resume work at a moment's notice. By contrast, most modern laptops tend to overheat if left running, so it's best to turn them off or put them into standby or hibernation mode.

After choosing a partition, you may be offered the chance to format it. Unless you need the partition to be accessible by older operating systems, such as Windows 98 or Windows Me, select the **Format The Partition Using The NTFS File System** option (not the Quick option), and press **ENTER** to format the partition.

After the formatting, installation continues. You will need to:

1. Choose networking settings in the Networking Settings dialog box. You'll usually want to choose the **Typical Settings** option.

2. Specify how the PC will connect to the Internet (if at all): through a modem, through a DSL or cable broadband connection, or through a local area network (LAN).

3. Choose whether to activate Windows (you can wait up to 30 days if you prefer to make sure that XP works okay on your PC) and whether to register it (which is required for support, but is otherwise optional).

4. Set up an account for each user of the PC. (You can set up additional accounts later, at which point you can apply passwords to the accounts.)

Shut Down Your PC

After you finish working in Windows, close Windows as follows:

1. Click the **Start** button, and click **Turn Off Computer**. The Turn Off Computer dialog box appears.

2. Click **Turn Off**. Windows closes and switches off your PC. (If your PC has older power-management features, you may receive the message "It is now safe to turn off your computer." Press the power button to turn your PC off manually.

Alternatives to Shutting Down

Instead of shutting down your PC, you can log off, switch users, restart, or put your PC into standby or hibernation mode.

LOG OFF

TIP

To log off quickly using the keyboard, press ⊞+L.

Log off to end your user session, close all your applications, and display the logon screen so that someone else can log on. To log off:

1. Click the **Start** button, and click **Log Off**.

2. Click **Log Off** in the Log Off Windows dialog box (shown here).

NOTE

You usually need to restart your PC only if Windows has become unstable or programs have crashed. You also need to restart Windows after installing certain updates or software, but these items usually offer to restart Windows automatically.

SWITCH USERS

Switching users keeps your user session active and your applications open but displays the logon screen so that someone else can log on. Your user session keeps running in the background. When you log on again, your applications are as you left them. To switch users:

1. Click the **Start** button, and click **Log Off**.

2. Click **Switch User** in the Log Off Windows dialog box.

RESTART YOUR PC

To restart your PC to reload Windows:

1. Click the **Start** button, and click **Turn Off Computer**.

2. Click **Restart** in the Turn Off Computer dialog box.

USE STANDBY OR HIBERNATION MODE

Put your PC into standby or hibernation mode to freeze your computing session at its current stage and (for hibernation mode) save it to your hard drive so that you can resume your session later. Laptop PCs tend to offer better standby or hibernation capabilities than desktop PCs so that you can pack up your work and go at a moment's notice, but most desktop PCs can use standby or hibernation modes too.

To use standby mode:

1. Click the **Start** button, and click **Turn Off Computer**.
2. Click **Stand By** in the Turn Off Computer dialog box.

To use hibernation mode:

1. Click the **Start** button, and click **Turn Off Computer**.
2. Press **SHIFT** to change the Stand By item in the Turn Off Computer dialog box to a Hibernate item, and then click that item.

Depending on your PC, you may also be able to invoke standby mode by pressing a custom button on the keyboard or by pressing the PC's power button. See Chapter 9 for instructions to configure how XP responds to the power button, the sleep button, and to your closing the lid of a laptop PC.

NOTE

Desktop computers tend to offer only hibernate mode, while laptop computers initially offer standby mode, and then, by pressing **SHIFT**, you can use hibernate mode. The difference between the two is that standby mode is a special low-power state that preserves the battery but does not fully shut down the computer. You can more quickly return to whatever you were doing. Hibernate mode fully shuts down the computer, but in such a way that you can return to exactly what you were doing when you shut down, just more slowly than with standby mode. Many laptop computers go into standby mode automatically when you close the lid.

Chapter 2

Working with Windows XP

In this chapter you'll learn the essentials of working with Windows. First, you'll learn to work with the major components of the Windows interface: windows, dialog boxes, menus, and toolbars. After that you'll learn to customize your Windows desktop for speed, comfort, and aesthetics. You'll then see how to manage files and folders using Windows Explorer and how to burn CDs to back up or transfer files.

Use the Windows Interface

The major components of the Windows interface are the desktop, windows, and dialog boxes. You'll need to use these components to take almost any action in Windows.

Work with the Desktop

The desktop (see Figure 2-1) takes up most of the screen and is the background against which you do your work.

TIP

This chapter (and the rest of the book) discusses Windows XP, but most of the information applies to earlier versions of Windows as well.

- When you open a program, it appears in a window on the desktop; you can resize the window so that it takes up more or less space, and you can adjust its position relative to other open windows.

- When you open a dialog box, it appears in a rectangular area on the desktop, usually in front of the program to which it refers.

- The taskbar (which contains the Start button) appears at the bottom of the desktop by default. You can drag it to the other three edges of the desktop if you prefer.

- You can position icons for files and folders on the desktop so that you can access them quickly.

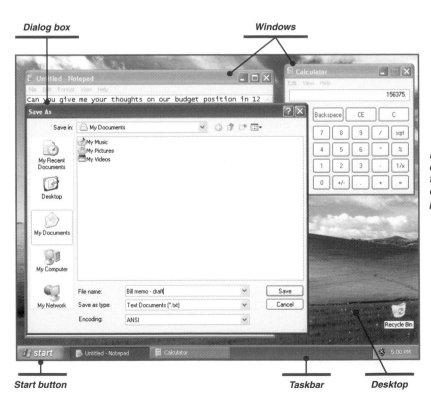

Dialog box   *Windows*

Start button   *Taskbar*   *Desktop*

Figure 2-1: Windows and dialog boxes appear on the desktop. You can drag them to different positions.

Work with Windows

A window represents a running application or an open document in a running application. Almost all windows have menus that enable you to take actions using the mouse or the keyboard, and almost all windows can be resized by dragging their sizing handles in the lower-right corner or by dragging one of their borders. Figure 2-2 shows you the key components of a typical window and explains how to use them.

TIP

If a window's title bar isn't visible because the window is positioned so that its top is off the top edge of the screen, move the window back by pressing **ALT+SPACEBAR**, **M**, and then **DOWN ARROW** or another arrow key to move the window. Press **ENTER** or **ESC** when the window is suitably placed.

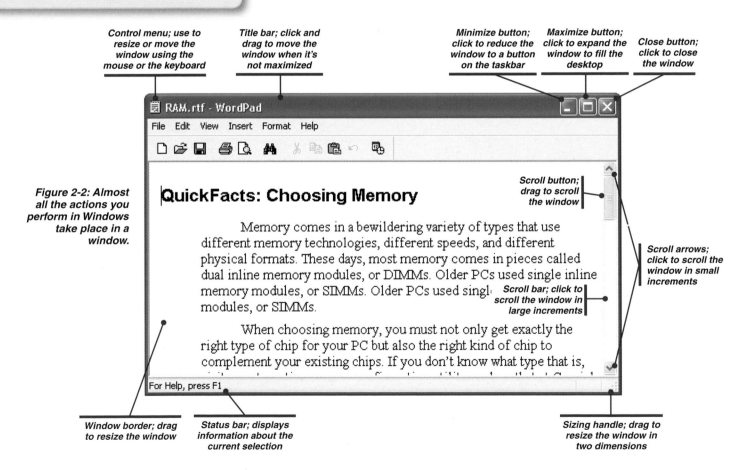

Control menu; use to resize or move the window using the mouse or the keyboard

Title bar; click and drag to move the window when it's not maximized

Minimize button; click to reduce the window to a button on the taskbar

Maximize button; click to expand the window to fill the desktop

Close button; click to close the window

Figure 2-2: Almost all the actions you perform in Windows take place in a window.

Scroll button; drag to scroll the window

Scroll arrows; click to scroll the window in small increments

Scroll bar; click to scroll the window in large increments

Window border; drag to resize the window

Status bar; displays information about the current selection

Sizing handle; drag to resize the window in two dimensions

RAM.rtf - WordPad

File   Edit   View   Insert   Format   Help

QuickFacts: Choosing Memory

Memory comes in a bewildering variety of types that use different memory technologies, different speeds, and different physical formats. These days, most memory comes in pieces called dual inline memory modules, or DIMMs. Older PCs used single inline memory modules, or SIMMs. Older PCs used singl... modules, or SIMMs.

When choosing memory, you must not only get exactly the right type of chip for your PC but also the right kind of chip to complement your existing chips. If you don't know what type that is,

For Help, press F1

CHANGE A WINDOW'S STATE

A window can be in one of three states:

- A **maximized** window occupies the whole of your desktop except for the taskbar area. To maximize a window, click the **Maximize** button.

- A **normal** window can be any size to which you drag it using the sizing handle or any of its borders. To change a maximized window to a normal window, click the **Restore Down** button that replaces the Maximize button when you maximize the window.

- A **minimized** window is a window shrunk down to a button on the taskbar. In a normal or maximized window, click the **Minimize** button to minimize the window. Click the button on the taskbar to restore the window to its previous size.

ARRANGE MULTIPLE WINDOWS

You can open multiple windows at once and arrange them on the desktop as you need by dragging them manually or by right-clicking open space in the taskbar and choosing the appropriate command from the shortcut menu:

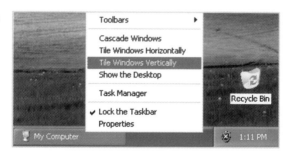

TIP

To undo a cascade or tile arrangement, right-click open space in the taskbar, and choose **Undo Cascade** or **Undo Tile**.

- **Cascade Windows** arranges the windows so that you can see the title bar of each.

- **Tile Windows Horizontally** arranges the non-minimized windows in a horizontal arrangement so that all of them are visible and each occupies roughly the same amount of space.

- **Tile Windows Vertically** arranges the non-minimized windows in a vertical arrangement so that all of them are visible and each occupies roughly the same amount of space.

- **Show The Desktop** hides all open windows and dialog boxes so that you can see the desktop. Right-click open space in the taskbar, and choose **Show Open Windows** to restore the windows to their previous arrangement.

MAKE A WINDOW ACTIVE

Only one window can be active at any given time. The active window receives the keystrokes you type using the keyboard. To make a window active, click it or click its taskbar button. The active window has a different color than other windows; the color depends on the Windows color scheme you're using, but it's usually darker so that it stands out. The taskbar button for the active window is also a different color than the other taskbar buttons.

CLOSE A WINDOW

To close a window, click its **Close** button, or open the **File** menu and click either **Close** or **Exit** (depending on the application to which the window belongs).

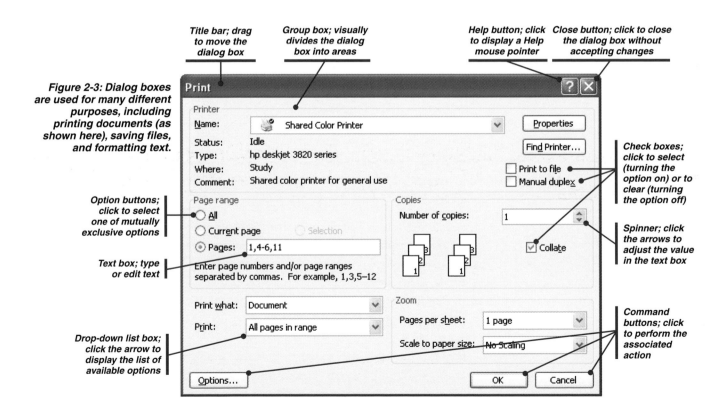

Figure 2-3: Dialog boxes are used for many different purposes, including printing documents (as shown here), saving files, and formatting text.

Title bar; drag to move the dialog box

Group box; visually divides the dialog box into areas

Help button; click to display a Help mouse pointer

Close button; click to close the dialog box without accepting changes

Check boxes; click to select (turning the option on) or to clear (turning the option off)

Option buttons; click to select one of mutually exclusive options

Spinner; click the arrows to adjust the value in the text box

Text box; type or edit text

Drop-down list box; click the arrow to display the list of available options

Command buttons; click to perform the associated action

Work with Dialog Boxes

A dialog box is a fixed-size rectangle that contains features called *controls* for taking actions or setting preferences. Figure 2-3 shows a dialog box that uses many of the standard Windows controls.

The common controls in dialog boxes are:

- The **title bar** contains the name of the dialog box and is used to drag the dialog box around the desktop. (You may need to move a dialog box so that you can see the part of the window or desktop that it is obscuring.)
- **Tabs** let you select from among several pages of controls in a dialog box.
- A **drop-down list box** opens a list from which you can choose one item that will be displayed when the list is closed.
- **Option buttons**, also called *radio buttons* (because only one can be selected at a time, like the station buttons on a radio), let you select one from among mutually exclusive options.
- A **text box** lets you enter and edit text.
- **Command buttons** perform functions such as closing the dialog box and accepting changes to the settings (the OK button), or closing the dialog box and discarding the changes (the Cancel button).
- A **spinner** lets you select from a sequential series of numbers.
- A **slider** lets you select from several values.
- **Check boxes** let you turn features or options on (by *selecting* the check box, placing a check mark in it) or off (by *clearing* the check box, removing the check mark from it).
- **Group boxes** are lines used to separate distinct parts of the dialog box—for example, to group related controls.
- The **Help button** changes the mouse pointer to a question mark with which you can click an item that you want to learn more about. (Help is available for only some items in dialog boxes.)

Some dialog boxes include an Apply button that you can click to make the changes you've chosen so far take effect without closing the dialog box.

NOTE

Complex programs may have dozens or even scores of toolbars. In most programs, you can toggle the display of a toolbar by clicking the **View** menu, clicking **Toolbars**, and then clicking the name of the toolbar on the submenu. You may also be able to toggle the display of a toolbar by right-clicking any toolbar that's displayed, and then clicking the toolbar name on the resulting menu.

TIP

Some programs treat the menu bar as a toolbar and allow you to reposition it.

Work with Menus and Toolbars

The primary way to issue commands in Windows is to use menus and toolbars. Menus appear on the menu bar at the top of a window. To use a menu:

- Click the menu name using the mouse so that the menu appears, and then click the appropriate command on it.

  –Or–

- Press **ALT** and then press the menu's underlined letter to display the menu. You can then press **DOWN ARROW** to select the menu and press **ENTER** to invoke it, or simply press the underlined letter (if there is one) to select the menu item and invoke it.

A toolbar typically appears at the top of a window, just below the menu bar, but can often be dragged to another edge of the window or dragged into the window so that it floats freely. To use a toolbar, click the button that represents the action you want to take. If the toolbar button is graphical, you can often display a ScreenTip containing information about it by hovering the mouse pointer over the button for a moment without clicking, as shown here.

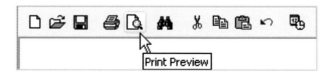

Customize XP

XP lets you customize many different aspects of its look and behavior. This book shows the default look you get when you install a fresh copy of XP onto a computer. If your computer's manufacturer installed XP for you, or if you upgraded from another version of Windows, XP may look different.

To configure XP quickly to suit you, follow the steps in this section.

Change How Your Screen Looks

The look of your screen should be both pleasing and easy for you to read. There are three major areas that you can change: the screen resolution and color quality, the desktop background and icons, and the screen saver.

CHANGE THE RESOLUTION AND COLOR QUALITY

First, set the resolution and color qualities that work best with your monitor.

1. Right-click open space on the desktop, and click **Properties**. The Display Properties dialog box appears.

2. Click the **Settings** tab (see Figure 2-4).

3. Drag the **Screen Resolution** slider to adjust the resolution, and then click **Apply** to test the resolution. In the Monitor Settings dialog box (shown here), click **Yes** or **No** as appropriate.

Figure 2-4: Use the Settings tab of the Display Properties dialog box to set a comfortable resolution and color depth.

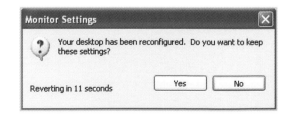

After changing the resolution and color depth, you may need to adjust a CRT (cathode-ray tube) monitor so that the picture appears as large as possible without overlapping any edges.

You can set a picture as your desktop background from Windows Explorer by right-clicking it and clicking **Set As Desktop Background**.

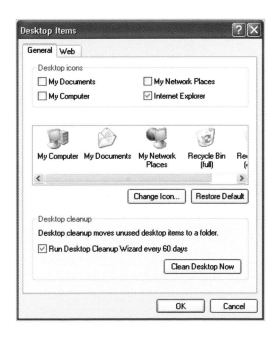

4. To adjust the color quality, open the **Color Quality** drop-down list, and select the quality that's best for you (probably the highest available for the resolution, you picked). Click **Apply** and make your choice in the Monitor Settings dialog box again.

5. If you have a CRT (cathode-ray tube) monitor that is flickering, increase the refresh rate: click **Advanced**, click the **Monitor** tab, choose a higher refresh rate in the **Screen Refresh Rate** drop-down list, and click **Apply**. Click **OK** to close the Advanced monitor and display adapter dialog box (leave the Display Properties dialog box open).

CHANGE THE DESKTOP BACKGROUND AND ICONS

With the Display Properties dialog box still open, choose a desktop background and the icons that appear on it.

1. Click the **Desktop** tab.

2. Select a picture you want to use in the Background list box.

- To choose another picture, click **Browse** and use the Browse dialog box to select the picture.

- To use a color rather than a picture, select **None** in the Background list box, and then choose the color in the Color drop-down list box.

3. In the Position drop-down list box, choose **Center**, **Tile**, or **Stretch** to make the picture fit your desktop.

4. Click **Customize Desktop** to display the Desktop Items dialog box.

5. Select or clear the check boxes in the Desktop Items area to control whether icons for My Documents, My Computer, My Network Places, and Internet Explorer appear on your desktop.

6. Click **OK** to close the Desktop Items dialog box.

NOTE

Depending on how you have it configured, XP displays different options for controlling what happens when you interrupt the screen saver. If the **On Resume**, **Display Welcome Screen** check box is available, select this check box if you want XP to display the Welcome screen (so that you have to log in again); clear this check box to go straight back into your session. If the **On Resume**, **Password Protect** check box is available, select this check box if you want security; clear this check box if you want to go straight back to work.

SET UP A SCREEN SAVER

A screen saver is a changing pattern that hides the on-screen display when you leave your PC unused for a specified length of time. Screen savers used to be needed to prevent static text images from burning into a CRT screen (hence the name), but are now mostly used for security or entertainment, as they aren't needed to prevent harm to LCDs or to modern CRTs. To change the screen saver:

1. In the Display Properties dialog box, click the **Screen Saver** tab (see Figure 2-5).

2. Select a screen saver in the Screen Saver drop-down list box.

3. Click **Preview** to see the screen saver full-screen. Move the mouse to cancel the preview.

4. Click **Settings** and use the resulting dialog box to set any configurable options in the screen saver.

5. Change the **Wait** text box to specify how many minutes' inactivity XP should allow before starting the screen saver.

Figure 2-5: Configure a screen saver to hide your screen after a specified interval.

Change How Objects Look

With Windows you can change not only how the screen looks, but also how objects and icons look on the screen.

CHANGE THE APPEARANCE OF OBJECTS

You can change the appearance of Windows objects in two ways:

- Click the **Themes** tab in the Display Properties dialog box, and select a different theme in the Theme drop-down list box. For example, choose **Windows Classic** to apply the look used for Windows 98, Me, and 2000 instead of the Windows XP theme.

- Click the **Appearance** tab in the Display Properties dialog box, and use the controls to change the style of windows and buttons, the color scheme, and the font size. Click **Advanced** to access options that give you more control over the look of items.

After you finish working in the Display Properties dialog box, click **OK** to close it.

ORGANIZE THE ICONS ON YOUR DESKTOP

To organize the icons on your desktop, right-click your desktop, and use the options on the Arrange Icons By submenu.

- To arrange icons automatically, select **Auto Arrange**. Display the submenu again, and choose **Name**, **Size**, **Type**, or **Modified** to specify the arrangement.

- To arrange icons manually, clear **Auto Arrange**, redisplay the submenu, and clear **Align To Grid**. Then drag the icons to where you want them.

NOTE

Whether and how you organize the icons on your desktop is entirely up to you. Some people use desktop icons as a major means of navigation in XP. Other people prefer to open their program windows full-screen, which makes the desktop inaccessible; if you do this, you may prefer to keep your icons on the Start menu or on the Quick Launch toolbar rather than on the desktop.

Customize the Start Menu and the Taskbar

The two primary controls in Windows are the Start menu and the taskbar. There are several customization steps you can take with both of these controls.

CUSTOMIZE THE START MENU

To make the Start menu as useful as possible, configure it so it shows what you need.

1. Right-click the **Start** button, and click **Properties** to open the Taskbar And Start Menu Properties dialog box.

2. Click the top **Customize** button to open the Customize Start Menu dialog box.

3. On the General tab (see Figure 2-6), choose between large and small icons; specify the number of programs to show in the frequently used programs area; and choose whether to show an Internet item and an E-mail item, and the programs associated with them, on the Start Menu.

4. Click the **Advanced** tab (see Figure 2-7), and use the options to specify how the Start menu behaves, which items appear on it, and how they appear.

5. Click **OK** to close the Customize Start Menu dialog box.

Figure 2-6: Choose basic Start menu options on the General tab of the Customize Start Menu dialog box.

Figure 2-7: On the Advanced tab of the Customize Start Menu dialog box, choose which items to include and how they appear.

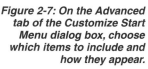

QUICKSTEPS

CUSTOMIZING THE TASKBAR FROM THE DESKTOP

You can customize the taskbar from the desktop.

• Right-click the notification area or open space on the taskbar, and click **Lock The Taskbar** to turn locking on or off.

• With locking off, move the mouse pointer over the border between the taskbar and the desktop so that the mouse pointer turns into a two-headed arrow. Drag up to increase the number of rows of taskbar buttons; drag down to decrease it.

• With locking off, drag from open space in the taskbar to a different edge of the desktop to move the taskbar there.

• To set the date or time, double-click the clock in the notification area, and use the options in the Date And Time Properties dialog box. The Internet Time tab lets you automatically synchronize your PC's time with a time server on the Internet.

CUSTOMIZE THE TASKBAR

You can also customize the taskbar.

1. Click the **Taskbar** tab in the Taskbar And Start Menu Properties dialog box (see Figure 2-8).

2. In the Taskbar Appearance area, choose whether to:

   • **Lock The Taskbar** so that you can't move it by accident.

   • **Hide The Taskbar** when you're not using it. (This frees up desktop space. To summon the taskbar, move the mouse pointer to the edge of the screen where the taskbar is hiding.)

   • **Keep The Taskbar On Top** of other windows rather than letting other windows hide it.

   • **Group Similar Taskbar Buttons** to reduce the number of buttons.

   • **Display The Quick Launch Toolbar**, a toolbar that contains icons for launching programs.

3. In Notification Area, choose whether to:

   • **Show The Clock** (this is usually helpful).

   • **Hide Inactive Icons automatically**. To manage icon behavior, click **Customize**, use the options in the Customize Notifications dialog box, and then click **OK**.

4. Click **OK** to close the Taskbar And Start Menu Properties dialog box.

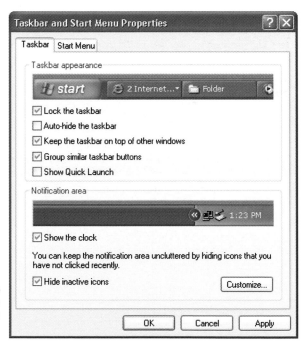

Figure 2-8: Customize the taskbar so that it behaves in your preferred way.

UNDERSTANDING FOLDERS

All the data stored on your hard drive is kept in files, which are contained in folders. A folder is a special type of file that acts as a container for files or other folders. Folder is another term for *directory*, a term used in older, non-graphical operating systems, such as DOS and UNIX.

ROOT FOLDERS, FOLDERS, AND SUBFOLDERS

The *root folder* is the master folder on a drive and contains all the files and other folders stored on that drive. The other folders are contained within and can be said to "branch off" the root folder in the form of an inverted tree. Windows represents the root folder as a drive icon and encourages you to think of it as a drive. For clarity, this book follows that convention.

A *subfolder*, or *child folder*, is a folder stored inside another folder (its *parent folder*, or *containing folder*). Usually, these terms are used only when precision is required; plain "folder" is the normal description.

SYSTEM FOLDERS

Windows XP includes many system folders to keep its programs, functions, and data organized. To discourage you from disturbing these files and perhaps causing problems in Windows, XP hides most of its system files from you. XP stores most of its files in the Windows folder on the boot drive, the drive from which your PC starts (typically the C: drive). XP stores other vital files in the root folder of the boot drive. XP stores programs in the Program Files folder.

Continued...

Manage Files and Folders Using Windows Explorer

When you use a program in Windows, the program uses your PC's memory (RAM) to store the data temporarily so that it can manipulate it. Memory stores data only while you're working with it and only while the PC is running. For example, if you open the WordPad program that comes with Windows XP and use it to write a letter, the data is stored in memory. When you close WordPad, the data is removed from the memory so that the memory can be used to store other data. When you shut down your PC, all the data is removed from the memory.

If you want to store data permanently so that you can use it later, you *save* it to the hard disk or another disk. So, normally, after writing a letter in WordPad, you'll save it to a disk so that you can keep it rather than losing it when you close WordPad.

When you save information to a disk, you save it in a named *file* that you place within a folder. (See the QuickFacts "Understanding Folders" for details on folders.)

To manage files and folders in Windows, you use the program called Windows Explorer. Windows Explorer usually manifests itself as a window, but it also runs the desktop, which functions as a special-purpose Windows Explorer window.

Use the My Computer Window

My Computer is a special view in Windows Explorer that displays the drives and major hardware (such as scanners and cameras) attached to your PC.

1. Click the **Start** button. The Start menu is displayed.
2. Click **My Computer**. The My Computer window opens.

UNDERSTANDING FOLDERS *(Continued)*

Your PC manufacturer may also have stored vital files on your hard drive. For example, many manufacturers put a folder (often with a name such as i386) containing the XP installation files on the hard drive rather than supplying an XP CD.

USER FOLDERS

XP provides a set of folders for each user (see "Manage Files and Folders Using Windows Explorer" in this chapter) along with links for easily accessing these folders.

Figure 2-9 shows an example of the My Computer window. The My Computer window for your PC will have different contents depending on the drives and hardware attached to the PC.

Hard disk (drive C:)   **Floppy drive (drive A:)**

Task pane; provides links for taking actions related to the selected object

Task pane; contains links to other folders you may want to access quickly

Details pane; provides information about the selected object

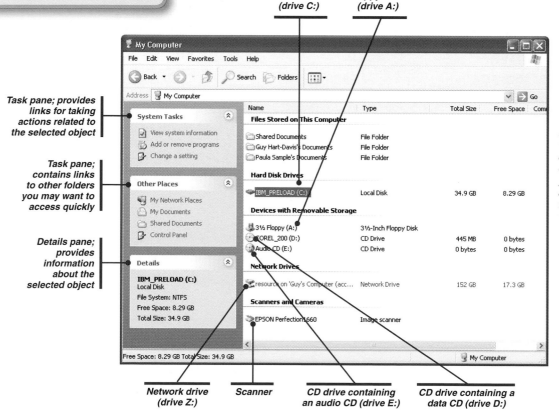

Network drive (drive Z:)   **Scanner**   **CD drive containing an audio CD (drive E:)**   **CD drive containing a data CD (drive D:)**

Figure 2-9: My Computer provides an overview of your computer and lets you open the drives and folders you see to find files stored within them.

TIP

You can expand or collapse a task pane or the Details pane by clicking the title bar.

USE THE TASK PANES AND THE DETAILS PANE

Windows Explorer displays three panes on the left side of its window by default:

- The top task pane contains links for actions you can take on the selected object.
- The middle task pane contains links to other folders you may want to access from this folder.
- The Details pane at the bottom displays information about the selected object.

NAVIGATE USING THE FOLDERS PANE

Instead of displaying the task panes, you can display the Folders pane (shown on the left in Figure 2-10), which shows a tree diagram of the folder hierarchy. To display the Folders pane, click the **Folders** button on the toolbar.

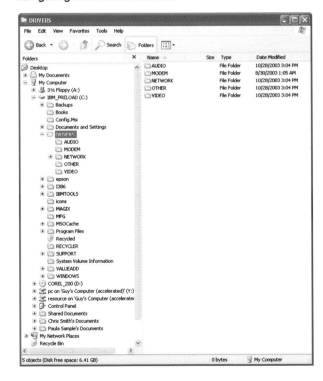

Figure 2-10: The Folders pane provides another way of navigating from folder to folder.

To navigate using the Folders pane:

- Double-click a folder to display its contents.
- Click a + sign to expand a collapsed item.
- Click a – sign to collapse an expanded item.

To hide the Folders pane, click the **Folders** button again, or click the **X** in the upper-right corner of the pane.

IDENTIFY LOCAL DRIVES

As you can see in Figure 2-9 (earlier in this chapter), each drive is assigned a drive letter, which is designated as a capital letter followed by a colon.

- Drive A: is the floppy drive.
- Drive C: is the PC's first (and in this case only) hard drive. Subsequent hard drives are assigned the letters D:, E:, and so on.
- Drive D: is usually the PC's first optical drive (CD or DVD). If the PC has two or more hard drives, the first optical drive gets the next letter (for example, E: if there are hard drives C: and D:) rather than getting D:.
- Drive E: is the PC's second optical drive (if it has one).

NOTE

My Computer's default view is to display the drives and folders broken up into categories: Files Stored On This Computer, Hard Disk Drives, Devices With Removable Storage, Network Drives (if you have any), and Scanners And Cameras.

NOTE

Many hardware manuals assume that your CD drive is drive D:. If your CD drive has another letter assigned, you'll need to substitute that letter when following such instructions. If in doubt as to which drive is which, open the **My Computer** window and read the descriptions.

IDENTIFY NETWORK DRIVES

Beyond these local drives and devices, your PC may have network drives attached, as the PC in Figure 2-9 does. Windows XP by default automatically assigns drive letters to network drives, starting with Z: and working backward through the alphabet.

Your PC may also have other local drives attached, such as a removable memory drive (for example, a CompactFlash drive or Memory Stick drive), or an Iomega Zip or Rev removable disk. Such drives are assigned letters after the last optical drive. For example, in the PC shown in Figure 2-9 (earlier in this chapter), such a drive would be assigned the letter F.

To see what a drive contains, double-click it. Figure 2-11 shows an example of the contents of a CD. From here, you can double-click one of the folders or files to open it, or simply click the **Up** button to move back up to your My Computer window.

Figure 2-11:
Double-click a
drive to display
its contents.

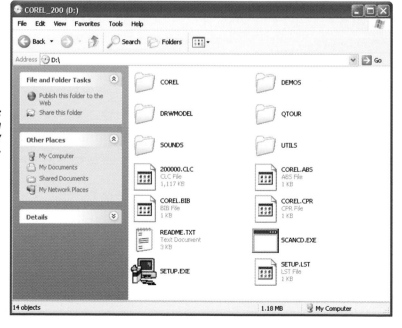

Check the Amount of Space on a Drive

To see how much space is left on a drive:

1. Click the **Start** button, and click **My Computer** to open the My Computer window.

2. Right-click the drive (move the mouse pointer over the drive's icon or name, and click the right mouse button), and click **Properties** from the context menu. The Properties dialog box for the drive appears. Figure 2-12 shows an example of the Properties dialog box for a hard drive.

3. Examine the Used Space and Free Space readouts and the pie chart that shows the proportion of used space and free space.

4. Click **OK** to close the Properties dialog box.

TIP

From the Properties dialog box for a drive, you can change the drive's name by typing in the text box at the top. You can also verify which file system the drive is using by looking at the File System readout. Windows XP's standard file system for local hard drives is NTFS (NT File System). Removable drives may use the FAT32 file system, which can be read by Windows 98 and Windows Me (these OSs cannot read NTFS).

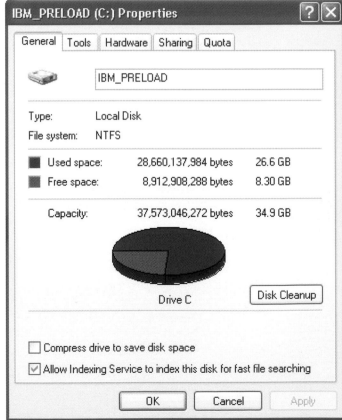

Figure 2-12: Use the Properties dialog box for a drive to check how much space is available on it.

1

UICKSTEPS

USING DISK CLEANUP TO FREE UP DISK SPACE

These days, the hard drives on new PCs are large enough to hold impressive quantities of files. If you store a lot of graphics, music files, and video files on your hard drive, however, you may fill it up. Files that you delete take up space in your Recycle Bin until you empty it.

Apart from the files that you create, Windows and its accessory programs need a fair amount of space on your hard drive. Windows needs between 1 and 2 GB for permanently storing its files and up to 1 GB of space to use as *virtual memory*, temporary storage space for data that won't fit in RAM. Internet Explorer, the Web browser, needs space to store temporary files—files containing data you've downloaded and that you may need again.

The easiest way to free up space is to remove files that you've created and that you no longer need. For example, after creating and finishing a movie, you might back up all its files to a DVD and then remove the originals from your hard disk to make space.

Windows also offers an automated tool called Disk Cleanup that can remove certain types of old files for you. To free up space:

1. Click the **Start** button, click **All Programs**, and then click **Accessories**. Click **System Tools**, and click **Disk Cleanup**. The Disk Cleanup dialog box appears (see Figure 2-13).

2. Select the check boxes for the items you want to delete.

3. Click **OK**.

If you need to free up more space, click the **More Options** tab, and choose to remove optional Windows components or installed programs you don't use, or remove all System Restore data (see Chapter 10) except for the last restore point.

Use Files and Folders

The files and folders on a hard drive represent the primary storage facility for all the information that you work with and want to keep. Your ability to navigate through the structure of folders and files and create, select, rename, and search these elements determines, to a large extent, how easily you can use your computer.

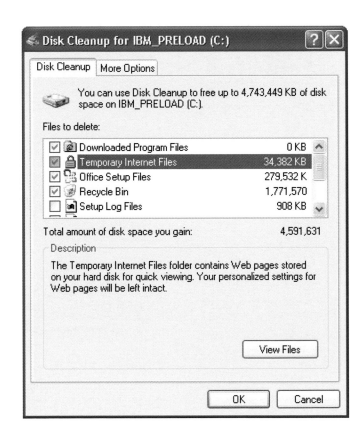

Figure 2-13:
Use Disk Cleanup to remove unnecessary old files and create free space on your disk.

NAVIGATE XP'S FOLDER STRUCTURE

To help you manage your files and folders, Windows XP automatically builds a structure of folders for you to keep your files and folders in. The key folders have links on your Start menu by default so that you can access them quickly.

- **My Documents** is the default folder for saving documents that aren't pictures, music files, or videos. For example, if you save a file in the WordPad word-processing program that comes with Windows XP, WordPad suggests using the My Documents folder.
- **My Music** is the default folder for saving music files.
- **My Pictures** is the default folder for saving picture files—anything from photographs to pictures you create using the Paint program that comes with Windows XP.
- **My Videos** is the default folder for saving video files you create (for example, by using the Windows Movie Maker program that comes with Windows XP). This folder doesn't have a link on the Start menu unless you choose to add it.

To open one of these folders, click the **Start** button, and click the appropriate link.

CREATE A FOLDER

You can create folders within these folders (or within other folders) as needed so that you have storage locations for your files. To create a folder:

1. In a Windows Explorer window, open the folder in which you want to create the new folder.
2. Click the **File** menu, click **New**, and then click **New Folder**. A new folder is displayed with its default name highlighted.
3. Type a name for the folder.
4. Press **ENTER** to apply the name. Double-click the folder to open it.

CHANGE THE FOLDER VIEW

Depending on the contents of the folder, Windows Explorer offers five or six different views. You can change the view using the View button on the toolbar or from the View menu.

- **Filmstrip** view is available only for folders containing pictures. It displays a filmstrip of icons across the bottom of the window with a larger preview of the selected picture above it.

- **Thumbnails** view displays a thumbnail preview of each picture or video file and so is good for working with these file types. It's less useful for documents, spreadsheets, and other text-based files.

- **Tiles** view displays a medium-sized icon for each object.

- **Icons** view shows a small icon for each object.

- **List** view shows a tiny icon and the name for each object. List view is best for browsing folders that contain many objects.

- **Details** view shows columns of information, such as the name, size, type, and date modified. You can sort the files by clicking a column heading; click again to reverse the sort order.

SELECT FILES OR FOLDERS

You can select files and folders by clicking and dragging.

- To select a single file or folder, click it.

- To select multiple contiguous files or folders, drag a selection rectangle around them, as shown here. Alternatively, click the first file or folder, hold down **SHIFT**, and click the last file or folder.

- To select multiple noncontiguous files or folders, click the first file or folder, hold down **CTRL**, and click each of the other files or folders you want to select.

RENAME A FILE OR FOLDER

To rename a file or folder that's not selected:

- Click the name once, pause, and click again (don't double-click). Type the new name, and press **ENTER**.

  –Or–

- Right-click the name, choose **Rename**, type the new name, and press **ENTER**.

TIP

To select all the files in a folder, click the **Edit menu,** and click **Select All**; or press **CTRL+A**. To select all the files in a folder except one, select that file, click the **Edit** menu, and click **Invert Selection**.

DELETING FILES AND FOLDERS

When you don't need a file or folder any more, delete it. Windows places objects you delete in the Recycle Bin, a special folder, in case you need to recover them.

If the Recycle Bin becomes full, Windows automatically deletes the oldest objects without consulting you. To keep this from happening, you should empty the Recycle Bin from time to time.

DELETE A FILE OR FOLDER

With the file or folder in view:

- Click the icon to select it, press **DELETE**, and click **Yes** to confirm the deletion.

   –Or–

- Right-click the icon, click **Delete**, and click **Yes** to confirm the deletion.

RECOVER A DELETED FILE OR FOLDER

If you just deleted a file or folder using Windows Explorer, open **Edit** and click **Undo Delete**.

If you deleted the file or folder a while ago:

1. Double-click the **Recycle Bin** on the desktop. The Recycle Bin is displayed.

2. Right-click the icon for the file or folder, and choose **Restore**.

Recycle Bin

PERMANENTLY DELETE A FILE OR FOLDER

If you're sure you want to delete a file or folder permanently:

- Click the icon, hold down **SHIFT** while you press **DELETE**, and click **Yes** to confirm the deletion.

   –Or–

- Double-click the **Recycle Bin** on the desktop to open it, right-click the icon for the file or folder, click **Delete**, and click **Yes** to confirm the deletion.

Continued...

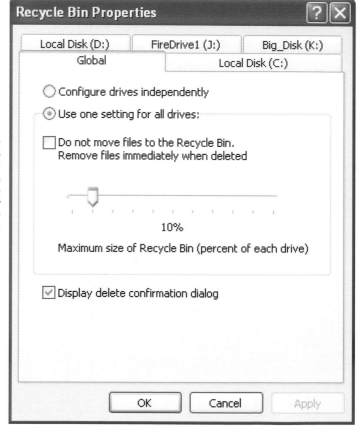

Figure 2-14: You can configure the Recycle Bin to use the same percentage of space on each drive, or configure each drive independently.

DELETING FILES AND FOLDERS

(Continued)

EMPTY THE RECYCLE BIN

1. Double-click the **Recycle Bin** on the desktop. The Recycle Bin is displayed.

2. In the Recycle Bin Tasks pane, click **Empty The Recycle Bin**. The Confirm Multiple File Delete dialog box appears.

3. Click **Yes**.

   –Or–

   Right-click the **Recycle Bin** on the desktop, and click **Empty The Recycle Bin** on the shortcut menu.

CONFIGURE THE RECYCLE BIN

To change the amount of space the Recycle Bin takes up:

1. Right-click the **Recycle Bin** on the desktop, and click **Properties**. The Recycle Bin Properties dialog box appears (see Figure 2-14).

2. If your PC has multiple hard drives and you want to set different amounts of Recycle Bin space on each, select the **Configure Drives Independently** option button, and use the slider on each tab to set the percentage of the drive available to the Recycle Bin. Otherwise, ensure the **Use On Setting For All Drives** option button is selected, and then drag the slider on the Global tab.

3. If you don't want to use the Recycle Bin, select the **Do Not Move Files To The Recycle Bin** check box. (This is strongly discouraged because it enables you to delete files instantly even when you've made a mistake.)

4. If you don't want to see deletion confirmation messages, clear the **Display Delete Confirmation Dialog** check box.

5. Click **OK** to close the Recycle Bin Properties dialog box.

SEARCH FOR FILES AND FOLDERS

When your PC contains many files and folders, you may have to search to find the one you need.

1. Click the **Start** button, and click **Search**. The Search Results window opens.

2. Click the **All Files And Folders** link in the What Do You Want To Search For? pane. The search criteria pane is displayed (see Figure 2-16).

3. Enter all or part of the file name or a word or phrase in the file. (You can also enter both if necessary.)

4. In the Look In drop-down list box, specify the drive or folder to search—for example, the My Documents folder.

5. If necessary, use the When Was It Modified? section, the What Size Is It? section, or the More Advanced Options section to set more specific search options. For example, you might search for files of more than 5 MB modified in the last week.

6. Click **Search**. The search begins. Files and folders that match your criteria are listed in the detail pane.

7. If Windows Explorer finds too many files, you can refine the search criteria and search again.

8. Double-click a search result to open it, or right-click a result and click **Open Containing Folder** to open the folder that contains the result.

9. After you finish searching, click the **File** menu, and click **Close** to close the Windows Explorer window.

Figure 2-16: Use XP's Search feature to find files or folders.

COPYING AND MOVING FILES AND FOLDERS

Windows XP offers several ways to copy and move files and folders. The following are the most consistent and easiest ways of copying and moving.

COPY FILES OR FOLDERS

1. Select the files or folders you want to copy.

2. Click the **Edit** menu, and click **Copy To Folder**. The Copy Items dialog box appears (see Figure 2-15).

3. Navigate to the destination folder by double-clicking each drive and folder. If necessary, you can create a new folder inside the current folder by clicking **Make New Folder** and typing the name for the new folder.

4. Click **Copy**. The dialog box closes, and the files or folders are copied.

MOVE FILES OR FOLDERS

1. Select the files or folders you want to move.

2. Click the **Edit** menu, and click **Move To Folder**. The Move Items dialog box appears. This dialog box is functionally the same as the Copy Items dialog box, except that it moves the files or folders instead of copying them.

3. Navigate to the destination folder. If necessary, you can create a new folder inside the current folder by clicking **Make New Folder**, typing the name for the new folder, and pressing **ENTER**.

4. Click **Move**. The dialog box closes, and the files or folders are moved.

COPY FILES OR FOLDERS TO A FLOPPY DISK

1. Insert a formatted floppy disk into your PC's A: drive.

2. Select the files or folders you want to copy.

3. Click the **File** menu, click **Send To**, and then click **3½ Floppy (A:)**. The files or folders are copied to the floppy disk.

Most floppy disks are sold preformatted, but you may sometimes need to format (or reformat) a floppy disk.

Continued...

Figure 2-15: Use the Copy Items dialog box to specify the destination for files or folders you're copying.

To do so, click the **Start** button, click **My Computer**, right-click **3½ Floppy (A:)**, choose **Format**, click **Start** in the Format 3½ Floppy dialog box, and then click **OK**.

COPY FILES OR FOLDERS TO A RECORDABLE CD

1. Select the files or folders you want to copy.

2. Click the **File** menu, click **Send To**, and then click **CD Drive**. The CD Drive item shown on the Send To menu represents a writable CD drive. (Read-only CD drives do not appear on this menu.)

3. Follow the procedure described in "Record or Burn a CD," later in this chapter, to burn the files or folders to the CD.

NOTE

If you want to choose which action to take for a particular content type each time you insert a disk, select the **Prompt Me Each Time To Choose An Action** option button. If you want to insert a removable disk without Windows reacting, select the **Select An Action To Perform** option button, but select the **Take No Action** "action."

Control What Happens When You Insert a Removable Disk

Windows' AutoPlay feature can automatically take a specified action when you insert a removable disk (for example, a CD or a memory card). To configure AutoPlay:

1. Click the **Start** button, and click **My Computer**.

2. Click the removable drive you want to affect.

3. Click the **File** menu, and click **Properties**. The Properties dialog box for the drive appears.

4. Click the **AutoPlay** tab (see Figure 2-17).

5. In the top drop-down list, select the content type. The options depend on the drive type. A recordable CD drive offers Music Files, Pictures, Video Files, Mixed Content, Music CD, and Blank CD. The Actions list box displays the available choices.

Figure 2-17: By configuring AutoPlay for a drive, you can tell Windows how to handle removable media.

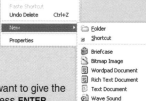
6. In the Actions group box, if you want to take a predetermined action, make sure the **Select An Action To Perform** option button is selected, and then click the action in the list box.

7. Repeat steps 5 and 6 to specify how to handle other content types.

8. Click **OK** to close the Properties dialog box.

Once you've done this, Windows will take the action you specified when you insert a removable disk in the drive. If you chose to be prompted for the action, a dialog box appears that offers you a choice of actions.

Create Shortcuts

Shortcuts allow you to quickly access files or folders from places other than where the files or folders are stored. For example, you can start a program from the desktop even though the actual program file is stored in another folder. To create a shortcut:

- Drag a program file (one with an .exe extension) to a different folder—for example, from a Windows Explorer window to the desktop.

  –Or–

- Right-click and drag any file or folder to a different folder, and then choose **Create Shortcuts Here** from the shortcut menu.

After creating the shortcut, you can rename it as you would any other object.

Create Your Own CDs

If your PC has a CD recorder (often called a CD *burner*), you can use XP's features for burning CDs. XP can create audio CDs that you can play in almost any CD player and data CDs that you can use for archiving data or transferring data from one PC to another.

NOTE

The icon for a shortcut has an upward-pointing arrow in its lower-left corner:

TIP

Use CD-R discs when you want to create a permanent CD—for example, an audio CD or a data archive. Use CD-RW discs when you want to store data temporarily and then replace it. For example, you might use seven CD-RW discs for backup, one for each day of the week, erasing and overwriting each when its day comes around again. Rewritable CDs cost a little more than recordable CDs.

Prepare to Record a CD

To create your own CDs, you need to have recordable CDs to use and you must select the files or music you want to put on one.

BUY RECORDABLE CDS

First, you'll need suitable CDs for your burner. There are three main considerations:

- **Recordable or rewritable** These days, most CD burners can handle both recordable discs (CD-R; discs that can be written to only once) or rewritable discs (CD-RW; discs that can be erased and written to again multiple times).

- **Capacity** Both CD-R and CD-RW discs come in several capacities; 650 MB and 700 MB are the most widely used capacities. 650 MB is enough space for 74 minutes of CD-quality audio; 700 MB holds 80 minutes.

- **Speed** CDs come in different maximum speed ratings. Check the speed of your CD burner and buy accordingly.

SEND FILES TO A CD

Before burning a CD, you need to copy the files you want on the CD to a temporary storage area that represents the CD.

1. Open a Windows Explorer window, and browse to the folder that contains the files you want to copy to the CD. For example, click the **Start** button, and click **My Documents**.

2. Select the files you want to copy.

3. Right-click the selection, click **Send To**, and click **CD Drive**. (Your CD drive may have a different description, such as CD-RW Drive.) The files are copied to the temporary storage area, and a balloon is displayed above the notification area to alert you to their presence.

> ⓘ **You have files waiting to be written to the CD.**
> To see the files now, click this balloon.

4. Click the balloon to open a Windows Explorer window showing the contents of the storage area (see Figure 2-18).

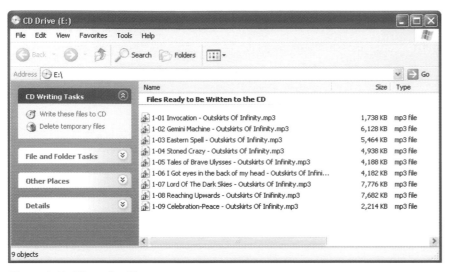

Figure 2-18: XP copies files to a temporary storage area in preparation for burning them to a CD.

Record or Burn a CD

After you've copied all the files to the storage area:

1. Click **Write These Files To CD** in the CD Writing Tasks pane. The CD Writing Wizard starts (see Figure 2-19).

2. Type the name for your CD in place of the default name (the current date). You can use up to 16 letters.

3. If you want the wizard to close after burning the CD, select the **Close The Wizard After The Files Have Been Written** check box.

4. Click **Next**. The wizard writes the files to the CD and then ejects it.

5. Click **Finish**.

6. Remove the CD from the drive, and label it. Then reinsert it and ensure that the files have been burned correctly.

NOTE

If you're burning music files to a CD, the procedure is different. See "Burn an Audio CD."

Figure 2-19: Name your CD and choose whether to close the wizard when it has finished.

BURN AN AUDIO CD

To burn an audio CD, follow steps 1 through 4 in the previous section. Then:

1. The wizard asks if you want to make an audio CD. Select the **Make An Audio CD** option button.

2. Click **Next**. The wizard starts Windows Media Player and sends the CD's files to it as a playlist (see Figure 2-20).

3. Rearrange the songs into a better order, if necessary, by dragging them.

4. Click **Copy Music**. Windows Media Player converts any compressed tracks to uncompressed audio, writes them to the CD, and ejects the CD.

5. Remove the CD from the drive, and label it. Then put it back in the drive, and make sure it works.

Figure 2-20: The CD Writing Wizard uses Windows Media Player to create an audio CD.

ERASE A CD-RW DISC

Before you can use a CD-RW disc again, you must erase it.

1. Insert the CD in your CD burner.

2. Click the **Start** button, and click **My Computer** to open a My Computer window.

3. Right-click the icon for the CD burner, and click **Erase This CD-RW**. The CD Writing Wizard starts.

4. Click **Next**. The wizard erases the files from the CD, and then the Completing the CD Writing Wizard dialog box appears.

5. Click **Finish**.

You can then write files to the CD as you did before.

NOTE

To burn DVDs in Windows, you must have a DVD burner and compatible DVD-burning software. Two of the leading DVD-burning programs are Roxio Easy DVD Creator and Nero Ultra 6. Most DVD burners come with DVD-burning programs, but sometimes these programs are stripped-down versions designed to encourage you to buy the full version.

Chapter 3

Connecting to and Using the Internet

The Internet provides a major means of worldwide communications between both individuals and organizations, as well as a major means of locating and sharing information. For many, having access to the Internet is the primary reason for having a computer.

To use the Internet, you must have a connection to it, either through a dial-up connection or a broadband connection. You can then send and receive e-mail, access the World Wide Web, and use Instant Messaging.

Connect to the Internet

You can connect to the Internet using a telephone line, a TV cable, or a satellite link. With a telephone line, you can connect through either a *dial-up* connection or a DSL (digital subscriber line) connection (see comparison in Table 3-1). DSL, cable TV, and satellite connections are called *broadband* connections because of

TABLE 3-1: COMPARISON OF DIAL-UP AND DSL CONNECTIONS

FEATURE	DIAL-UP	DSL
Cost	Average $20/month	Average $40/month
Speed	Up to 53 Kbps* download**, 33 Kbps upload	Most common: 768 Kbps download, 128 Kbps upload
Connection	Dial up every time	Always connected
Use of line	Ties up line, may need a second line for voice or fax	Line can be used for voice and fax while connected to the Internet

Kbps is Kilobits (thousands of bits, 1 or 0) per second
** Download is transferring information from the Internet to your computer

TABLE 3-2: REPRESENTATIVE SPEEDS, COSTS, AND RELIABILITY FOR INTERNET CONNECTIONS

SERVICE	DOWNLOAD SPEED	UPLOAD SPEED	MONTHLY COST	RELIABILITY
Dial-Up	53 Kbps	33-6 Kbps	$20	Fair
DSL	768 Kbps	128 Kbps	$40	Good
Cable Internet	1 Mbps	500 Kbps	$40	Good
Satellite Internet	1 Mbps	150 Kbps	$60	Fair

NOTE

To connect to the Internet, you must have an existing account with an Internet service provider (ISP), and you must know your ISP's phone number for your modem to dial. You also need to know the user name and password for your account. If you want to use Internet mail, you must know your e-mail address, the type of incoming mail server (POP3, IMAP, or HTTP), the names of the incoming and outgoing mail servers, and the name and password for the mail account (these may be the same as those for the ISP account). This information is provided by your ISP when you establish your account.

their higher (than dial-up) speeds and common setup (see comparison in Table 3-2). You must have access to at least one of these forms of communication in order to connect to the Internet. You must also set up the Internet connection.

Set Up Communications

Communications is the physical link between your PC and the Internet. To set up communications, you must first choose between a dial-up and a broadband connection. With a dial-up connection, you must first install and configure a modem.

INSTALL A MODEM

If a modem came with your PC or if one was already installed when you upgraded to Windows XP, your modem should already be installed and you don't need to do anything more. Skip ahead to "Set Up a Dial-Up Connection." Otherwise, to install the modem:

1. For an internal modem, install it in your PC. For an external modem, attach it to your PC via the serial cable or USB (universal serial bus) cable. Most USB modems draw power through the USB cable, while serial modems require their own power supply. Connect the phone line to the modem. If the modem has a power switch, turn it on.

2. Click the **Start** button, and click **Control Panel**. In Category View, click **Printers And Other Hardware**, and then click **Phone And Modem Options**. (In Classic View, double-click **Phone And Modem Options**.) The Phone And Modem Options dialog box appears.

CAUTION

At this writing, there is increasing competition between DSL services offered by telephone companies and cable Internet services offered by TV cable companies. This has caused the DSL side to increase speeds and decrease prices, while the cable side is offering low introductory prices. Do not depend on Table 3-2 to make your final decision. Check your own local services, both DSL and cable, and look at the total cost for a year, not just the low introductory price. Also, get a realistic idea of the actual average speed you should experience. Cable Internet is similar to a party line where everybody shares the same line, so while the line is rated at 3 Mbps, you will seldom, if ever, get that speed. Ask for a written statement of the actual average speed you will see.

NOTE

See Chapter 6 for instructions on upgrading, installing, and configuring hardware.

NOTE

The first time you open Phone And Modem Options dialog box, the Location Information dialog box appears. Select your country, type the area code, specify any carrier code and numbers to dial for accessing an outside line, and choose between tone and pulse dialing. Then click **OK** to display the Phone And Modem Options dialog box.

3. Click the **Modems** tab. If the list shows Unknown Modem, select that and click **Remove**. If the list shows a modem by name, as shown below, XP has identified and installed your modem. Skip to "Set Up a Dial-Up Connection."

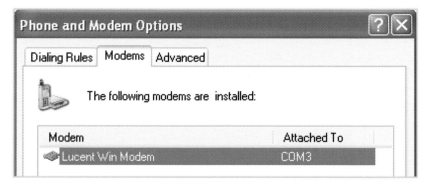

4. Click **Add** to open the Add Hardware Wizard, and click **Next**. If only the correct modem is displayed, skip the next step. If several modems are shown, select the check box for the correct modem, clear the other check boxes, and skip the next step. If the wrong modem or Unknown Modem is shown, select it and click **Change**. If no modem is found, click **Next**.

5. If you have a disk or CD containing XP drivers for your modem, click **Have Disk**, insert the disk, select the drive, click **OK**, select the manufacturer and model, and click **OK**. If you don't have a disk, select **Standard Modem Types** under Manufacturer and the speed of your modem under Model, and then click **Next**.

6. Select the COM (communications) port to which the modem is connected (see the Note), and click **Next**.

7. When the wizard tells you that your modem has been installed successfully, click **Finish** to close the wizard, and then click **OK** to close the Phone And Modem Options dialog box.

Figure 3-1: A dial-up connection requires a user name, password, and phone number.

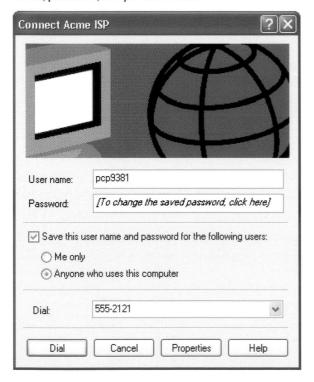

SET UP A DIAL-UP CONNECTION

With a modem installed and working, you can set up a *dial-up connection* that uses the modem to connect via your phone line to a computer at your ISP.

1. If the Control Panel isn't open, click the **Start** button, and then click **Control Panel**. If the Control Panel is open, click **Back**.

2. In Category View, click **Network And Internet Connections**, and then click **Network Connections**. In Classic View, double-click **Network Connections**.

3. Click **Create A New Connection**. The New Connection Wizard starts. Click **Next**.

4. Select the **Connect To The Internet** option button, and click **Next**. Select the **Set Up My Connection Manually** option button (see "Configure an Internet Connection" for other options), and click **Next**. Select the **Connect Using A Dial-Up Modem** option button, and again click **Next**.

5. Type the name for your connection (this can be any name that suits you; descriptive is usually better), and click **Next**. Type the phone number to dial, and again click **Next**.

6. Type the user name and password (twice) given to you by your ISP. (See the Note at the beginning of this chapter on what you need to connect to the Internet.) Choose whether anyone else can use this user name and password and whether this is the default Internet connection. Click **Next**.

7. The wizard tells you that you have successfully set up the dial-up connection. If you would like a shortcut on the desktop so that you can quickly open this connection, select the **Add A Shortcut For This Connection To My Desktop** check box. Click **Finish**. An icon for the connection is displayed in the Network Connections window, and the Connect dialog box appears (see Figure 3-1).

8. Review the information in the Connect dialog box, and then click **Dial**. You should hear your modem dialing and going through the *handshaking* (beeps and pinging sounds) with the equipment at your ISP's end. When the connection is established, XP displays a pop-up message giving the connection speed in the notification area.

9. To disconnect, right-click the connection icon in the notification area, and click **Disconnect**.

NOTE

Sometimes a DSL or TV cable connecting device is called a "modem," but it is not an analog-to-digital converter, which is the major point of a **mo**dulator-**dem**odulator. For this reason, this book doesn't describe DSL and cable connecting devices as modems.

NOTE

Because Internet Explorer comes built into XP and is the default browser, this book assumes that you will use Internet Explorer as your browser.

SET UP A BROADBAND CONNECTION

A broadband connection—which uses a DSL phone line, a TV cable, or a satellite connection—is normally made with a device that connects to your local area network (LAN) and allows several computers on the network to use the connection. (See Chapter 8 for instructions on setting up a network.) With a network set up, your computer connected to the network, and a broadband service connected to the network, your computer is connected to the broadband service. There is nothing else you need to do to set up a broadband connection.

Configure a Connection

You may already have configured your Internet connection in the process of establishing either a dial-up connection or a broadband connection. The easiest way to check that is to try to connect to the Internet by clicking the **Start** button and clicking **Internet**.

If an Internet web page is displayed, your connection is configured and working, and you need do no more. If Internet Explorer doesn't display an Internet web page and you know that your dial-up or broadband and network connections are working properly, you need to configure your Internet connection.

1. If Internet Explorer did not connect to the Internet and the New Connection Wizard did not start, start the New Connection Wizard: click the **Start** button, click **All Programs**, click **Accessories**, click **Communications**, and then click **New Connection Wizard**.

2. Click **Next**, verify that the **Connect To The Internet** option button is selected, and click **Next** again. If you have an ISP you want to use and they have given you a CD, select that option. If you have an ISP but no CD, select the **Set Up My Connection Manually** option button. If you don't have an ISP, select the **Choose From A List Of Internet Service Providers (ISPs)** option button. Whether using the CD option or choosing from a list, follow the instructions on the screen to complete the setup. If you select the manual option, take the following steps to complete the process.

TIP

If you think your modem has been set up properly, yet it is not connecting when you open Internet Explorer, look at the Internet Options in Internet Explorer by clicking the **Tools** menu, clicking **Internet Options**, and then clicking the **Connections** tab. See if you have a dial-up connection specified and that it dials the connection. If not, make the necessary corrections.

3. Choose how you want to connect to the Internet, as shown in Figure 3-2.

- If you will use a modem, leave the **Connect Using A Dial-Up Modem** option button selected, and then click **Next**.

- If you will use a broadband connection (such as DSL or a cable connection), determine whether you have to sign on. If so, select the **Connect Using A Broadband Connection That Requires A User Name And Password** option button, and then click **Next**.

- If you will use an always-on broadband connection, select the **Connect Using A Broadband Connection That Is Always On** option button, click **Next**, click **Finish**, and then skip to step 6.

4. Enter the name of your ISP, which will serve as the name of this connection, and click **Next**. If necessary, enter the phone number of the data connection to your ISP, and click **Next**.

5. Enter the user name and password (twice) given to you by your ISP, choose whether to make this the default Internet connection and whether to use this account name and password for any user of this PC, and click **Next**. You are shown a summary of the connection details. If the details are not correct, click **Back** and make the necessary corrections. When the details are correct, click **Finish**.

6. Click the **Start** button again, and click **Internet**. If prompted, click **Connect** and then click **Dial**. If you still do not connect to the Internet, you may need to reinstall your modem (see "Install a Modem," earlier in this chapter). If you are using a broadband connection, you may need to troubleshoot network problems (see Chapter 8).

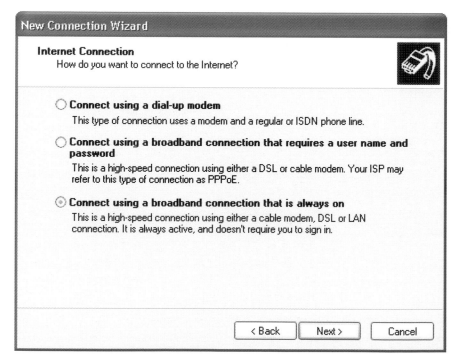

Figure 3-2: Most broadband connections are always on and don't require you to specify a user name and password in the New Connection Wizard.

Use the Web

The *World Wide Web*, usually called simply the *Web*, is the sum of all the web sites in the world. Web sites range from enormous corporate sites (such as IBM's web site), news sites (such as CNN), and online stores (such as Amazon.com) all the way down to minute sites promoting an individual's hobbies, opinions, or skills.

To access the Web, you use a web browser. Most copies of XP come with Microsoft's Internet Explorer web browser built-in and configured as the default browser. This section assumes you have Internet Explorer running. To start Internet Explorer:

● Click the **Start** button, and click **Internet**.

–Or–

● If the Quick Launch toolbar (the icon area next to the Start button)

Launch Internet Explorer Browser
Finds and displays information and Web sites on the Internet.

is displayed, click the **Internet Explorer** icon on the Quick Launch toolbar.

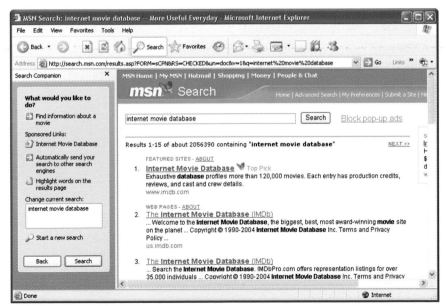

Figure 3-3: The results of a search using Search Companion in Internet Explorer.

Search the Internet

You can search the Internet in two ways: using the search facility built into Internet Explorer and using an independent search facility on the Web.

SEARCH FROM INTERNET EXPLORER

1. In Internet Explorer, click **Search** on the toolbar to open Search Companion.

2. In the text box, type what you want to search for, and click **Search**. The list of matching web sites is shown in the right-hand pane of Internet Explorer. Figure 3-3 shows an example.

3. Click the link of your choice to go to that site.

TIP

When you enter search criteria, place double quotation marks around them to return only results that contain the literal phrase you type. For example, searching for lightbulb jokes returns results that include the words "lightbulb" and "jokes," both together and separately, whereas searching for "lightbulb jokes" returns only results that contain that phrase.

SEARCH FROM AN INTERNET SITE

There are many independent Internet search sites. One of the most popular is Google. To access Google:

1. In Internet Explorer, click the icon to the left of the Address bar to select the current address (as shown here), type www.google.com, and either click **Go** or press **ENTER**.

2. In the text box, type what you want to search for, and click **Google Search**. The list of matching web sites is shown in a full web page, as illustrated in Figure 3-4.

3. Click the link of your choice to go to that site.

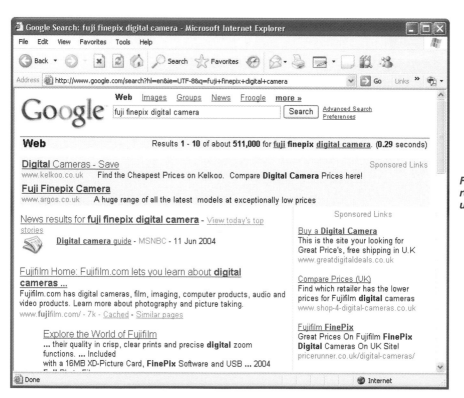

Figure 3-4: The results of a search using Google.

BROWSING THE INTERNET

Browsing the Internet refers to the use of a web browser, such as Internet Explorer, to go from one site to another to see the sites' content. You can browse to a site by directly entering a site address, by clicking a link to a site on another site, or by using the browser controls. First, open your browser by clicking the **Start** button and clicking **Internet**.

GO TO A SITE DIRECTLY

To go directly to a site:

1. Open your browser and click the icon to the left of the Address bar to select the current address.

2. Type the address of the site you want to open, and either click **Go** next to the Address bar or press **ENTER**.

USE SITE NAVIGATION

Site navigation is the use of a combination of links and menus on one web page to locate and open another web page, either on the same site or on another site.

- **Links** can be words, phrases, sentences, or graphics that take you to another page when clicked. Links are often underlined—if not initially, then when you hover the mouse pointer over them. When you move the mouse pointer over a link, the mouse pointer changes to a hand with the forefinger pointing upward.

- **Menus** contain one word or a few words, in either a horizontal or vertical list, that take you to a linked page when you click them. When you move the mouse pointer over a menu, the mouse pointer changes to a hand with the forefinger pointing upward.

Continued...

Access Your Favorite Sites

When you find a web site that you would like to be able to return to quickly, use Internet Explorer's Favorites feature to save it and then easily reopen it.

SAVE A FAVORITE SITE

To add a site to your Favorites list:

1. In Internet Explorer, navigate to the site.

2. Click the **Favorites** menu, and click **Add To Favorites**. The Add Favorite dialog box appears.

3. Edit the name in the text box (or type a new name) so the name will remind you of the site.

4. Click **OK** to add the Favorite.

OPEN A FAVORITE SITE

To open a Favorite site you have saved, click the **Favorites** menu, and click the site you want.

Use the Links Bar

The Links bar allows you to create buttons for sites you frequently access—for example, news or sports sites you go to every day.

ADD A SITE TO THE LINKS BAR

To add a site to your Links bar:

1. In Internet Explorer, navigate to the site you want to add.

2. Drag the icon on the left of the Address bar to the location in the Links bar where you want to place the link.

OPEN A LINK

To open a link, click it on the Links bar in Internet Explorer.

Change Your Home Page

When you first start Internet Explorer, it automatically displays a specific web page called your *home page*. (You can also display your home page by clicking the **Home** icon on the toolbar.) To change your home page:

1. Navigate to the site you want to use as your home page.

2. Click the **Tools** menu, and click **Internet Options**. The Internet Options dialog box appears.

3. On the General tab, under Home Page, click **Use Current**. The web page currently displayed becomes your new home page.

4. Click **OK** to close the Internet Options dialog box.

Access Your Web History

Internet Explorer keeps a history of the web pages you visit so that you can easily return to a site you've visited in the past. You can set the length of time to keep sites in that history; Internet Explorer clears the sites after the period you specify. You can also clear your history manually.

USE THE HISTORY FEATURE TO REVISIT A PAGE

To use the History feature to return to a page you've visited recently:

1. In Internet Explorer, click **History** on the toolbar to open the History pane.

2. Click the day, web site, and web page you want to open, as shown in Figure 3-5.

Figure 3-5: You can use the History feature to find a site or page that you visited in the recent past.

ORGANIZING FAVORITE SITES

If you add many Favorite sites, it can become hard to find easily the one you want. Internet Explorer provides three ways to organize your Favorite sites.

REARRANGE FAVORITES ON THE LIST

The items on your Favorites list are in the order you added them unless you drag them to a new location or sort the list.

- Click the **Favorites** menu, and drag the desired site to the location in the list where you want it to appear.

  –Or–

- Click the **Favorites** menu, right-click an item, and choose **Sort By Name** to sort the list alphabetically.

PUT FAVORITES IN FOLDERS

The Favorites list comes with several default folders installed by XP and by your PC's manufacturer. You can also add further folders for categorizing your Favorites, and you can put sites in folders.

1. In Internet Explorer, navigate to the site you want to add to your Favorites list.

2. Click the **Favorites** menu, and click **Add To Favorites**.

3. Edit the name in the text box as needed, click **Create In**, select the folder to use, and click **OK**.

CREATE NEW FOLDERS

To create your own folders within the Favorites list:

1. In Internet Explorer, click the **Favorites** menu, and click **Organize Favorites**.

2. Click **Create Folder**, type a name for the folder, and press **ENTER**.

3. Drag the desired Favorites to the new folder, and then click **Close**.

SET AND CLEAR HISTORY

You can set the length of time to keep your web history, and you can clear your history manually.

1. In Internet Explorer, click the **Tools** menu, and click **Internet Options**. The Internet Options dialog box appears.

2. On the General tab, use the **Days To Keep Pages In History** spinner to set the number of days. Alternatively, click **Clear History** to clear all your history immediately.

3. Click **OK** to close the Internet Options dialog box.

Copy Internet Information

You'll sometimes find information on the Internet that you want to copy—a picture, some text, or a web page.

COPY A PICTURE FROM A WEB PAGE

To copy a picture from the open web page to your hard drive:

1. Right-click the picture you want to copy, and click **Save Picture As**. The Save Picture dialog box appears.

2. Locate the folder in which you want to save the picture.

3. Click **Save**.

COPY TEXT FROM A WEB PAGE

To copy some text from the open web page to a text editor or word processor:

1. Drag across the text to select it.

2. Right-click the selection, and click **Copy**.

3. Open or switch to the text-editing application (for example, Notepad) or the word processor (for example, Microsoft Word). Open the document in which you want to paste the text.

4. Right-click where you want the text, and click **Paste**.

Open Link
Open Link in New Window
Save Target As...
Print Target

Show Picture
Save Picture As...
E-mail Picture...
Print Picture...
Go to My Pictures
Set as Background
Set as Desktop Item...

Cut
Copy
Copy Shortcut
Paste

Add to Favorites...

Properties

COPY A WEB PAGE FROM THE INTERNET

To store a copy of the open web page on your hard drive:

1. Click the **File** menu, and click **Save As**. The Save Web Page dialog box appears.

2. Select the folder in which to save the page, enter the file name you want to use, and click **Save**.

Play Internet Audio and Video

You can play audio and video files from the Internet directly from a link on a web page or by using the separate Windows Media Player program.

Many web pages have links to audio and video files, such as those shown in the Yahoo! Movies page in Figure 3-9. To play such a file, simply click its link. If you have more than one audio or video player installed, Internet Explorer asks you which player you want to use. Make that choice, and the player opens and plays the requested file.

For instructions on playing Internet radio and other audio with Windows Media Player, see Chapter 5.

Figure 3-9: Click an audio or video link on a web page to play the audio or video file.

CONTROLLING INTERNET SECURITY

Internet Explorer allows you to control several aspects of Internet security to help keep your browsing sessions safe. To configure security settings, open the Internet Options dialog box by clicking the **Tools** menu and clicking **Internet Options**.

CATEGORIZE WEB SITES

Internet Explorer allows you to categorize web sites into four zones: Internet (sites that are not classified in one of the other ways), Local Intranet, Trusted Sites, and Restricted Sites, as shown in Figure 3-6.

From the Internet Options dialog box:

1. Click the **Security** tab. Click the **Internet** zone. Note its definition.

2. Click **Custom Level**. Select the elements in this zone that you want to disable, enable, or be prompted for before using. Alternatively, select the level of security you want for this zone (High, Medium, Medium-Low, or Low), and click **Reset**. Click **OK** when you're finished.

3. Click each of the other zones where you can identify either groups or individual sites to place in a particular zone.

HANDLE COOKIES

Cookies are small files containing text data that web sites store on your computer so that they can identify your PC when you return to the web site. Cookies have a positive side: they can save you from having to enter your name and ID frequently. Many e-commerce web sites (sites where you can execute a payment transaction over the Web) require cookies for their shopping carts and payment mechanisms to work at all.

Continued…

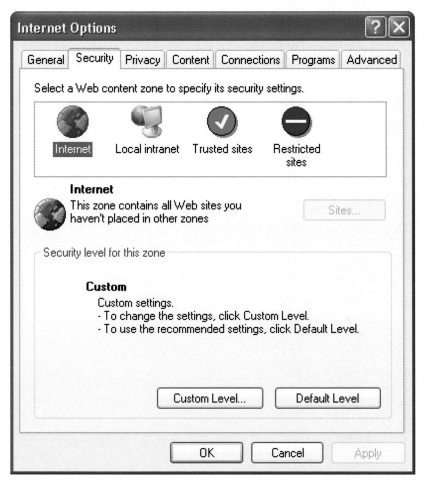

Figure 3-6: You can increase your security by using the controls on the Security tab of the Internet Options dialog box to categorize web sites into security zones.

CONTROLLING INTERNET SECURITY *(Continued)*

Cookies can also be dangerous, enabling web sites to identify you when you do not want them to be able to do so and potentially letting outsiders access sensitive information on your PC. Internet Explorer lets you determine the types and sources of cookies you will allow and what those cookies can do on your PC (see Figure 3-7).

From the Internet Options dialog box:

1. Click the **Privacy** tab. Select a privacy setting by dragging the slider up or down.

2. Click **Advanced** to open the Advanced Privacy Settings dialog box. If you want, select the **Override Automatic Cookie Handling** check box, and choose the settings you want to use.

3. Click **OK** to return to the Internet Options dialog box.

CONTROL CONTENT

You can control the amount of bad language, nudity, sex, and violence that Internet Explorer displays. These content controls work only for sites that have ratings; be aware that many sites do not have ratings, no matter how offensive their content.

From the Internet Options dialog box:

1. Click the **Content** tab. Click **Enable** to open the Content Advisor dialog box (see Figure 3-8).

2. Select the category you want to affect, and drag the slider to the level you want to allow. Repeat for the other categories.

3. Click **OK** to close the Content Advisor dialog box.

Continued...

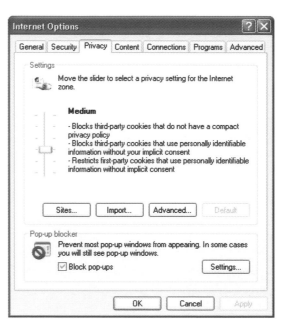

Figure 3-7: Determine how you will handle cookies that web sites want to store on your PC.

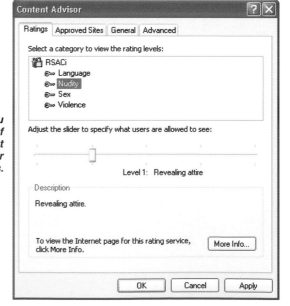

Figure 3-8: You can set the level of offensive content allowed in four categories.

Use E-Mail

E-mail has been described as the "killer application" for the Internet—the feature for which users feel they simply must have Internet access. XP includes Outlook Express, a powerful e-mail application.

Establish an E-Mail Account

To send and receive e-mail, you must set up an e-mail account with an ISP and configure Outlook Express to use that account. The section, "Configure an Internet Connection," earlier in this chapter, discussed how to set up an account with an ISP and listed the information you need, including:

- Your e-mail address
- The type of mail server the ISP uses (POP3, IMAP, or HTTP)
- The addresses of the incoming and outgoing mail servers
- The user name and password for your Internet account or e-mail account

After obtaining this information and establishing your Internet connection, set up your e-mail account in Outlook Express.

1. Click the **Start** button, and click **E-Mail**. (If **Outlook Express** is not your default e-mail program, click the **Start** button, select **All Programs**, and click **Outlook Express**) Outlook Express launches the Internet Connection Wizard so that you can enter your details.

2. Type the name you want people to see in your messages, and then click **Next**.

3. Type your e-mail address, and click **Next**.

4. Select the type of mail server used by your ISP, type the addresses of your ISP's incoming and outgoing mail servers, and click **Next**.

5. Type your account name and password, and specify whether you want Outlook Express to remember your password so that you don't have to enter it each time you sign on to the mail server. Click **Next**, and then click **Finish**.

Use the next three sections—"Create and Send E-Mail," "Receive E-Mail," and "Respond to E-Mail"—to test your setup.

NOTE

If Outlook Express detects another e-mail program on your PC, it prompts you to import your messages and Address Book from that program. If you're switching from that other e-mail program to Outlook Express, you will typically want to import your messages and Address Book into Outlook Express so that you can use them.

Create and Send E-Mail

To create and send an e-mail message:

1. Open **Outlook Express** and click **Create Mail** on the toolbar. The New Message window opens, similar to the one in Figure 3-10.

2. Start typing a name in the **To** text box. If your Address Book contains a match for the name (see the QuickSteps "Using the Address Book" in this chapter), Outlook Express will suggest the match, and you can accept the suggestion by pressing **ENTER**. If Outlook Express doesn't suggest a match or if the suggested match is wrong, type the rest of the e-mail address.

3. To send the message to more than one primary addressee, type a semicolon (;) after the first addressee, and then type a second address, as in step 2.

4. To send the message to secondary addressees for whom the message is intended as information, press **TAB**, and then type the second addressee (and, if necessary, subsequent addressees) in the Cc text box, just as you did in the To text box.

5. Press **TAB** to move the insertion point to the Subject text box. Type the subject, press **TAB** to move the insertion point to the message box, and type your message.

6. When you have completed your message, click **Send**. If you've finished working with Outlook Express, close it.

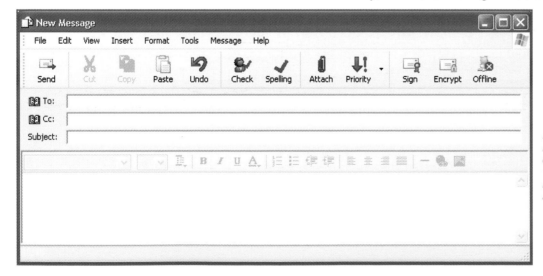

Figure 3-10: Sending an e-mail message is a swift and easy way to communicate with people who may not be online at the same time as you.

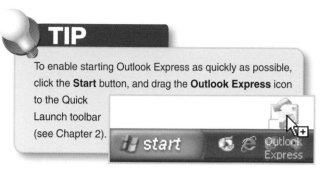

Receive E-Mail

Depending on how Outlook Express is set up, it may automatically download any e-mail that has been sent to you when you establish a connection to your ISP. If not, or if you need to establish a dial-up connection to your ISP manually, do so and then click **Send/Recv**.

In any case, Outlook Express will place the e-mail you receive in your Inbox. To open and read your e-mail:

1. Open **Outlook Express** and click **Inbox** in the Folders list to open your Inbox, which contains all of the messages that you have received and haven't yet deleted. (Depending on your configuration, Outlook Express may display the Inbox by default when it opens.)

2. Click a message in the Inbox to read it in the Preview pane at the bottom of the window, or double-click a message to open the message in its own window, as shown in Figure 3-11.

3. Print or delete a message in either the Inbox or its own window by clicking the appropriate button on the toolbar. Close Outlook Express if you have finished working with it.

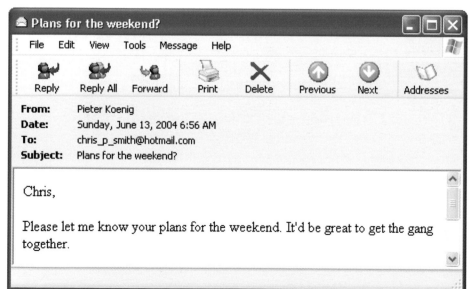

Figure 3-11: You can read messages in the Preview pane in the Inbox, but you can see more of a message by opening it in its own window.

Normally, the contents of your Inbox are sorted by date, with the oldest message at the top and the most recent message at the bottom. You can sort your Inbox by any of the columns by clicking the column heading. The first time you click, the column is sorted in ascending order (alphabetically, earliest date first, or smallest number first). The second time you click, the column is sorted in descending order (reverse alphabetically, latest date first, or largest number first).

From	/	Subject
✉ **Hotmail Staff**		**Welcome to MSN Hotmail**
Pieter Koenig		Plans for the weekend?

Not all e-mail programs can successfully receive HTML messages, so some recipients may receive versions of your messages that are hard to read. Most e-mail programs released since 2000 can send and receive HTML without problems.

Respond to E-Mail

You can respond to messages you receive in three ways by first clicking the message in your Inbox and then:

- Clicking **Reply** to send a response to just the person who sent the original message

- Clicking **Reply All** to send a response to all the addressees (both To and Cc) in the original message

- Clicking **Forward** to relay a message to people not shown as addressees of the original message

When you take any of these actions, Outlook Express displays a window similar to the New message window, in which you can add or change addressees and the subject, and add a message. Click **Send** when you have completed the reply or forwarded message and are ready to send it.

Apply Formatting to Messages

The simplest e-mail messages are sent in plain text—text without any formatting. These messages are compact, so they take minimal bandwidth, can be received quickly, and can be received and read by e-mail programs that don't support formatting.

If you want, you can send messages that are formatted using HTML (Hypertext Markup Language), the formatting language used to create most web sites. You can use formatting either for a single message or for all the messages you send.

APPLY FORMATTING TO AN INDIVIDUAL MESSAGE

To apply formatting to an individual message you're creating in Outlook Express, click the **Format** menu, and click **Rich Text (HTML)**.

APPLY FORMATTING TO ALL MESSAGES

To apply formatting to all messages you create in Outlook Express:

USING THE ADDRESS BOOK

The Address Book, shown in Figure 3-12, allows you to collect addresses and other information about your contacts, the people with whom you correspond or otherwise interact. To open the Address Book, click **Addresses** on the Outlook Express toolbar.

ADD A NEW ADDRESS

To add a new address to the Address Book:

1. Click **New** on the toolbar, and click **New Contact**. The Properties dialog box for the contact appears.

2. Enter as much of the information that you have that you want to store. For e-mail, you must enter a name and an e-mail address. You can have several e-mail addresses for each contact. Type each e-mail address in the E-Mail Address text box, and then click **Add**.

3. After entering the information, click **OK** to close the Properties dialog box for the contact.

   –Or–

   Right-click an e-mail address in an e-mail message, and click **Add To Address Book**. This creates a new contact and opens the Properties dialog box so that you can add such further information as you have about the contact.

ADD A GROUP OF ADDRESSES

To add a group of addresses that you want to be able to send a single message to:

1. Click **New** on the toolbar, and click **New Group**. The Properties dialog box for the group appears.

2. Type the group name, and click **Select Members**. The Select Group Members dialog box appears. Use the controls in the dialog box to select contacts in the Address Book and add them to the group.

3. After adding contacts to the group, click **OK** to close the Select Group Members dialog box, and click **OK**.

4. Click **Close** to close the Address Book.

1. Click the **Tools** menu, and click **Options**. The Options dialog box appears.

2. Click the **Send** tab.

3. Click **HTML** under Mail Sending Format.

4. Click **OK**.

CONVERT A FORMATTED MESSAGE TO PLAIN TEXT

After starting a formatted message, to convert it to plain text:

1. In the New Message window, click the **Format** menu, and click **Plain Text**.

2. In the dialog box warning you that you will lose any current formatting, click **OK**.

SELECT A FONT AND A COLOR FOR ALL MESSAGES

To use a particular font and font color on all HTML messages you send:

1. In Outlook Express, click the **Tools** menu, and click **Options**.

2. Click the **Compose** tab. In the Compose Font area, click **Font Settings** opposite Mail.

3. Select the font, style, size, effects, and color that you want to use for all your messages, and then click **OK**.

4. Click **OK** to close the Options dialog box.

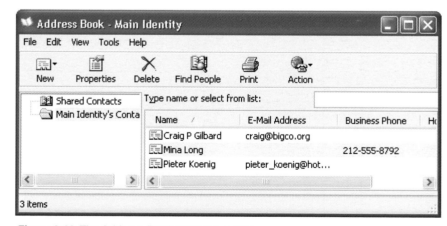

Figure 3-12: The Address Book provides a place to store information about your contacts.

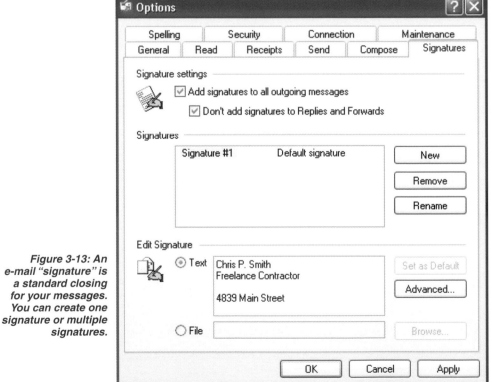

TIP

If you have several e-mail accounts, you may want to use a different signature for each account. Select the first signature, and click **Advanced** on the Signatures tab of the Options dialog box. The Advanced Signature Settings dialog box appears. Select the accounts for which to use this signature, and click **OK**. Repeat the process for your other signatures.

ATTACH A SIGNATURE

To attach a *signature,* or canned closing, to all of the e-mail messages you send:

1. In Outlook Express, click the **Tools** menu, and click **Options**.

2. Click the **Signatures** tab (see Figure 3-13), and click **New**. Under Edit Signature, type the signature text you want to use; or click **File**, browse to the file that contains the text for the signature, click the file, and click **Open**.

3. Click **Add Signatures To All Outgoing Messages**. Ensure that **Don't Add Signatures To Replies And Forwards** is selected so that replies and forwarded messages you send do not receive a signature.

4. Click **OK**.

Figure 3-13: An e-mail "signature" is a standard closing for your messages. You can create one signature or multiple signatures.

Options

Spelling	Security	Connection	Maintenance
General	Read	Receipts	Send	Compose	Signatures

Signature settings

☑ Add signatures to all outgoing messages

☑ Don't add signatures to Replies and Forwards

Signatures

Signature #1	Default signature

New
Remove
Rename

Edit Signature

◉ Text

Chris P. Smith
Freelance Contractor

4839 Main Street

Set as Default
Advanced...

○ File

Browse...

OK   Cancel   Apply

Attach Files to Messages

You can attach and send files, such as documents or pictures, with e-mail messages.

1. In Outlook Express, click **Create Mail** on the toolbar to open a new message.

2. Click **Attach** to display the Insert Attachment dialog box. Select the file you want to send, and click **Attach**.

Attach

3. Address, type, and send the message as you normally would.

Receive Attached Files

When someone sends you a file attached to a message, you can save the file:

1. Open your **Inbox**.

2. Click the message in the message list so that it appears in the preview pane.

3. Click the **paper clip** icon at the right end of the bar above the preview pane, and click **Save Attachments** to display the Save Attachments dialog box.

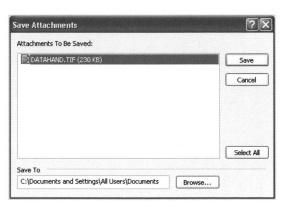

4. Verify that the folder in the Save To box is the location where you want to save the file. If necessary, change it by clicking **Browse**, selecting the folder you want, and clicking **OK**.

5. Click the file in the Attachments To Be Saved list, and then click **Save**.

NOTE

Microsoft also makes MSN Messenger, another instant-messaging program. MSN Messenger is a little different from Windows Messenger, but the two programs can exchange messages. Whether they can also send and receive audio and video and share applications depends on the versions of both programs involved.

Use Instant Messaging

Windows Messenger is an application for *instant messaging*, or *IM*—instantly sending and receiving messages with one or more people who are online at the same time as you. Instant messaging is often referred to as "chat" or "online chat," and the people with whom you chat are called your "contacts."

Beyond text messages, Windows Messenger also lets you have audio-only or audio-and-video conversations with one contact at a time, providing an inexpensive form of telephony and videoconferencing.

Set Up Windows Messenger

Windows Messenger is installed automatically with XP. Depending on which version of XP you have, Windows Messenger may automatically start when

you start XP, or it may display the Windows Messenger dialog box, shown here, either the first time you start XP or the first time you run Windows Messenger manually. If you want to use Windows Messenger, select the **Allow Windows Messenger To Connect To The Internet** option button, and click **OK**.

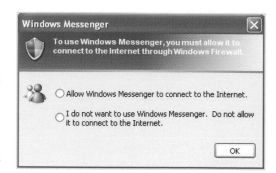

ESTABLISH A PASSPORT

To use Windows Messenger, you must have an online account called a Microsoft Passport. You create a Microsoft Passport automatically when you set up a Hotmail account or an MSN account, so if you have one of these accounts, you already have a Microsoft Passport. If you don't have a Microsoft Passport, Windows Messenger walks you through the process of acquiring one.

1. Click the **Start** button, click **All Programs**, and click **Windows Messenger**.

2. Click the **Click Here To Sign In** link to start the .NET Passport Wizard. Click **Next**.

3. If you already have an e-mail account, click the **Yes** option button; otherwise, either go to "Establish an E-Mail Account," earlier in this chapter, and establish an e-mail address before completing the .NET Passport Wizard, or click the **No. I Would Like To Open An MSN Hotmail E-mail Account** option button, and work through the process of opening an MSN Hotmail account.

4. If you already have a Microsoft Passport, click the **Yes. I Want To Sign In With My Passport** option button, and click **Next**. Skip to step 6.

NOTE

Windows Messenger doesn't normally create a permanent record of your chats, but you can save a chat by clicking the **File** menu, clicking **Save As**, specifying the location and file name, and then clicking **Save**.

If you chose not to associate your Microsoft Passport with your XP user account, you must enter your Passport details manually each time you sign in to Windows Messenger.

5. If you don't have a Microsoft Passport, click the **No. I Want To Register My E-Mail Address With Passport Now** option button, and click **Next** twice. Enter the information requested, click **Agree**, and when you are told you have successfully registered your e-mail address, close your browser. You are returned to the .NET Passport Wizard. Click **Back**, click **Yes. I Want To Sign In With My Passport**, and click **Next**.

6. Enter your e-mail address and your Microsoft Passport password, and then click **Next**.

7. If you want XP to automatically use your Microsoft Passport to sign you into web sites that use Passport, select the **Associate My Passport With My Windows User Account** check box. If you prefer to log in manually, clear this check box. Click **Next**.

8. Click **Finish** to close the wizard.

SIGN IN TO WINDOWS MESSENGER

With your Microsoft Passport established, you can sign in to Windows Messenger by clicking the **Click Here To Sign In** link in the Windows Messenger window.

ADD CONTACTS TO WINDOWS MESSENGER

The first time you sign in to Windows Messenger, your contacts list will be empty, as in Figure 3-14. You must add contacts in order to communicate with them.

1. Click **Add A Contact** in the tasks pane at the bottom of the Windows Messenger window to start the Add A Contact wizard. If you know your contact's e-mail address, select the **By E-Mail Address Or Sign-In Name** option button, and click **Next**. Enter the e-mail address, and click **Next**. Depending on the person's status, different things will occur:

   - If the person has a Microsoft Passport, you will be told you were successful in establishing the contact.

   - If the person is logged on to Windows Messenger, you will be told you can chat with the contact.

   - If the person isn't logged on, you will be told you can send an e-mail message asking your contact to sign on.

   - If the person doesn't have a Microsoft Passport, you will be told you can send an e-mail message telling your contact about Passport and how he or she can get one.

2. In any of the preceding cases, click **Next**, add your own message to the canned message, and click **Finish** to close the Add A Contact wizard.

3. If you don't know your contact's e-mail address, click the **Search For A Contact** option button, and click **Next**. Enter the required information as best you can, and click **Next**. If there is more than one person who fits your criteria, select the correct one, and click **Next**. You are told the person was found, but you cannot immediately add him or her to your contact list due to the privacy policy. You can send the person an e-mail message by clicking **Next**, typing your message, and clicking **Finish** to close the Add A Contact wizard.

When you add a contact, the contact receives a message. Similarly, when someone else adds you to his or her contact list, Windows Messenger lets you choose whether to allow the person to contact you or block the person from contacting you, as shown here. You can also choose whether to add the person to your contact list.

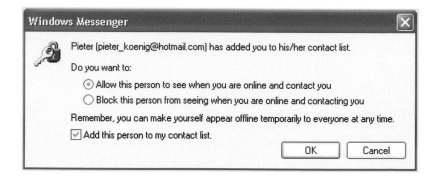

Figure 3-14: You must add contacts to Windows Messenger before you can communicate with other people.

3

PERSONALIZING MESSENGER

Windows Messenger offers many configuration options. To display the Options dialog box, click the **Tools** menu, and click **Options** (see Figure 3-15).

PERSONAL TAB OPTIONS

Type your name as you want it to appear, and choose the font used for your instant messages.

PHONE TAB OPTIONS

Add any phone numbers—home, work, or cellular—that you want your contacts to be able to view.

PREFERENCES TAB OPTIONS

This tab contains the most important settings:

- Whether XP starts Windows Messenger automatically when you log on
- Whether Windows Messenger runs in the background when you close its window or whether it signs you out and stops running
- Whether and how quickly Windows Messenger changes your status to Away
- Whether Windows Messenger can receive messages using Microsoft's handwriting technology, Ink
- Whether Windows Messenger displays alerts and plays sounds when your contacts come online or send you messages
- Whether running a program full-screen blocks alerts and sets your status to Busy
- The folder in which Windows Messenger stores files other people send you

Continued...

Send and Receive Instant Messages

You can send and receive text messages and files with several contacts at a time, either in the same conversation or in separate conversations. You can have only one audio or audio-and-video chat at a time and only with one contact.

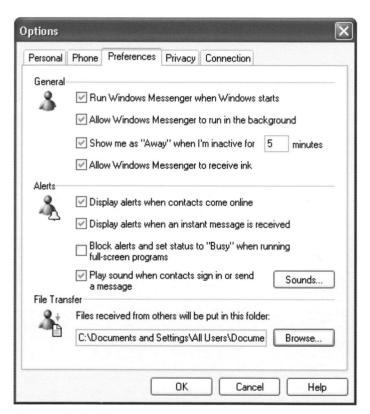

Figure 3-15: The Windows Messenger Options dialog box includes options for controlling when and how Windows Messenger runs, who can contact you and who is blocked, and which of your phone numbers you share with your contacts.

PERSONALIZING WINDOWS MESSENGER *(Continued)*

PRIVACY TAB OPTIONS

This tab enables you to control who can contact you and what actions Windows Messenger can take on your behalf:

- Use the **My Allow List** and **My Block List** to control which contacts can see your online status and send you messages.

- Choose whether to be alerted when other people add you to their contact list.

- Choose whether to enter your password manually when a web site requests your Microsoft Passport or allow Windows Messenger and XP to supply it automatically (the default).

- Choose whether to block Windows Messenger from downloading extra tabs (add-on features).

CONNECTION TAB OPTIONS

Windows Messenger automatically detects your Internet connection, so you shouldn't need to change the options on this tab unless Windows Messenger doesn't work. (In this case, ask your network administrator which settings to choose.) The message "You are currently connected to .NET Messenger Service using a direct connection (no firewall)" on this tab is poorly phrased. It doesn't mean that Windows Firewall has stopped working.

SEND A MESSAGE TO A CONTACT

To send a message to a contact who is online:

1. Double-click the contact to open a Conversation window.

2. Type a message in the text box. To add an emoticon, or "smiley," click **Emoticons** and then click the emoticon in the drop-down list.

3. Press ENTER or click **Send**.

4. If your contact replies, the Conversation window shows who said what (see Figure 3-16).

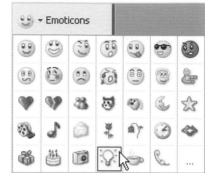

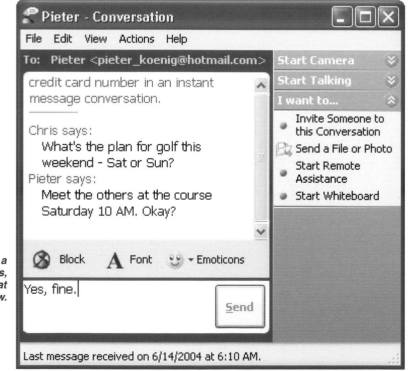

Figure 3-16: When a conversation is in progress, you can see who said what in the Conversation window.

RECEIVE A MESSAGE

When a contact tries to start a conversation with you, Windows Messenger displays a pop-up window above the notification area. Click this pop-up window to open the Conversation window with the contact so that you can reply.

SEND A FILE

To send a file to a contact you're chatting with:

- Drag the file from a Windows Explorer window (or the desktop) to the Conversation window.

  –Or–

- Click **Send A File Or Photo** in the I Want To list, select the file in the resulting Send A File dialog box, and click **Open**.

Whichever method you use, your contact receives a message that you want to send the file. Your contact can choose whether to accept the file or reject it.

RECEIVE A FILE

When a contact sends you a file, Windows Messenger prompts you to accept it or decline it. Click the appropriate link. If you choose to receive it, Windows Messenger receives the file and displays a link that you can click to access it directly.

HAVE AN AUDIO CONVERSATION

If your PC includes a sound card, speakers, and a microphone, you can have an audio conversation over the Internet with one of your contacts.

- From an existing Conversation window with that contact, click **Start Talking**.

  –Or–

- To start a new conversation, click **Start A Voice Conversation** in the main Windows Messenger window, select the contact, and click **OK**.

NOTE

If Windows Messenger displays a warning that files may contain harmful viruses or scripts, read the message, ensure you've taken adequate precautions, select the **Don't Show Me This Message Again** check box, and click **OK**.

NOTE

Files you receive via Windows Messenger are stored in the folder specified under File Transfer on the Preferences tab of the Options dialog box (click the **Tools** menu, and click **Options**). The default folder is My Documents\My Received Files.

NOTE

The first time you have an audio or video conversation, you must complete the Audio And Video Tuning Wizard (which starts automatically) to make sure that your PC is configured correctly for audio and/or video.

CAUTION

Application sharing and the Whiteboard use an older Microsoft communications program called NetMeeting. When you try to use either of these capabilities, XP may display a Security Alert dialog box telling you that Windows Firewall has blocked the program from receiving unsolicited information. Click **Unblock This Program**, and click **OK**.

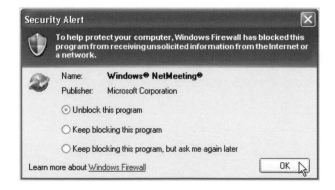

HAVE AN AUDIO-AND-VIDEO CONVERSATION

If your PC has a video camera or web cam as well as a sound card, speakers, and a microphone, you can have an audio-and-video conversation over the Internet with one of your contacts.

- From an existing Conversation window with that contact, click **Start Camera**.

  –Or–

- To start a new conversation, click **Start A Video Conversation** in the main Windows Messenger window, select the contact, and click **OK**.

SHARE AN APPLICATION OR A WHITEBOARD

You can share an application with one or more contacts in an existing conversation by clicking **Start Application Sharing**. For example, to work with your associates on a budget workbook, you could open the workbook in Excel and then share Excel via application sharing so that your colleagues could see it and work with you on it. Only the computer that's sharing the application must have the application installed. In this example, your associates wouldn't need to have Excel on their PCs to be able to work with you.

Windows Messenger also enables you to share its Whiteboard with other users. Whiteboard is an enhanced version of the Microsoft Paint accessory application (which is discussed in Chapter 5) with which you can draw or display pictures with annotations. To start sharing the Whiteboard, click **Start Whiteboard**. You can then use the Whiteboard to brainstorm, share pictures, or sketch out ideas during your conversation.

Chapter 4

Installing and Using Programs

Once you've got your PC set up and configured the way you want, you're likely to spend most of your time using programs to accomplish tasks. As discussed in the previous chapter, Windows XP comes with programs for accessing the Internet, sending e-mail, and other functions. For other tasks, you can use the programs that come with XP or install other software.

This chapter introduces you to some of the capabilities that you'll find built into XP and the programs that come with it. The chapter also describes the ways in which you're most likely to want to go beyond these capabilities and suggests how to find software that will help you to do so.

Run and Stop Programs

The standard way of running a program is to click the **Start** button, locate the item for the program you want to run, and click the item. You can also start a program in several other ways.

NOTE

When you try to open a program using the Run dialog box, XP searches through a preset list of folders for the program. If XP can't find the program, it displays an error message instead of running the program. When this happens, you need to type the folder path before the program name. You can type the path anyway if you prefer, but usually it's easiest to type just the program name unless XP displays the error message.

TIP

You can use the Run dialog box to open folders, documents, and URLs (Internet addresses) as well as programs.

Figure 4-1: The Command Prompt window enables you to run text-only programs and older programs, and also execute commands that you type.

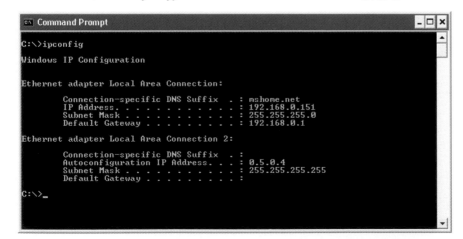

Run a Program Using Run

XP includes various system tools that don't have Start menu items because you're meant to run them only in special circumstances. For example, the program Msconfig controls what happens during the Windows startup process (see Chapter 10). To run such programs, use the Run dialog box.

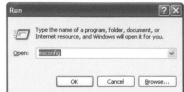

1. Click the **Start** button, and click **Run**. The Run dialog box appears.

2. Type the name of the program, and press **ENTER**.

Run a Program from the Command Prompt

Some of XP's system programs, and some older programs, need to be run from the Command Prompt window. For example, Ipconfig lets you examine the details of your network connection (see Chapter 8). To run such a program:

1. Click the **Start** button, click **All Programs**, click **Accessories**, and then click **Command Prompt**. The Command Prompt window opens (see Figure 4-1).

2. Type the program name, and press **ENTER**. The program runs or opens.

3. When you have finished using the Command Prompt window, click its **Close** button to close it.

Stop a Program

To stop a program:

● Click the **Close** button in the upper-right corner of the window.

–Or–

● Click the **File** menu, and then click **Exit**.

–Or–

● Press **ALT+F4**.

SWITCHING AMONG PROGRAMS

You can switch among your open (started) programs by clicking a window, using the taskbar, or "CoolSwitching," pressing the **ALT+TAB** key combination.

SWITCH PROGRAMS BY CLICKING A WINDOW

If you can see the program to which you want to switch, click its window to make it active.

SWITCH PROGRAMS USING THE TASKBAR

Click the taskbar button for the window you want to make active.

If the window's button has been collapsed into a group of similar buttons to enable the buttons to fit on the taskbar at a readable size, click the group button, and then click the window you want.

SWITCH PROGRAMS USING THE KEYBOARD

To switch programs using the keyboard, use the "CoolSwitch," or **ALT+TAB** method.

1. Hold down **ALT** and press **TAB**. The task list is displayed.

   D:\Documents and Settings\All Users\Docume...

2. Still holding down **ALT**, keep pressing **TAB** until you select the program you want.

3. Release **ALT**. XP makes the selected program active.

Meet XP's Included Programs

XP comes with a set of programs that can take care of basic computing needs. Because these programs are supplied with most copies of XP, it can be hard to distinguish which are features of XP and which are separate programs. For example, while Windows Explorer (discussed in Chapter 2) is considered a built-in and irremovable component of XP, and Internet Explorer (discussed in Chapter 3) is considered a built-in but substitutable component, programs such as Outlook Express and Windows Messenger (both discussed in Chapter 3) are considered separate programs. The main difference is that it's possible for your PC manufacturer to have substituted different programs for Internet Explorer, Outlook Express, Windows Media Player and Windows Messenger.

Table 4-1 lists the programs you're likely to find included on a PC running XP.

TABLE 4-1: PROGRAMS INCLUDED WITH XP

NAME	USE	DISCUSSED IN
Address Book	Store addresses and other contact details	Chapter 3
Calculator	Perform basic or scientific calculations	Chapter 4
Command Prompt	Issue advanced commands	Chapter 4
Notepad	Create and edit text documents without formatting	Chapter 4
Paint	Create and edit pictures	Chapter 5
Windows Movie Maker	Import video from a DV camcorder, edit it, and create your own movies	Chapter 5
WordPad	Create and edit text documents with simple formatting and objects (such as pictures)	Chapter 4
Windows Media Player	Play CDs, digital audio, video, and DVDs; listen to Internet radio; burn CDs	Chapter 5
Windows Messenger	Send and receive instant messages and files; hold video and audio chats; share applications	Chapter 3
Backup	Back up data for safekeeping and restore it after disaster strikes	Chapter 7
Character Map	Insert special characters in documents you create using other programs	Chapter 4
MSN Explorer	Access the Internet, Web, and e-mail through an integrated interface	Not discussed

Create Text Documents

Whether you use your PC for work or play, you're likely to want to create text documents: business proposals, memos, letters, schedules, recipes—anything from a few words up to many hundred pages.

Choose a Word Processor

XP includes two tools for creating text documents:

- Notepad (shown on the left in Figure 4-2) is a *text editor*—a program for creating and editing files that contain only unformatted text. Notepad is good for writing quick notes but not for creating documents that require formatting.

- WordPad (shown on the right in Figure 4-2) is a simple *word processor*—a program for creating documents that include limited formatting. WordPad documents can contain *objects*, or items created in other programs, such as pictures, charts, sounds, or video clips.

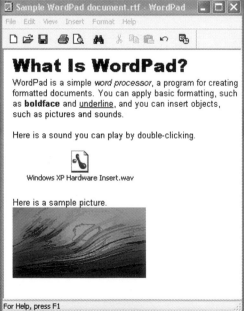

If you create more than even a few documents, you'll probably need a more advanced word processor than WordPad. The main word processors to consider are:

Figure 4-2: Notepad (on the left) can create only unformatted-text documents, while WordPad (on the right) can create documents with formatting, pictures, and inserted objects.

Figure 4-3: A full-featured word processor, such as Microsoft Word, enables you to create a wide variety of text documents.

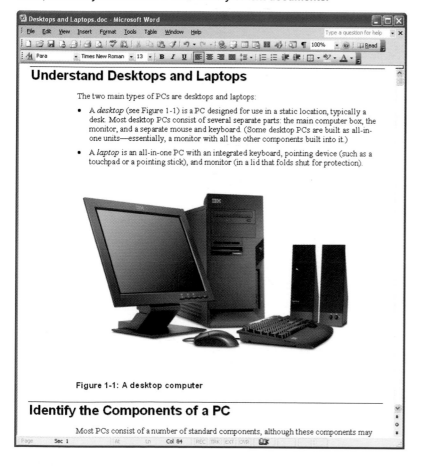

• **Microsoft Word** is the industry-standard word processor for Windows. Word (see Figure 4-3) offers a full set of features and is widely used. You can buy Word on its own, but it's prohibitively expensive. Instead, look for Word bundled with Microsoft Works, a basic suite of programs suitable for home or light office use, or buy Word as part of Microsoft Office, Microsoft's industry-leading productivity suite. Several versions of Microsoft Office are available with different sets of programs—for instance, Microsoft Office Professional Edition includes the Access database program, which is typically used only in business settings. If you are a student or teacher, you may qualify for an academic edition of Office at a considerable discount.

• **Lotus Word Pro** is a word processor from IBM's Lotus division. Word Pro is part of Lotus SmartSuite, a productivity suite that competes with Microsoft Office. Word Pro is a powerful word processor, and SmartSuite is typically less expensive than Microsoft Office, but most people find neither a compelling buy unless SmartSuite comes bundled with a new PC. (This is most likely to happen when you buy an IBM PC.)

• **Corel WordPerfect** is the latest version of WordPerfect, the leading word processor of the late 1980s. WordPerfect is the linchpin product in Corel WordPerfect Office, another productivity suite that competes with Microsoft Office. WordPerfect is a powerful word processor, and WordPerfect Office is usually around half the price of Microsoft Office. Some PC manufacturers bundle WordPerfect Office with their PCs.

• **OpenOffice.org** is a freeware productivity suite that includes a word processor (called Writer), a spreadsheet (called Calc), a presentation program (called Impress), a drawing program (called Draw), and database connectivity tools. OpenOffice.org has fewer features and less polish than Word, but it offers enough features to meet most home and many business needs. You can download OpenOffice.org from the OpenOffice.org web site, www.openoffice.org.

• **Sun StarOffice** is a productivity suite based on OpenOffice.org but sold and supported as commercial software. Like OpenOffice.org, StarOffice has fewer features and less polish than Word (and the other Microsoft Office applications), but it offers enough features to meet most home and many business needs. StarOffice is much less expensive than Microsoft Office and comes bundled with some inexpensive PCs.

UNDERSTANDING FREEWARE AND SHAREWARE

Commercial software is relatively straightforward: you pay for either a shrink-wrapped box or a file that you download. You then have certain limited rights to install the software on one or more computers (depending on what you bought). A typical commercial software package offers a limited amount of support but no compensation for any loss of data incurred if the software doesn't work the way it's supposed to.

Some software authors choose to share the fruits of their labors with other people for free. The programs they create are called *freeware*, and you can use them freely without paying. Some authors ask you to make a donation toward their costs if you like the program; such software is sometimes called *donationware*.

Other software authors provide full or lightly restricted versions of their software for download and evaluation. If you like the software enough to keep using it, you're supposed to pay the author for it (and you may have to pay in order for it to keep working). Such software is called *shareware* and is a popular way for software authors to distribute their work without incurring the large costs associated with commercial production.

TIP

WordPad doesn't offer the Close command, but you can close the open document without closing WordPad by starting a new document: click the **File** menu, click **New**, choose the document type in the **New** dialog box, and click **OK**.

Create a Text Document

Whichever word processor you use, the process of creating a text document is the same. This example uses WordPad.

1. Start the word processor. To open WordPad, click the **Start** button, click **All Programs**, click **Accessories**, and then click **WordPad**.

2. Most word processors automatically open a new blank document when you start them. If necessary, click the **File** menu, and click **New** to create a new document.

3. Enter the text of your document by typing it or copying it from another source and pasting it into your document.

4. Insert any other objects your document needs. For example, in WordPad, you might insert pictures or sounds.

5. Format the document using the available formatting options. For example, in WordPad, you can select the font and the font size; make text bold, italic, underlined, or a particular color; and apply left, center, or right alignment to any paragraph.

6. When you want to save the document, click the **File** menu, and click **Save**. The Save As dialog box appears. Choose the location, type the name for the file, and click **Save**.

7. You can view how the document will look when it is printed. Click the **File** menu, and click **Print Preview** to preview the document for gross layout errors. Press **ESC** to cancel the preview.

8. Print the document by clicking the **File** menu, and clicking **Print**. The Print dialog box appears. Choose your printing options, and then click **Print**.

9. In Word Pad, or in another word processor that doesn't have a Close command, click the **File** menu, and click **Exit** to close the document and the word processor. In most word processors, you can click the **File** menu, and click **Close** to close the document but leave the word processor open for creating other documents.

QUICKSTEPS

INSERTING SPECIAL CHARACTERS

Many word processors include custom commands for inserting symbols and special characters. For example, in Microsoft Word, you click the **Insert** menu, click **Symbol**, and then work in the Symbol dialog box.

To insert special characters in other applications, use Character Map.

1. Click the **Start** button, click **All Programs**, click **Accessories**, click **System Tools**, and then click **Character Map**. Character Map opens (see Figure 4-4).

2. Select the font for the special character in the Font drop-down list.

3. Double-click the character to copy it to the Clipboard.

4. Click the **Close** button to close Character Map.

5. Activate the program in which you want to insert the character, right-click at the appropriate location, and click **Paste**.

TIP

In many cases, the best time to buy a suite of productivity software is when you buy your PC. So if you're thinking about buying a new PC, explore your options for buying a productivity suite with it and compare the cost to that of buying the suite separately.

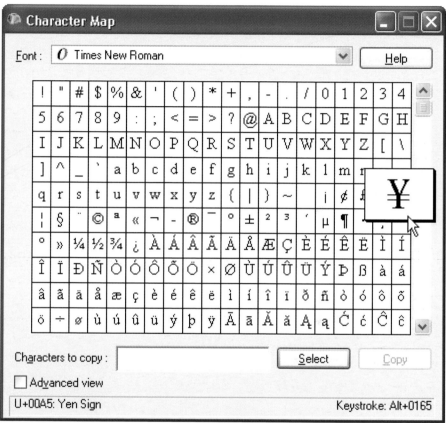

Figure 4-4: Character Map enables you to insert special characters in a document in any Windows application.

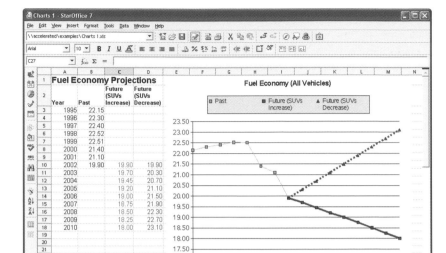

Figure 4-5: Spreadsheet programs are for analyzing data and presenting it effectively.

Create Other Office Documents

To create office documents other than text documents, you must install additional programs on XP. The three types of programs you're most likely to need for standard office work are:

- **Spreadsheet programs**, such as Microsoft Excel, Lotus 1-2-3, Corel Quattro Pro, OpenOffice.org Calc, and the Spreadsheet module in StarOffice (shown in Figure 4-5), enable you to organize, calculate, summarize, and present data. Typical uses of spreadsheets include planning and tracking budgets, analyzing sales, and charting results.

- **Presentation programs**, such as Microsoft PowerPoint, Lotus Freelance Graphics, Corel Presentations (see Figure 4-6), OpenOffice.org Impress, and the Presentation module in StarOffice, let you quickly create visually impressive presentations for business or social purposes. You can show your presentations using a PC or a slide projector.

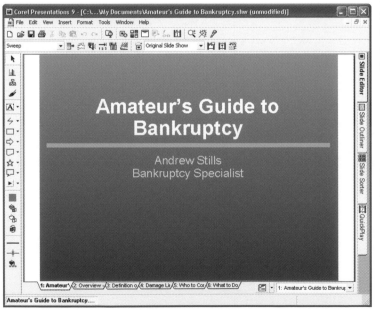

Figure 4-6: Presentation programs enable you to put together simple or complex presentations on any subject.

![clock icon] **QUICKSTEPS**

PERFORMING CALCULATIONS

XP's Calculator hides a powerful scientific calculator behind its default appearance as a basic calculator.

1. Click the **Start** button, click **All Programs**, click **Accessories**, and then click **Calculator**. Calculator opens.

2. To switch to Scientific mode (see Figure 4-7), click the **View** menu, and then click **Scientific**. (To switch back, click the **View** menu, and then click **Standard**.)

3. Type the numbers and mathematical signs, or click the buttons to enter them and perform calculations.

4. To copy a calculation to another program, click the **Edit** menu, and then click **Copy**. Activate the other application, right-click at the appropriate location, and then click **Paste**.

5. Click the **Close** button to close Calculator.

- **Database programs**, such as Microsoft Access, Lotus Approach, and Corel Paradox, enable you to store large amounts of data in databases that you can search and query for particular data. Databases tend to be used in business settings; few homes and home offices require full-scale databases. You can create small databases in spreadsheet programs or store your data in an address book program (such as XP's Address Book, discussed in Chapter 3) or a personal information manager (PIM) program.

Beyond these office-standard programs, you can find other programs for just about any computer-based task you need to perform, be it creating illustrations, laying out publications, designing web sites, or managing a company's relationships with its customers.

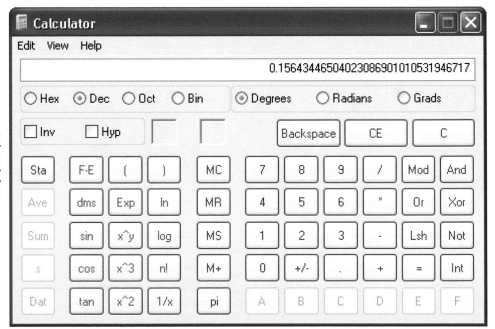

Figure 4-7: The Scientific view of the Calculator provides enough advanced functions for some mathematical and scientific usage.

Install and Remove Programs

Before you can use a new program, you must get a copy of the program and install it on your PC. These days, there are two main ways of getting programs:

- Buy a retail package from a physical or online store. Almost all such programs come on CDs. (Some large programs come on a DVD rather than using multiple CDs.)

  –Or–

- Download a program from the Web using a web browser (for example, Internet Explorer, discussed in Chapter 3). You can buy commercial software for download from online stores. You can also find shareware and freeware programs on software-distribution sites.

Install a Program from a CD

To install a program from a CD:

1. Insert the CD.

2. If XP doesn't automatically launch the CD's installation program, click the **Start** button, click **My Computer**, right-click the CD drive, and click **AutoPlay** to launch the installation program.

3. Follow the instructions in the installation program for accepting the license agreement; entering any product key or security code required; and choosing options, such as the folder in which to install the program and which components to include. Figure 4-8 shows a typical installation program for a Microsoft product.

4. After the installation program finishes you'll usually need to click **Finish** or **OK** to close it. If you need to restart XP, the installation program will prompt you to do so. Save any unsaved work before letting the installation program restart XP.

Figure 4-8: Most installation programs follow a standard series of steps that include choosing whether to install the entire program or just some of its components.

TIP

Unless you are specifically told otherwise, always save a program you're downloading to your hard drive rather than opening it via download. That way, if there is a problem when you try to install the program, you can restart the installation without having to download the program a second time.

NOTE

If the downloaded file is zipped, you will need to extract its contents. Double-click the file to display its contents in a Windows Explorer window, and then drag them to your desktop. Double-click the resulting file to start the installation. If extracting the contents of the zipped file results in a folderful of files, double-click the file named **setup.exe**.

Download and Install a Program

To download and install a program from the Web:

1. Click the **Start** button, and click **Internet** to open Internet Explorer.
2. Locate the web site that contains the program you want to download. Purchase the program, if necessary, and click the link for the download.
3. The File Download dialog box appears (see Figure 4-9), asking whether you want to open the program or save it to your PC. Click **Save**. The Save As dialog box appears. Select the folder in which to store the downloaded file—your Desktop folder is usually the most convenient location—and click **Save**.
4. When you are told the download is complete, click **Close**. Close the Internet Explorer window if it is still open.
5. If you saved the downloaded file to your desktop, double-click the file to start the installation. If you saved the file elsewhere, open a Windows Explorer window to that folder, and then double-click the file.
6. Follow the instructions in the installation program for accepting the license agreement; entering any product key or security code required; and choosing options, such as the folder in which to install the program and which components to include.
7. After the installation program finishes installing the program, you'll usually need to click **Finish** or **OK** to close the installation program. If you need to restart XP, the installation program prompts you to do so. Save any unsaved work before letting the installation program restart XP.

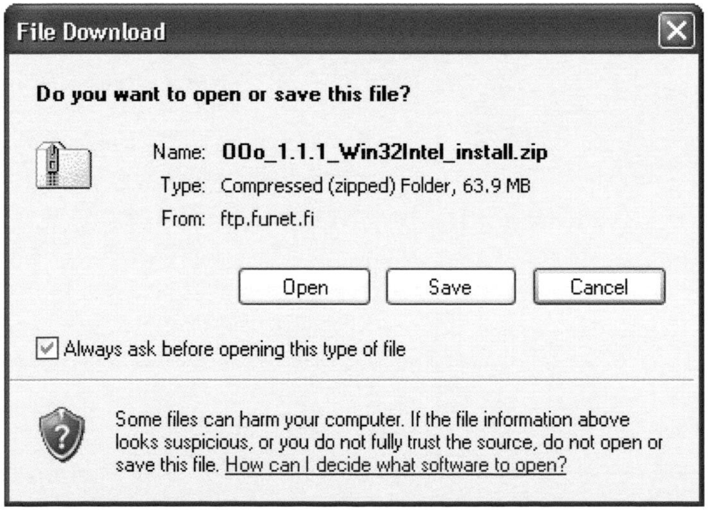
File Download
Do you want to open or save this file?
Name: OOo_1.1.1_Win32Intel_install.zip
Type: Compressed (zipped) Folder, 63.9 MB
From: ftp.funet.fi
Open
Save
Cancel
Always ask before opening this type of file
Some files can harm your computer. If the file information above looks suspicious, or you do not fully trust the source, do not open or save this file. How can I decide what software to open?

Figure 4-9: When the File Download dialog box asks you whether to open or save the program, click Save.

QUICKSTEPS

STARTING A PROGRAM AT LOGON

If you always use a program when using XP, make XP start the program automatically when you log on.

1. Click the **Start** button, click **All Programs**, right-click the menu item for the program, and click **Copy**.

2. On the All Programs menu, right-click **Startup** and click **Open All Users**. A Windows Explorer window opens showing the Start Menu\Programs\ Startup folder. Programs in this folder are started automatically when you log on.

3. Right-click open space in the folder, and then click **Paste** to paste the copied item.

4. Click **Close** to close the Windows Explorer window.

The next time you log in, XP starts the program automatically.

Figure 4-10: If a program doesn't have a custom uninstall option, use the Add Or Remove Programs window to remove it.

Remove a Program

When you install a program, the installation program typically puts files in many folders, not just in the folder you designated. The installation program also creates entries in the XP registry, a central database of configuration settings. When you remove a program, you must do so in a way that removes all files and registry settings.

To remove a program:

1. Close all open programs.

2. Click the **Start** button, click **All Programs**, and display the program's folder on the Start menu to see if the program has a custom uninstall option. If it does (as in the example here), click the uninstall option and follow the instructions on the resulting screens.

3. If the program doesn't have an uninstall option and the All Programs menu is still open, click your name at the top of the Start menu to close the All Programs menu. Then, in any case, assuming the Start menu is still open, click **Control Panel**. In Category View, click **Add Or Remove Programs**; in Classic View, double-click **Add Or Remove Programs**. The Add Or Remove Programs window opens (see Figure 4-10).

4. Click the program you want to remove, and click **Remove** or **Change/ Remove** (which button is shown depends on the program). Follow the on-screen procedure for removing the program. The details of the procedure depend on the program you're removing; you may be asked to choose between removing the entire program and removing only some parts of it.

5. When the program has been removed, click **OK** to close the notification dialog box (see the example here). Click **Close** to close the Add Or Remove Programs window, and then click **Close** to close the Control Panel window.

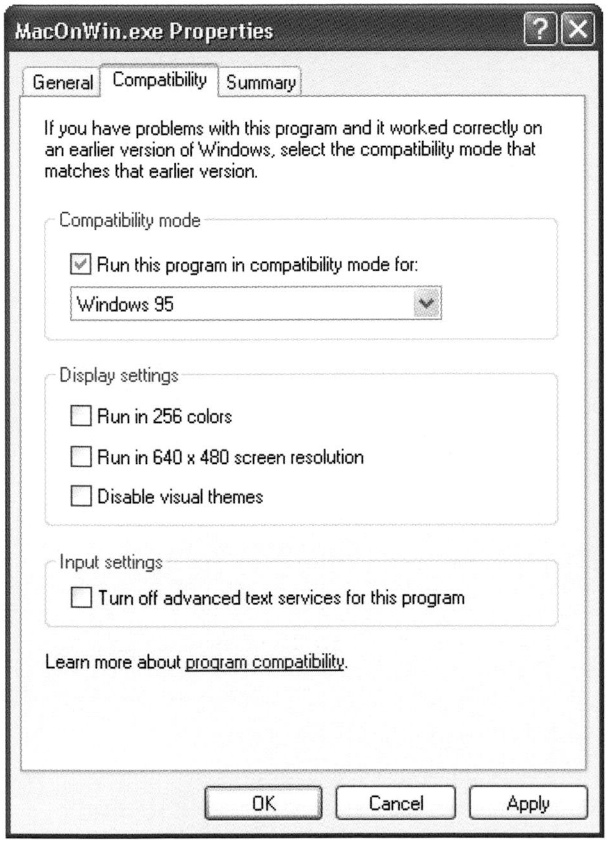

MacOnWin.exe Properties

General | **Compatibility** | Summary

If you have problems with this program and it worked correctly on an earlier version of Windows, select the compatibility mode that matches that earlier version.

Compatibility mode

☑ Run this program in compatibility mode for:

Windows 95 ▾

Display settings

☐ Run in 256 colors

☐ Run in 640 x 480 screen resolution

☐ Disable visual themes

Input settings

☐ Turn off advanced text services for this program

Learn more about program compatibility.

OK | Cancel | Apply

Figure 4-11: To make older programs run on XP, you may need to set Compatibility Mode, lower the color depth, or reduce the screen resolution.

Configure Programs

After installing most current or recent programs, you can run them simply by clicking their entries on the Start menu. You may need to configure some older programs, however, before they will run on XP. You also often need to set configurable options in your programs so that they work the way you want them to.

Use Compatibility Mode to Run Older Programs

Because XP is based on very different software than Windows 95, Windows 98, and Windows Me, some programs designed for those versions of Windows won't run properly on XP. To make them work, you must use XP's Compatibility Mode, which provides the environment that the program expects to find.

To set up Compatibility Mode for a program:

1. Click the **Start** button, click **All Programs**, and locate the menu item for the program.

2. Right-click the menu item, and click **Properties** to display the Properties dialog box for the program.

3. Click the **Compatibility** tab (see Figure 4-11).

4. Select the **Run This Program In Compatibility Mode For** check box, and select the operating system in the drop-down list box: Windows 95, Windows 98/Windows Me, Windows NT 4.0 (Service Pack 5), or Windows 2000.

5. For programs that are many years old, and for some games, you may need to experiment with the options under Display Settings to reduce color depth to 256 colors, reduce the screen resolution to 640 × 480 pixels, or disable XP's visual themes.

6. Click **OK** and then try to run the program. If it fails to run and displays an error message, try different compatibility settings.

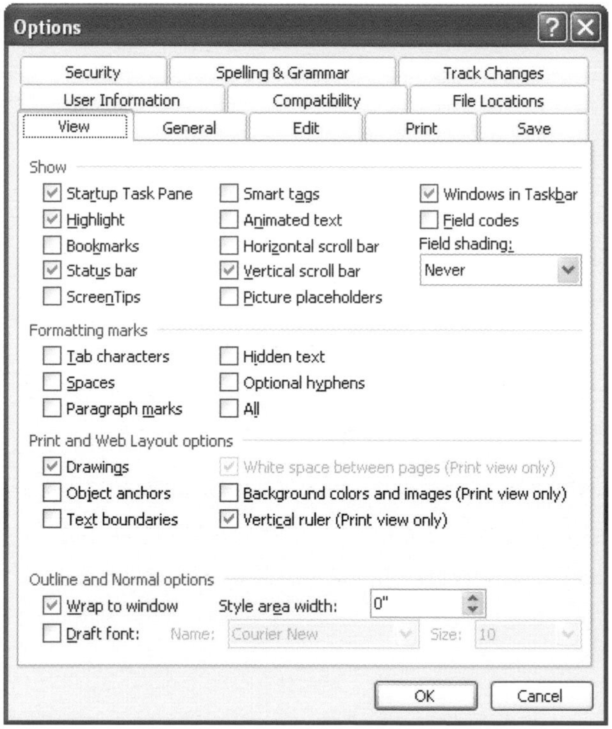

Set Configurable Options

Most complex programs contain many configurable options that you can change to control the way the program behaves. The standard location for configurable options in Windows programs is the Options dialog box, which you typically access by clicking the **Tools** menu, and clicking **Options**. Figure 4-12 shows the Options dialog box for Microsoft Word 2003, which contains 11 tabs with options for controlling everything from the screen elements that the program displays to the way it converts documents created in other word processors.

Set Program Startup Options

You may also want to configure how a program starts.

1. Click the **Start** button, click **All Programs**, and locate the menu item for the program.

2. Right-click the menu item, click **Properties** to display the Properties dialog box for the program, and then click the **Shortcut** tab.

3. In the Target text box, you can add to the command for starting the program any specific *switches*, or command modifiers, that you want to apply. For example, you can make Microsoft Word create a new document based on a particular template by using a /t switch and the template name (with no spaces between the two).

4. To create a shortcut key for running the program, click the **Shortcut Key** text box, and then press the desired key. XP creates a shortcut using **CTRL+ALT** and that key. For example, if you press **S**, XP creates the shortcut **CTRL+ALT+S**.

5. To control the initial window size for the program, choose **Normal Window**, **Maximized**, or **Minimized** in the Run drop-down list box.

6. Click **OK** to close the Properties dialog box.

Figure 4-12: You can configure the appearance and behavior of most Windows programs by using their Options dialog boxes.

Chapter 5
Installing and Using Audio and Video Hardware

Most PCs include powerful audio and video capabilities that Windows XP enables you to use with minimal effort. This chapter shows you how to use those capabilities to listen to CDs and Internet radio, copy CDs to your PC, and watch videos and DVDs. The chapter also shows you how to attach a digital camera (so that you can import pictures from it), a scanner (so that you can scan physical documents into your PC), a DV camcorder (so that you can import video), and a printer (for printing any text or graphical documents).

CHOOSING A DIGITAL CAMERA

There are three key factors to consider when choosing a digital camera:

- **Resolution** Camera resolution is measured in megapixels, or millions of pixels, by multiplying the horizontal resolution of the camera's sensor by the vertical resolution. For example, 2048 × 1536 resolution gives approximately 3 megapixels. The important number is effective pixels, which is usually substantially lower than the total pixel number that is normally quoted. Higher resolutions enable you to make larger prints without graininess. You can enlarge 2-megapixel pictures to 8 × 6 inches, 3-megapixel pictures to 10 × 8 inches, and 5-megapixel pictures to around 13 × 10 inches.

- **Lens zoom** Digital cameras use two types of zoom: optical zoom moves the lens elements and delivers full quality, while digital zoom enlarges the pixels to create the effect of zoom. Optical zoom is the important measurement, but you will sometimes want to use digital zoom as well to zoom in on faraway objects.

- **Memory type and capacity** Digital cameras typically use removable memory cards, such as CompactFlash, Secure Digital, and Memory Stick. If you already have devices that use one of these types of cards, you may prefer that type; otherwise, all the types work well. Most cameras come with a small memory card; buy a larger card when you buy the camera so that you can take plenty of photos before needing to download them to your PC.

NOTE

Some older digital cameras connect directly to your PC via a serial cable. Serial cables transfer data far more slowly than USB, so if you have the choice between USB and serial, choose USB.

Connect Cameras, Scanners, and Printers

Before you can work with video hardware, you must connect it to your computer. This section shows you how to connect a digital camera, a web cam, a video camera, a scanner, and a printer.

Connect Cameras and Scanners

XP makes the process of connecting cameras and scanners to your PC as straightforward as possible. The process is different for different types of cameras—digital still cameras, web cams, and video cameras—and for scanners.

CONNECT A DIGITAL CAMERA

How you connect a digital camera to your PC depends on the camera model and the medium it uses to store the pictures.

- If your digital camera has fixed (nonremovable) storage, you typically connect it directly to your PC via a USB (Universal Serial Bus) cable.

  -Or-

- If your digital camera has a removable memory card, you remove the memory card and insert it in a card reader attached to your PC via a USB port. Depending on the camera, you may also be able to connect it directly to your PC via a USB cable.

When you plug in the USB cable or insert the memory card in the card reader, XP detects the camera or card as a removable disk drive, as shown here. You can then access the contents of the camera or the memory card using Windows Explorer.

CONNECT A WEB CAM

Almost all web cams connect to your PC via USB. Simply plug the web cam's connector into a USB port on your PC or a USB hub attached to your PC.

XP recognizes many USB web cams and automatically loads drivers for them, as shown here. For some web cams, you may need to supply the drivers.

CONNECT A DV CAMCORDER

To connect a DV camcorder to your PC, you typically need a FireWire port on the PC. "Import Video from a DV Camcorder," later in this chapter, discusses how to add a FireWire port to your PC (if necessary) and how to import video from your camcorder.

CONNECT A SCANNER

To create high-quality pictures of hard-copy photographs and other documents, use a scanner. With optical character recognition (OCR) software, you can also use a scanner to enter the text from hard-copy original documents, either typed or printed, on to your PC without retyping all the text. If you don't have a scanner, see the "Choosing a Scanner" QuickFacts for advice on choosing one.

Most modern scanners are Plug and Play devices (you plug them in, Windows detects them automatically, and you can start to use them).

1. Connect the scanner to your PC via the USB port or the parallel port. (If you have a choice between the two, choose USB.) If the scanner is Plug and Play, XP displays a Found New Hardware pop-up message above the notification area.

CHOOSING A SCANNER

For scanning photos and documents, your best buy is typically a *flatbed scanner*—a scanner that has a flat sheet of glass on which you place the object to be scanned. The scanner's lens then moves along the area occupied by the object to capture its image. Flatbed scanners deliver good scanning for most general purposes and start at less than $50. Most modern flatbed scanners connect via USB 2.0, which is the most convenient form of connection for PCs.

The other three main types of scanners are *sheet-fed scanners* (ones that feed the document past the scanner lens), *slide scanners* (specialized scanners for scanning film and slides), and *drum scanners* (high-quality scanners in which the paper being scanned is wrapped around the inside of a drum on which the scanner's lens revolves).

The measurement of a scanner's quality is its resolution, which is given in horizontal and vertical measurements in dots per inch (dpi). Entry-level scanners now start at 1200 X 1200 dpi, which is more than enough for scanning text documents. For scanning pictures, look for 2400 X 2400 dpi; for professional quality, look for 4800 X 4800 dpi. Make sure that this resolution is optical (produced by the scanner's hardware) rather than interpolated, in which the scanner's software doubles the optical resolution by adding extra rows of pixels between the real rows.

If you need to produce text versions of scanned documents, you'll need OCR software. Many scanners include "lite" versions of OCR software, but you may need to buy more powerful software if you scan many text documents. If you have Microsoft Office 2003, you can use the OCR feature built into the Microsoft Office Document Imaging program.

2. If you haven't permitted XP to connect automatically to Windows Update, the Found New Hardware Wizard starts, asking for permission to connect. Select the **Yes, This Time Only** option button or the **Yes, Now And Every Time I Connect A Device** option button, as appropriate, and then click **Next**.

3. Insert the installation CD for the scanner, if you have one, and then click **Next**. The Found New Hardware Wizard searches for the software and installs it if it finds it.

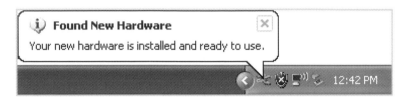

4. Click the **Start** button, and click **Control Panel**. In Category View, click **Printers And Other Hardware**, and then click **Scanners And Cameras**. In Classic View, double-click **Scanners And Cameras**. The Scanners and Cameras window opens. If your scanner is listed in the window, installation is complete; skip the rest of these steps.

5. Click **Add An Imaging Device**. The Scanner And Camera Installation Wizard starts. Click **Next**.

6. With the device's CD (if any) still in your PC's CD drive, click **Have Disk**. If a driver appears, complete the installation and close the Scanner And Camera Installation Wizard. If you cannot find the driver, cancel the Scanner And Camera Installation Wizard, and use the manufacturer's installation program on the disk. If you don't have a disk, see if the Manufacturer and Model lists in the wizard include a driver for your device. If not, download a driver from the manufacturer's web site, and run the Scanner And Camera Installation Wizard again.

Install a Printer

Sooner or later, you'll probably need to print documents from your PC. First, you must install a printer.

How you install a printer depends on whether it's a local printer (one attached directly to your PC) or a network printer and on whether the printer supports the Plug and Play specification, which enables the PC to detect the printer.

CHOOSING A PRINTER

Printers come in two main types:

- **Inkjet printers** spray ink from tiny nozzles on to the paper as it is fed through the printer. Most inkjet printers can print in color as well as in black and white and produce printouts of a high enough quality for most use. Inkjets start at less than $40, and most consumer printers are inkjets. Higher-quality (and more expensive) inkjets use more colors of ink and can print photos well.

- **Laser printers** use a laser to create the image. Laser printers are usually more expensive than inkjet printers and are typically used in companies, although there are some "personal" laser printers at lower prices. For business purposes, most companies use monochrome laser printers for black-and-white documents, reserving their color laser printers for color documents.

When buying a printer:

- If you need to print photos, buy a high-quality inkjet printer and special photo paper.

- If you need to produce many high-quality black-and-white business documents, buy a monochrome laser printer.

- Factor the cost of ink (for inkjet printers) or toner (for laser printers) refill cartridges into the cost of the printer. If you use an inkjet extensively, refills may soon cost more than the printer did.

- If you need to network the printer, buy a printer that connects via Ethernet (see Chapter 8) rather than the standard USB connection. If you're planning a wireless-only network, consider either a printer that includes a wireless connection or a wireless access point that offers a printer connection.

- If you also need to scan, photocopy, and fax items, consider a multifunction printer that includes these capabilities.

OPEN THE PRINTERS AND FAXES WINDOW

To work with printers and faxes, use the Printers And Faxes window in the Control Panel.

1. Click the **Start** button, and click **Control Panel**.

2. In Category View, click **Printers And Other Hardware**, and then click **Printers And Faxes**. In Classic View, double-click **Printers And Faxes**. The Printers And Faxes window opens.

For quick access to the Printers And Faxes window, XP Professional includes a Printers And Faxes link on the Start menu by default; this section assumes your Start menu includes the Printers And Faxes link. To add this link in XP Home Edition:

1. Right-click the **Start** button, and click **Properties**. The Taskbar And Start Menu Properties dialog box appears.

2. On the Start Menu tab, click the top **Customize** button, and click the **Advanced** tab.

3. Scroll down in the Start Menu Items list box, and select the **Printers And Faxes** check box.

4. Click **OK**, and then click **OK** again.

CONNECT THE PRINTER

Before installing the printer in XP, connect the printer to your PC or network.

1. If necessary, unpack the printer and assemble it.

2. Load the printer with ink or toner and with paper.

3. Connect the printer to your PC or to the network.

    - Most recent consumer printers connect via USB.

    - Older consumer printers connect via a parallel port (see Chapter 1).

    - Most network printers connect via Ethernet to a network switch or hub (see Chapter 8).

    - For a wireless printer, you don't need to establish a physical connection provided you have a wireless access point (see Chapter 8).

4. Plug the printer into an electrical outlet, and turn it on.

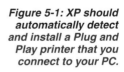

Some printers include custom software utilities for automating printer installation, calibrating the printer, and managing your printouts. If your printer includes a custom installation utility, you may not need to take the steps described here.

NOTE

If the Found New Hardware Wizard displays the message "Cannot install this hardware," go to the next section, "Install a Local Other Printer."

INSTALL A LOCAL PLUG AND PLAY PRINTER

To install a Plug and Play printer, connect it to your PC, as described in the previous section. Then:

1. Start XP if it isn't running. XP should detect and automatically install the new printer. You'll see a balloon message when XP detects the printer.

   > ⓘ **Found New Hardware** ☒
   >
   > HEWLETT-PACKARDDESKJET 3820
   >
   > 1:22 AM

2. If the Found New Hardware Wizard starts and prompts you to allow it to connect to Windows Update to search for software, click the **Yes**, **Now And Every Time I Connect A Device** option button if you have a broadband Internet connection, or click the **Yes**, **This Time Only** option button if you have a dial-up Internet connection. If your printer included a CD, insert it in your PC's CD drive. Click **Next** and follow the steps of the wizard. Typically, your best choice is to allow XP to install the software automatically.

3. Click the **Start** button, and click **Printers And Faxes**. The Printers And Faxes window opens, showing the printer you installed. Hover the mouse pointer over the printer to display its status, as shown in Figure 5-1. (If your printer isn't listed in the Printers And Faxes window, XP didn't install it. Go to the next section, "Install a Local Other Printer.")

Figure 5-1: XP should automatically detect and install a Plug and Play printer that you connect to your PC.

4. To check that the printer is working, click the printer, click **Set Printer Properties** in the Printer Tasks task pane, and then click **Print Test Page** on the General tab of the resulting Properties dialog box. If the test page prints satisfactorily, click **OK**; otherwise, click **Troubleshoot** and follow the suggestions.

5. Click **OK** to close the Properties dialog box, and then click **Close**.

INSTALL A LOCAL OTHER PRINTER

If your printer doesn't install automatically using the steps in the previous section, install it manually.

1. If your printer included a CD with software for XP, insert the CD in your PC's CD drive, and follow the on-screen instructions to install the printer. When the installation procedure is complete, click the **Start** button, and click **Control Panel**. In Category View, click **Printers And Other Hardware**, and then click **Printers And Faxes**; in Classic View, double-click **Printers And Faxes**. Click the printer and click **Set Printer Properties** in the Printer Tasks task pane, and then click **Print Test Page** on the General tab of the resulting Properties dialog box. If the test page prints satisfactorily, click **OK** and skip to step 8.

2. If your printer didn't include a CD, click the **Start** button, click **Printers And Faxes**, and then click **Add A Printer** in the Printer Tasks task pane. The Add Printer Wizard starts.

3. Click **Next**. The Local Or Network Printer page is displayed.

4. Select the **Local Printer Attached To This Computer** option button, clear the **Automatically Detect And Install My Plug And Play Printer** check box, and then click **Next**. The Select A Printer Port page is displayed.

5. Select the **Use The Following Port** option button, and select the port in the drop-down list box. Usually, you'll need to select **LPT1** for a printer attached to a parallel port, and **USB001** for a printer attached via USB.

6. Click **Next**. The Install Printer Software page is displayed.

7. Select the manufacturer and model of the printer you want to install. If you can't find your printer, click **Windows Update** to download the latest printer drivers, and then search for the manufacturer and model once more. After finding the correct printer, click **Next**. The Name Your Printer page is displayed.

8. Change the default name for the printer to a more helpful name, if you want; choose whether to use this printer as your default printer; and click **Next**. The Print Test Page page is displayed.

NOTE

If Windows Update doesn't produce a driver for your printer, download the driver from the printer manufacturer's web site, and then expand the file if it is compressed. On the Install Printer Software page, click **Have Disk**. Then use the resulting dialog boxes to specify the location where you saved the driver file, and select the printer.

9. Click **Yes** to print a test page, and then click **Next**. The Completing The Add Printer Wizard page is displayed, showing a summary of the selected settings (see Figure 5-2).

10. If there are any problems, click **Back** and correct them; otherwise, click **Finish**. The wizard installs the printer, sends your test page to the printer, and displays a dialog box asking if it printed satisfactorily.

11. If the test page printed satisfactorily, click **OK**; otherwise, click **Troubleshoot** and follow the suggestions.

12. Click **Close** to close the Printers And Faxes window.

Figure 5-2: To install a printer manually, you must specify the printer manufacturer and model and select the port into which the printer is plugged.

INSTALL A NETWORK PRINTER

A network printer is a printer made available to your PC via a network in one of three ways:

- The printer is connected to someone else's PC and has been shared.
- The printer is connected to a dedicated printer server.
- The printer is directly connected to the network through its own network interface.

The first two types of network printer are installed as described in the following section. The third type of printer is installed (usually automatically) as a local printer, as described in the previous two sections.

1. Click the **Start** button, click **Printers And Faxes**, and then click **Add A Printer** in the Printer Tasks task pane. The Add Printer Wizard starts.

2. Click **Next**. The Local Or Network Printer page is displayed.

3. Select the **A Network Printer, Or A Printer Attached To Another Computer** option button, and click **Next**. The Specify A Printer page is displayed.

4. Verify that the **Browse For A Printer** option button is selected, and click **Next**. The Browse For Printer page is displayed (see Figure 5-3).

5. Scroll through the list of computers and printers on your network to locate the printer you want. Select that printer and click **Next**. XP warns you that the other computer will automatically install a printer driver on your PC, as shown here.

6. Click **Yes**. The Default Printer page is displayed.

7. Choose whether to make this printer your default printer, and click **Next**. The Completing The Add Printer Wizard page shows you a summary of your settings.

8. Click **Finish** and then click **Close** to close the Printers And Faxes window.

Figure 5-3: A printer attached to another PC must be shared by that PC before you can use it.

NOTE

Before you can share a printer attached to your PC, you must run the Network Setup Wizard. If the Sharing tab of the printer's Properties dialog box displays a message saying that Windows has disabled remote access to your PC, click the **Network Setup Wizard** link, and follow the steps of the wizard. See Chapter 8 for more information.

SHARE YOUR PC'S PRINTER

You can share the printer attached to your PC so that other people on your network can print using it.

1. Click the **Start** button, and click **Printers And Faxes**. The Printers And Faxes window opens.

2. Click the printer and then click **Share This Printer** in the Printer Tasks task pane. The Sharing tab of the Properties dialog box for the printer is displayed.

3. Select the **Share This Printer** option button, type a descriptive name of no more than 12 characters in the Share Name text box, and click **OK**.

4. Click **Close** to close the Printers And Faxes window.

Print Documents and Photos

Most programs provide similar features for printing documents, although the specific options vary depending on the contents of the document the program produces. For example, Microsoft Word has different features for printing word-processing documents than Microsoft Excel has for printing spreadsheets because word-processing documents and spreadsheets have different features.

PRINT A DOCUMENT

To print a document other than a photo:

1. Open the program and open the document you want to print. Or, click the **File** menu, and click **Preview** to view the document in print preview. Check for errors and correct any that you find.

2. Click the **File** menu, and click **Print**. The Print dialog box appears. Figure 5-4 shows an example of a Print dialog box.

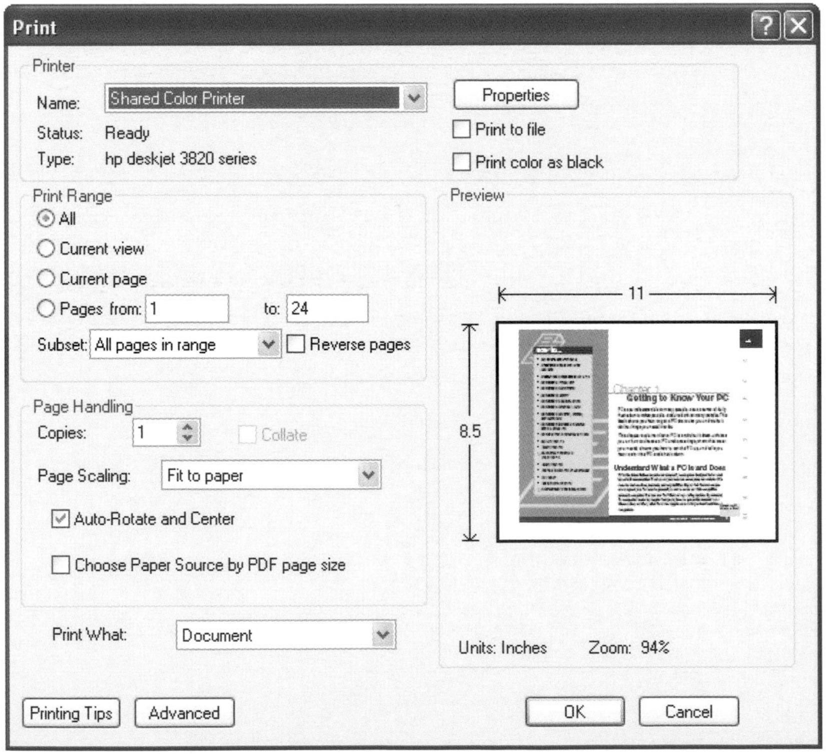

Figure 5-4: The controls in the Print dialog box vary from program to program, but most Print dialog boxes let you choose the printer, print range, and number of copies.

3. Choose the printer in the drop-down list.

4. Choose other options for printing (depending on the program). For example, you might choose to print only some pages.

5. Click **OK**.

PRINT A PHOTO

You can print a photo directly from a graphics program, such as Paint or Photoshop Elements, but XP also provides the Photo Printing Wizard.

1. Open a Windows Explorer window, and browse to the folder that contains the photos you want to print. For example, click the **Start** button, and click **My Pictures** to open your My Pictures folder.

2. Select the photos to print, and click **Print The Selected Pictures** in the Picture Tasks task pane. (If you select only one photo, the link is called **Print This Picture**.) The Photo Printing Wizard starts. Click **Next**. The Picture Selection page is displayed.

3. If you decide not to print some of the photos, clear their check boxes. (All the check boxes are selected by default.)

4. Click **Next**. The Printing Options page is displayed.

5. Select the printer and choose printing preferences, and then click **Next**. The Layout Selection page is displayed (see Figure 5-5).

6. Select the layout and the number of times to print each photo, and then click **Next**. The wizard prints your photos.

7. Click **Finish** to close the wizard.

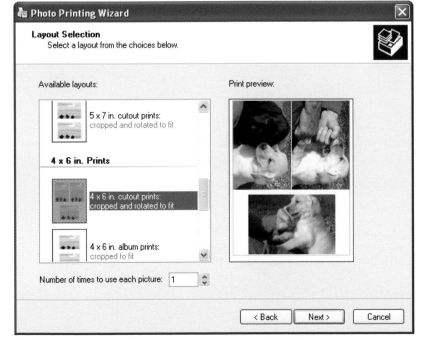

Figure 5-5: The Photo Printing Wizard enables you to print selected photos using various layouts.

Create and Import Pictures and Video

Once your video hardware is connected (as discussed earlier in this chapter), you can use XP's features and programs to work with pictures and video.

Work with Pictures Using Paint

XP's Paint accessory program is useful for creating simple illustrations, capturing still pictures from a web cam, and converting digital pictures from one format to another.

CREATE A PICTURE

To create a picture using Paint:

1. Click the **Start** button, click **All Programs**, click **Accessories**, and then click **Paint**. Paint opens.

2. Use the tools in Paint to create your picture (see Figure 5-6). Hover the mouse pointer over a tool to display a ScreenTip describing it.

3. Click the **File** menu, and click **Save As**. The Save As dialog box appears. Select the folder, enter the file name, and click **Save** to save the picture.

4. Click the **File** menu, and click **Exit** to close Paint and the picture.

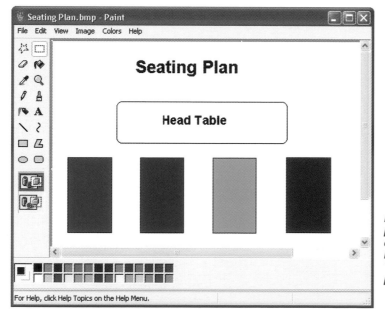

Figure 5-6: Paint offers preset shapes and colors for creating basic diagrams. You can also create pictures.

CHOOSING ILLUSTRATION PROGRAMS

If Paint doesn't provide the tools you need for graphical work, get a more advanced illustration program.

- **Paint Shop Pro** from Jasc Software, Inc. (www.jasc.com; around $100) provides powerful features for creating and editing graphics.
- **Photoshop Elements** from Adobe Systems, Inc. (www.adobe.com; around $120) is a stripped-down version of Photoshop, Adobe's market-leading graphics program.
- **Deneba Canvas** from ACD Systems of America, Inc. (www.deneba.com; around $400) is a professional-quality graphics program.
- **Photoshop** from Adobe Systems, Inc. (www.adobe.com; around $650, but less if purchased as part of Adobe Creative Suite) is the tool that most professionals use for editing graphics.

You can download evaluation versions of all these programs from the URLs provided.

CAPTURE STILLS FROM A WEB CAM

To capture still pictures from a USB web cam using Paint:

1. Connect your USB web cam to your PC as discussed in "Connect a Web Cam," earlier in this chapter.

2. Click the **Start** button, click **All Programs**, click **Accessories**, and then click **Paint**. Paint opens.

3. Click the **File** menu, and click **From Scanner Or Camera** to open the Capture Pictures From Video dialog box (shown in Figure 5-7 with pictures captured).

4. Aim the camera at your subject so that the picture in the Capture Pictures From Video dialog box shows what you want to capture.

5. Click **Capture**. Paint adds the captured picture to the list box on the right side of the dialog box. Click **Capture** again to capture further pictures as necessary.

6. In the list box, select the picture you want to keep.

7. Click **Get Picture**. Paint closes the Capture Pictures From Video dialog box and displays the picture in the Paint window.

8. Click the **File** menu, and click **Save**. The Save As dialog box appears.

9. Choose the folder, type the file name, and choose a suitable format in the Save As Type drop-down list (see the "Choosing the Best Picture Format" QuickFacts for advice), and then click **Save**.

10. If you've finished working with Paint, open the **File** menu, and click **Exit**.

Figure 5-7: Paint enables you to grab multiple still pictures from your web cam, choose the best, and save it as a picture.

CHOOSING PICTURE FORMATS

There are many different formats for digital pictures. These formats differ in the amount of data they save for the picture and the way in which they save it. Paint can open and save files in five of the most widely used formats.

BITMAP

Bitmap is a standard format that stores the details of the data contained in each pixel of the picture. Bitmaps are uncompressed, so they take up more disk space than most other graphics formats. Paint offers four grades of bitmap:

- Use Monochrome Bitmap when you want to convert a picture to black and white.
- Use 16 Color Bitmap when you want to strip a picture down to 16 colors. This sometimes gives desirable artistic effects, but typically wrecks any picture that contains complex colors.
- Use 256 Color Bitmap (8-bit) when you want to reduce a picture to 256 colors. The effects are better than 16 Color Bitmap, but changes most pictures considerably for the worse.
- Use 24-Bit Bitmap (more than 16 million colors) when you want to save as much data as possible about your picture; 24-bit bitmaps take up a considerable amount of space.

JPEG

JPEG (Joint Photographic Experts Group) is a graphics format widely used on the Web. JPEG uses *lossy compression*, compression that discards some of the data, to give a smaller file size. Use JPEG when you want to produce compact pictures with reasonable quality for Web use.

Continued...

CONVERT A PICTURE TO A DIFFERENT FORMAT

To convert a picture to a different format using Paint:

1. Click the **Start** button, click **All Programs**, click **Accessories**, and then click **Paint**. Paint opens.

2. Click the **File** menu, and click **Open**. The Open dialog box appears. Select the picture and click **Open**.

3. Click the **File** menu, and click **Save As**. The Save As dialog box appears.

4. Choose the format in the Save As Type drop-down list (see the "Choosing Picture Formats" QuickFacts for advice). If the new format uses the same extension as the current format, change the file name so that the new picture doesn't overwrite the old picture.

5. Click **Save**.

6. If you've finished working with Paint, click the **File** menu, and click **Exit**.

Work with Digital Pictures

XP makes it easy to import pictures from a digital camera and view them in Windows Explorer.

IMPORT PICTURES FROM A DIGITAL CAMERA

To import pictures from a digital camera:

1. Connect the digital camera or its memory card to your PC, as discussed in "Connect a Digital Camera," earlier in this chapter.

2. When XP detects a storage device, it may display the Removable Disk dialog box (see Figure 5-8). If not, click the **Start** button, click **My Computer**, right-click the entry for the storage device, and click **AutoPlay** to display this dialog box.

3. Click **Open Folder To View Files**, select the **Always Do The Selected Action** check box, and click **OK**. XP opens a Windows Explorer window showing the pictures or the folder containing them.

4. Select the pictures you want to transfer, click the **Edit** menu, and click **Copy To Folder**. Select the destination folder in the **Copy To Folder** dialog box, and click **Copy**.

5. Click the **Safely Remove Hardware** icon in the notification area, and then click the item for the removable disk drive on the resulting menu.

6. Detach the camera or remove the memory card from the card reader.

Figure 5-8: The easiest way to copy pictures from a digital camera or memory card to your PC is to select the Open Folder To View Files option in the Removable Disk dialog box.

TIP

If you are using a folder other than My Pictures and the View menu doesn't contain the Filmstrip command, you must customize the folder. Click the **Up** button to display the parent folder of the current folder. Right-click the folder that contains the pictures, and click **Properties** to display the Properties dialog box. Click the **Customize** tab, click **Photo Album (Best For Fewer Files)** in the Use This Folder Type As A Template drop-down list, and click **OK**. Double-click the folder to display the pictures.

VIEW PICTURES IN WINDOWS EXPLORER

To view pictures in Windows Explorer:

1. Open a Windows Explorer window, and browse to the folder that contains the pictures. For example, if the pictures are in your My Pictures folder, click the **Start** button, and then click **My Pictures**.

2. If the folder isn't automatically displayed in Filmstrip view (see Figure 5-9), click the **View** menu, and click **Filmstrip**.

3. Click **Previous Image** or **Next Image** to move from one picture to the next, or click the picture you want to display.

4. If a picture is on its side or upside-down, click it and click **Rotate Clockwise** or **Rotate Counterclockwise** until it is right-side up.

5. To view the pictures as a full-screen slideshow, click **View As A Slide Show** in the Picture Tasks pane. To create a slideshow of only some pictures, select them before clicking **View As A Slide Show**.

6. Click the **File** menu, and click **Close** when you have finished viewing your pictures.

Figure 5-9: Filmstrip view enables you to browse quickly through your pictures and rotate them as necessary.

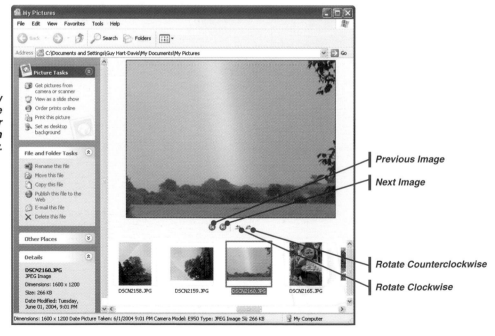

Previous Image

Next Image

Rotate Counterclockwise

Rotate Clockwise

Scan a Picture or Document

With your scanner connected and installed (as discussed in "Connect a Scanner," earlier in this chapter), you can scan a picture or a document.

1. Place the picture or document on the scanner, aligning it carefully with the guides.

2. Click the **Start** button, click **All Programs**, click **Accessories**, and then click **Scanners And Cameras Wizard** (this appears only if you have a scanner installed or camera attached). The Scanners And Cameras Wizard starts. Click **Next**. The Choose Scanning Preferences page is displayed (see Figure 5-10).

3. Choose your scanning preferences, and click **Next**. The Picture Name And Destination page is displayed.

NOTE

If you have multiple scanners or cameras, the Scanners And Cameras Wizard lets you choose which device to use.

4. Type the name for the group of pictures, select the file format (see the "Choosing Picture Formats" QuickFacts in this chapter), and choose the folder in which to store the picture. Click **Next** to start the scan.

5. After scanning, choose whether to publish the picture to a web site, order prints online, or do nothing beyond saving the picture. Click **Next** and then click **Finish**. The wizard opens a Windows Explorer window showing you the results of the scan so that you can open it for viewing, for editing, or for OCR.

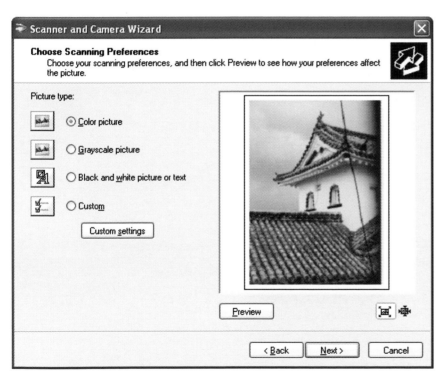

Figure 5-10: Click the Preview button to display a preview of the picture or document you're scanning, and select the appropriate Picture Type option button. Click the Custom Settings button if you need to adjust the default settings for that type.

Import Video from a Camcorder

If your PC has one or more FireWire ports, you can import video directly from a DV camcorder using Windows Movie Maker (which is usually included with XP) or another video program. A DV camcorder stores its data in a digital format that you can easily transfer to your PC. By contrast, an analog camcorder stores its data in an *analog format*—as a continuous but varying signal. To transfer analog footage from a camcorder to your PC, you need a video capture card that can create digital data from the analog signal.

FireWire is a standard technology for data transfer (it competes with USB), but most PCs use USB rather than FireWire. Some high-end PCs include FireWire, and if you're buying a PC with the intention of capturing video, you should ensure that FireWire is built into your PC. Otherwise, you'll need to add FireWire in one of these ways:

- Install a FireWire PCI card in a desktop PC.
- Insert a FireWire PC Card (see the example here) in a laptop PC.

See Chapter 6 for instructions on installing cards in your PC.

With a FireWire port available, you can capture video as follows:

1. With your computer turned on and Windows XP running, plug your DV camcorder into one of the FireWire ports on your PC, and turn on the camcorder. The Digital Video Device dialog box appears.

2. Verify that the **Record Video** item is selected, and click **OK**. XP launches Windows Movie Maker and opens the Video Capture Wizard, which walks you through the process of capturing the video.

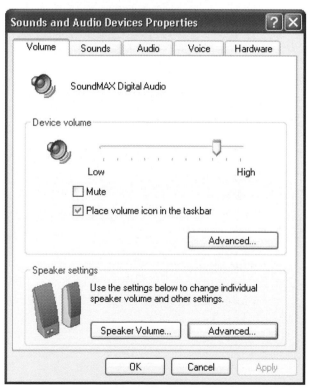

Listen To and Record Audio

Windows Media Player, a multimedia player that comes built into most copies of XP, enables you to play audio, video, and (with a hardware or software decoder) DVDs. Sound Recorder, a program included with XP, enables you to record audio from a microphone or another audio source.

Configure Your Audio Setup

When you set up your PC (see Chapter 1), you connected your external speakers (or a receiver or amplifier) to the line output of your sound card. You should now configure your audio setup.

> **NOTE**
>
> At this writing, the European Union is trying to force Microsoft to produce a version of XP without Windows Media Player. Even with Windows Media Player installed, some PC manufacturers configure XP to use another audio player, such as RealNetworks, Inc.'s RealPlayer, by default.

1. Click the **Start** button, click **Control Panel**, and then click **Sounds And Audio Devices**. The Sounds And Audio Devices Properties dialog box appears (see Figure 5-11).

   - In Category View, click **Sounds, Speech, And Audio Devices**, and then click **Sounds And Audio Devices**.

   - In Classic View, double-click **Sounds And Audio Devices**.

2. On the Volume tab, make sure the **Place Volume Icon In The Taskbar** check box is selected so that XP displays the Volume icon in the notification area.

Figure 5-11: Set the device volume, ensure the Volume icon is displayed in the notification area, and check your speaker placement.

TIP

To adjust the left-right balance of your audio, click **Speaker Volume** on the Volume tab of the Sounds And Audio Devices Properties dialog box, adjust the **Left** and **Right** settings as desired in the Speaker Volume dialog box, and then click **OK**.

3. Under Speaker Settings, click **Advanced**. The Advanced Audio Properties dialog box appears (see Figure 5-12). Select the appropriate speaker setup (for example, choose 7.1 Surround Sound Speakers if that's what you have), and click **OK**.

4. Click **OK** to close the Sounds And Audio Devices Properties dialog box.

SET THE VOLUME

You can control the volume at which audio plays in three ways:

- Use the volume control in the program that's playing sound.

- Use the volume control in the notification area or the master volume control to set the overall output volume for your PC.

- Use the physical volume control on your speakers or your receiver or amplifier to set the volume they produce.

If the Volume icon doesn't appear in the notification area, add it as described in "Configure Your Audio Setup."

Figure 5-12: Make sure XP knows which speaker setup you're using so that your audio sounds right.

Listen to CDs and Digital Audio

To listen to an audio CD:

1. Insert the CD.

2. If the AutoPlay dialog box doesn't appear, such as that shown here (the dialog box title may show the CD's name), click the **Start** button, click **My Computer**, right-click the CD drive, and click **AutoPlay**.

3. Click **Play Audio CD Using Windows Media Player**, and then click **OK**. Windows Media Player opens (see Figure 5-13) and starts playing the CD.

4. Use the playback controls to control the playback of the CD.

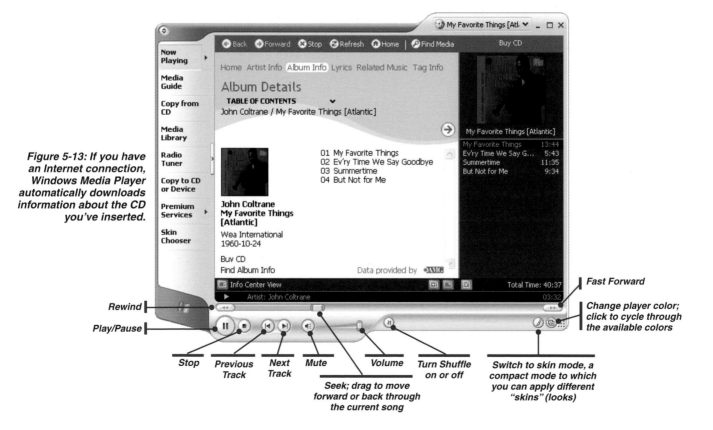

Figure 5-13: If you have an Internet connection, Windows Media Player automatically downloads information about the CD you've inserted.

Rewind

Play/Pause

Fast Forward

Change player color; click to cycle through the available colors

Stop | Previous Track | Next Track | Mute | Volume | Turn Shuffle on or off

Seek; drag to move forward or back through the current song

Switch to skin mode, a compact mode to which you can apply different "skins" (looks)

Copy Audio CDs to Your PC

Windows Media Player enables you to copy tracks from audio CDs to compressed audio files on your hard disk, to create and organize a library of your music, and to create recordable CDs containing selections of this music. To copy from a CD:

1. Insert the CD.
2. If the Audio CD dialog box doesn't appear, click the **Start** button, click **My Computer**, right-click the CD drive, and click **AutoPlay**.
3. Click **Copy Music From CD Using Windows Media Player**, and then click **OK**. Windows Media Player starts copying the music from the CD to your hard disk.

Listen to Internet Radio

Windows Media Player's Radio Tuner feature lets you listen to radio stations around the world that broadcast their programs across the Internet, either in addition to conventional broadcasting or instead of it. Internet radio works best over a broadband connection that delivers at least 128 Kbps (see Chapter 3 for details on Internet connections), but you can also listen to lower-quality radio broadcasts over a dial-up connection.

To start listening to Internet radio:

1. Click the **Start** button, click **All Programs**, and then click **Windows Media Player**.
2. Click the **Radio Tuner** tab on the left side.
3. Find a radio station in one of three ways:
   - Click a link in the Featured Stations list.
   - Click a link in the Find More Stations list, and use the resulting screen to browse by genre, search by keyword, or search by ZIP code.
   - In the Search text box, drag over **Search Keyword**, type the call letters of a radio station, and either press **ENTER** or click the **Search** arrow. The Search Results page is displayed.
4. After selecting a station, click the **Play** link.

TIP

To find radio stations that broadcast in a given language, at a specific speed, or on a particular band, click the **Use Advanced Search** link.

NOTE

Some radio stations don't have a Play link. Instead, you must click the **Visit Website To Play** link to open a web page showing the station, and then start it playing from there. Often, you must register with the station first.

TIP

You can also click the **Add To My Stations** link to add a radio station to your station list. You can then listen to it easily next time by opening **Radio Tuner**, clicking **My Stations,** and then clicking the station.

Record Audio

Sound Recorder, a small program included with XP, can record audio input through the line input or microphone input on your sound card. You must connect the audio source, tell XP which input to monitor, and trick Sound Recorder into overcoming a built-in limitation.

CONNECT THE AUDIO SOURCE

Connect the audio source to your sound card by using a cable with suitable connectors. For example, to connect a receiver output to a standard line input, you'll need a cable with two RCA plugs for the receiver end and a male-end stereo miniplug at the sound card end.

SPECIFY THE AUDIO SOURCE

Specify the audio source that Sound Recorder will record from.

1. Double-click the **Volume** icon in the notification area. The Volume Control window opens. (This window may have a different name, such as Play Control, depending on your PC's hardware.)

2. Click the **Options** menu, and click **Properties**. The Properties dialog box appears.

3. Click the **Recording** option button to display the list of devices for recording (see Figure 5-14).

Figure 5-14: Before you can record audio, you must tell XP which sound source to monitor.

4. Select the check box for each input device you want to be able to use. For example, select the **Line In** and **Microphone** check boxes.

5. Click **OK**. The Recording Control window opens. (This window may also have a different name and more channels, depending on your PC's hardware.)

6. Select the **Select** check box for the source you want to use.

7. Leave the Recording Control window open so that you can adjust the input volume on the input if necessary.

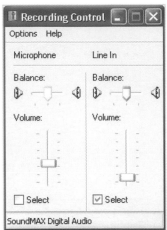

START SOUND RECORDER

Start Sound Recorder by clicking the **Start** button, clicking **All Programs**, clicking **Accessories**, clicking **Entertainment**, and then clicking **Sound Recorder**.

PREPARE SOUND RECORDER TO RECORD LONG FILES

Sound Recorder can record files up to 60 seconds long, but you can trick it into recording longer files.

1. In the Recording Control window, drag the **Volume** slider of your audio source all the way to the bottom to mute the sound source.

2. In Sound Recorder, click the **Record** button to start recording.

3. Let Sound Recorder run for 60 seconds, at which point it stops automatically.

4. Click the **File** menu, and click **Save**. The Save As dialog box appears.

5. Type the file name blank file, and press **ENTER** to save it.

6. Click the **Edit** menu, and click **Insert File**. The Insert File dialog box appears.

7. Click **blank file.wav** and click **Open** to insert it in the open version of the file. This adds another 60 seconds to the file's length, doubling it.

8. Repeat step 7 until the open file is longer than the longest audio segment you need to record.

9. Click the **File** menu, and click **Save** to save the file.

10. Click the **File** menu, and click **Exit** to close Sound Recorder.

11. In the Recording Control window, drag the **Volume** slider of your audio source back up to stop muting the input.

RECORD USING SOUND RECORDER

To record using Sound Recorder:

1. Click the **File** menu, and click **Open**. The Open dialog box appears.

2. Click **blank file.wav** and click **Open** to open it.

3. Click the **Record** button to start recording.

4. Start the audio playing.

5. Click the **Stop** button to stop recording.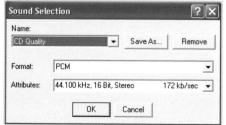

6. Click the **Rewind** button.

7. Click the **Play** button, listen to the sound, and check that the sound level is neither too high nor too low. (If it is, click **Rewind**, click **Record**, restart the audio, and record it again.)

8. Click the **File** menu, and click **Save As**. The Save As dialog box appears.

9. Specify the folder and name for the file.

10. Verify the format in the Save As Type drop-down list. If you need to change it, click **Change** and use the options in the Sound Selection dialog box to specify the format you want. For full-quality audio, select **CD Quality** in the Name drop-down list. This choice records the file as 16-bit stereo sampled at 44.1 kHz, making it sound perfect to human ears. The disadvantage to this format is that it takes up around 9 MB of disk space per minute of audio.

11. If you want to record another sound file, repeat steps 1 through 10. Otherwise, click the **File** menu, and click **Exit** to close Sound Recorder.

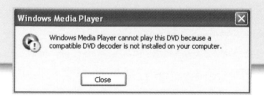

UNDERSTANDING DVD REGIONS

DVDs are encoded for eight different *regions* (geographical or notional areas) to enable the movie industry to control the release dates, pricing, and content of movies in different areas of the world.

- Most movies and DVDs are released in the U.S., Canada, and Japan first. Regional encoding helps prevent DVDs sold in these countries from spoiling movie ticket sales in countries with later release dates.

- People in Region 1 (the U.S., Canada, and U.S. Territories) typically pay less for DVDs than people in Region 2 (Europe, Japan, the Middle East, and South Africa) but more than people in Region 3 (Southeast and East Asia) and Region 6 (China).

- People temporarily in Region 8 (on international flights and cruises) get versions of movies with plane crashes and maritime disasters tactfully omitted.

To play a DVD, your DVD drive or player must be set for the right region. To Hollywood's dismay, you can get some multiregion DVD players, but almost all computer DVD drives are restricted to playing one region at a time. You can usually switch a drive from region to region, but only a limited number of times (five changes is typical) before it becomes locked with the last region setting.

If your DVD drive is set for the wrong region for a DVD you've inserted, Windows Media Player displays a message. Note the region you need, and click the **OK** button. The Properties dialog box for the DVD drive appears. Click the **DVD Region** tab, click the country in the list box, check that the readout in the New Region text box matches the required region, and then click **OK** to make the change.

Some DVDs are encoded without region restrictions. These *all-region DVDs* work on any DVD player or drive.

Watch Video Files and DVDs

You can also watch video files or video CDs using Windows Media Player; if your PC has a DVD drive, you can watch DVDs as well.

Watch Video Files

The easiest way to play a video file using Windows Media Player is to double-click the file in a Windows Explorer window (if the file is stored on a local drive) or click a link to the file in an Internet Explorer window (if the file is stored on the Internet). Windows Media Player starts automatically and begins playing the file. Use the playback controls to control playback in much the same way as to play a music file.

Watch DVDs

To watch a DVD using Windows Media Player, you must have a hardware or software DVD decoder. A hardware DVD decoder is part of your DVD drive or an add-in card to which the DVD drive is linked. A software DVD decoder is a program that enables Windows Media Player to decode the data on the DVD.

- Insert the DVD.

- If you bought your DVD drive separately, the package may have included a DVD decoder.

To watch a DVD using Windows Media Player:

1. Press the **eject** button on your PC to open the tray on your optical drive. Insert the DVD and press the **eject** button to close the tray.

2. XP recognizes the DVD and displays the AutoPlay dialog box.

3. Verify that the **Play DVD Video Using Windows Media Player** item is selected; select the **Always Do The Selected Action** check box, if appropriate; and then click **OK**.

4. To control the DVD playback, use the same controls as for playing a CD. Click the **View** menu, and click **Full Screen** to display the DVD playback full screen. (Alternatively, press **ALT+ENTER**.) Press **ESC** to return from full-screen mode to standard mode.

Chapter 6
Upgrading, Installing, and Configuring Hardware

No matter how well equipped your PC is when you buy it, you'll probably need to add hardware to it sooner or later to extend or improve its capabilities. This chapter explains how to establish which upgrades are possible for your PC, how to choose hardware, how to install or connect it physically to your PC, and how to get it working. This chapter also shows you how to perform the three hardware upgrades you're most likely to want to perform yourself: increasing your PC's memory, adding another hard drive, and adding an optical drive. It then explains how to add a PCI card to a desktop PC and how to install drivers for the hardware you install.

Beyond the hardware upgrades discussed in this chapter, Chapter 3 covers installing a modem; Chapter 5 covers connecting cameras, scanners, and printers; and Chapter 8 covers installing network adapters.

QUICKFACTS

UPGRADING THE MOTHERBOARD

Upgrading the motherboard is usually possible only for desktop PCs and not for laptop PCs. The motherboard must be the correct size for the PC case and must contain the appropriate number of PCI (Peripheral Component Interconnect) slots for the PCI cards you need to install. Depending on your needs, the motherboard may also have other features integrated into it, such as a graphics card, a sound card, and a network card. Having such features integrated reduces the number of PCI slots you need, but it also makes upgrading individual components of your PC more difficult.

A motherboard upgrade affects the whole PC and requires disconnecting most cables, removing almost all components, and reinstalling the components and reconnecting the cables. Consult a PC technician unless you are highly knowledgeable in this area.

Prepare to Install Hardware

Before you buy any hardware, you must be sure that it will work with your PC and that you can attach it to your PC.

- In most desktop PCs, you can upgrade almost any component from the *motherboard*, or *system board* (the main circuit board into which the processor, memory, and add-in cards are plugged) to the memory, hard drive, internal optical drives, sound card, graphics adapter, network adapter, and more.

- In most laptops, you can add memory but cannot change any other internal components without considerable expertise, expense, or trouble.

- You can add many external devices (such as hard drives, optical drives, and network adapters) to both desktop PCs and laptop PCs via USB, FireWire, and PC Card connections.

Connect Hot-Pluggable Hardware

Hot-pluggable devices are those you can plug in or unplug while Windows XP is running and have XP automatically load or unload the appropriate driver. FireWire, USB, and PC Card devices are almost always hot-pluggable. XP can sometimes detect serial devices (such as serial modems) and automatically load drivers for them, but such devices aren't normally considered hot-pluggable because some of them won't work unless they're plugged in when XP starts up.

All hot-pluggable devices connect to your PC from the outside, typically via USB ports, FireWire ports, or PC Card slots.

The first time you add a hot-pluggable device to your PC, the notification area displays a Found New Hardware pop-up window that mentions the type of connection the device uses. XP then examines the device and displays a second pop-up window in the notification area that gives the name of the device.

ADDING MEMORY

Adding memory, also known as RAM (random access memory), can be one of the most effective upgrades for your PC, because having plenty of memory enables your PC to run XP and your programs faster. XP will run with 128 MB, but 256 MB gives improved performance; 512 MB is enough for heavy single use or for multiple light users using Fast User Switching; and 1 GB or more is enough for multiple heavy users using Fast User Switching, the feature that enables you to switch among user sessions, as discussed in Chapter 1.

If the memory slots on your PC are accessible, the physical part of adding memory is relatively straightforward. (See the "Install Memory" section in this chapter.) You must get memory, however, that is the correct speed and type for your PC. You cannot mix and match memory types. Depending on your PC, you may have to install memory modules in matching pairs. If in doubt, consult your PC manufacturer's support center or a PC technician to determine what type of memory you need.

Before buying memory, check that your PC has a free memory slot. You may have to remove one or more of the installed memory modules in order to install higher-capacity memory modules.

After identifying the device, XP searches for a driver that will enable it to communicate with the device. "Supply a Device Driver Using the Found New Hardware Wizard," later in this chapter, discusses this process, which is often fully automatic.

Open a Desktop PC Case

To install hardware that's not hot-pluggable in a desktop PC, you must open the case and prepare to work inside it.

1. If XP is running, shut it down and turn off your PC.
2. Unplug the PC's power cord and any other cables (such as the keyboard and mouse cables) that could get in the way.
3. Unscrew the case or the relevant panel using a screwdriver for conventional case screws or your fingers for thumbscrews (screws with knurled, graspable sides—not instruments of torture).
4. Slide the case or panel off.
5. Before you touch anything inside the case, touch a metal object, such as your desktop PC case, to discharge any static you've built up.
6. Perform the desired operations inside the case; for example, install a drive or an adapter.
7. Replace the case or the panel.
8. Connect the cables you disconnected, and then restart the PC.

Install Memory

To add memory to a PC, follow these general steps, consulting your PC manufacturer's instructions for details:

1. If XP is running, shut it down and then turn off your PC.
2. Unplug the power cord. For a laptop PC, remove the battery.
3. For a desktop PC, open the case. For a laptop PC, open the memory compartment. Depending on the laptop PC, this usually means either lifting up the keyboard or un-screwing a memory hatch on the bottom of the laptop PC.

4. Before you touch anything inside the case, touch a metal object, such as your desktop PC case, to discharge any static you've built up. For a laptop PC, touch a metal object other than your laptop.

5. If you need to remove one of the installed memory modules to make space for a new one (as in the PC shown in Figure 6-1, where three memory modules fill all three available slots), use the PC manufacturer's instructions to identify which module is which. For most designs, you open the spring-loaded clips (the white tabs on either end of the modules in the figure) so that the module pops up at an angle, and then work it out of the slot with your fingers.

Figure 6-1: If all the memory slots on your PC are full, you will need to sacrifice one or more of your existing memory modules to make space for higher-capacity ones.

6. Slide the new module in at an angle so that it is firmly in the slot, and then push it gently until the spring-loaded clips click into place. Figure 6-2 illustrates installing a memory module in a laptop PC's memory compartment.

7. For a desktop PC, replace the case. For a laptop PC, close the memory compartment, and put the battery back in.

8. Connect the power cord, and then start your PC. Your PC typically will notice the memory automatically; however, on some PCs, you may need to access the BIOS settings (usually by pressing **DELETE** or **F2** during startup) and configure the PC to recognize the memory. Consult your PC manufacturer's documentation for instructions.

9. To check how much memory your PC has, click the **Start** button, right-click **My Computer**, click **Properties**, and check the readout near the bottom of the General tab of the System Properties dialog box. Click **OK** to close the dialog box.

Figure 6-2: When installing memory in a laptop, you typically open the memory compartment, slide in the memory module at a shallow angle, and then push it down gently until its latches click into place.

Add a Hard Drive

If you need more hard drive space than you currently have, you can often add a hard disk to your PC.

- On either a desktop PC or a laptop PC, you can replace your existing hard drive with a higher-capacity model. This option involves reinstalling XP and all your programs and transferring all the data and settings you want to keep, so it is best avoided unless you have no alternative.

- On most desktop PCs, you can install a second, third, or fourth internal hard drive to work alongside your existing drive or drives. The installation process involves mounting the drive in an empty drive bay in your PC, connecting an existing drive cable or installing a new one to the motherboard, and connecting an existing power cable to the power supply unit (see Figure 6-3). This process is relatively easy, but you may prefer to have a PC technician perform it for you to avoid any confusion.

- On either a desktop or a laptop PC, you can add an external USB 2.0 or FireWire hard drive. Provided that your PC has a USB 2.0 port or a FireWire port, this is usually the most convenient option for both desktop PCs and laptop PCs.

TIP

To transfer files and settings from your old hard drive to your new hard drive, you can use XP's Files And Settings Transfer Wizard (click the **Start** button, click **All Programs**, click **Accessories**, click **System Tools**, and then click **Files And Settings Transfer Wizard**). The Files and Settings Transfer Wizard can transfer Windows settings, program-configuration information, and specific files and folders. If you want to transfer all the data from your old hard disk to your new hard disk easily, consider a tool such as Symantec's Drive Image or Norton Ghost (both products are found at www.symantec.com and cost $69.95).

Drive bay

Hard drive

Power cable

Drive cable

Retaining screws

Figure 6-3: Secure the hard drive in the drive bay with screws, and connect the drive cable and the power cable (from the bundle of cables attached to the power supply) to the rear of the drive.

Set Up a New Hard Drive

After installing a new hard drive, you will normally need to initialize, partition, and format it.

INITIALIZE A NEW HARD DRIVE

1. Click the **Start** button, and then click **Run**. The Run dialog box appears.

2. Type <u>diskmgmt.msc</u> and press **ENTER**. The Disk Management window opens (see Figure 6-4).

3. If the new drive shows a red circle with a white bar, as shown with Disk 1 in the figure, right-click the drive and then click **Initialize Disk**. The Initialize Disk dialog box appears. Click **OK**. XP initializes the drive.

PARTITION A NEW HARD DRIVE

1. While still in the Disk Management window, for a drive that has been newly initialized, right-click the white box next to the drive, and click **New Partition**. The New Partition Wizard starts. Click **Next**. The Select Partition Type page appears.

2. Verify that the **Primary Partition** option button is selected, and then click **Next**. The Specify Partition Size page appears (see Figure 6-5).

3. Usually, it is most convenient to create one partition using all the space on the new drive. To do so, leave the default settings, and then click **Next**. If you want to create a smaller partition, change the **Partition Size In MB** value, and then click **Next**. The Assign Drive Letter Or Path page appears.

4. Verify that the **Assign The Following Drive Letter** option button is selected, and change the drive in the drop-down list if necessary.

Figure 6-4: Before you can use a newly installed hard drive, you usually need to initialize and format it first.

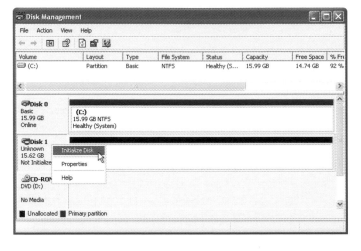

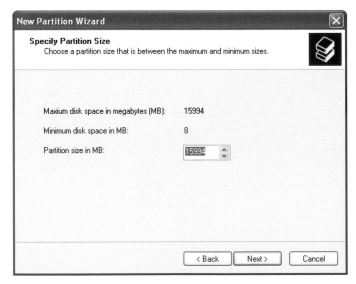

Figure 6-5: Format the new drive as a primary partition that takes up all the space on the new drive.

NOTE

Compression enables you to store more files on the drive, but it reduces drive performance slightly. If you have XP Professional, compression also prevents you from applying encryption to your files, because you cannot use both compression and encryption on the same files and folders.

FORMAT A NEW HARD DRIVE

1. Click **Next**. The Format Partition page appears (see Figure 6-6).

2. Verify that the **Format This Partition With The Following Settings** option button is selected, choose **NTFS** in the File System drop-down list box, and leave the **Allocation Size Unit** drop-down list set to Default.

3. Type a short name for the drive in the Volume Label box, for example, Drive2. Verify that the **Perform A Quick Format** check box is cleared (it's best to perform a full format of your new disk), and select the **Enable File And Folder Compression** check box if you want to use compression on the drive.

4. Click **OK**. On the Completing The New Partition Wizard page, verify your choices. If they're wrong, go back and fix them. Otherwise, click **Finish**. The wizard closes and begins formatting the drive.

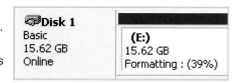

5. When the format is complete, click the **File** menu, and then click **Exit** to close the Disk Management window. You can then use your new drive to store files.

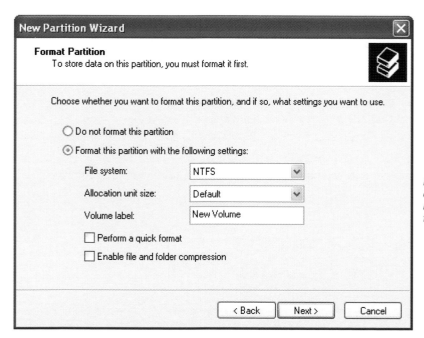

Figure 6-6: For most hard drives, you'll get optimum results using the NTFS file system.

NOTE

You also can get external optical drives that connect via SCSI or via a parallel port. These days, however, USB 2.0 or FireWire are far preferable means of connection for external drives because they're much faster than a parallel port, hot-pluggable, and easier than both SCSI and parallel-port connections.

Add a CD or DVD Drive

You can add a CD or DVD drive to your PC in the following three ways:

- Replace the existing drive on a desktop PC.
- Add a second internal drive to a desktop PC. If you have a free drive bay for a second optical drive and your existing drive is still functional, you may prefer to add the second drive instead so that you can work with two optical discs at once when necessary.
- Attach an external optical drive to either a desktop PC or a laptop PC via USB 2.0 or FireWire. In most cases, this is the easiest solution and the most flexible: you can disconnect the drive when you don't need it, and, if you have another PC, you can connect the drive to it when needed.

You can use the following steps to install an internal optical drive in conjunction with the manufacturer's specific instructions:

1. Turn off your PC, unplug the power cord, and remove the case or panel.
2. Before you touch anything inside the case, touch the case to discharge any static electricity.
3. Remove the cover from an unused drive bay at the front of the PC.
4. Slide the drive into the bay from the front, as shown here. You may want to slide it in beyond its final position so that the connectors on the back are easily accessible from the inside of the PC.

5. Connect a drive cable from the back of the optical drive to an existing drive cable or, if a new cable, plug it into a connector on your motherboard.

Audio cables (some drives use only one cable)

Drive cable

Power cable

6. Connect one or more audio cables (depending on the drive) from the audio outputs on the drive to your sound card.

7. Connect a power cable to the drive.

8. Slide the drive so that it is positioned flush with the front of the PC, and then screw it into place.

9. Close your PC, reattach the cables, and then restart it.

Install a PCI Card

Many add-on components for desktop PCs —sound cards, wired and wireless network adapters, and graphics adapters—are built as PCI cards. You install such a card in a PCI slot on your PC's motherboard (see Figure 6-7).

To install a PCI card:

1. Turn off your PC, unplug the power cord, and remove the case or panel.

2. Touch the case to discharge any static electricity.

3. If the opening at the back of the case next to the PCI slot is covered, unscrew and remove the metal tab (if it's screwed on) or break off the metal tab (if it's molded).

4. Remove the PCI card from its packaging, align it with the PCI slot, and press it into place.

5. Attach the PCI card's metal bracket to the case with a screw.

6. Close the case.

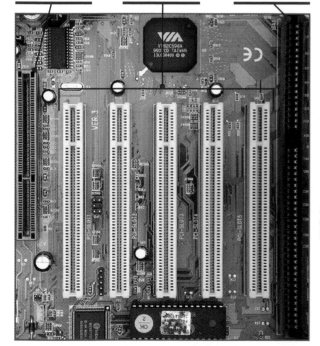

AGP slot; used for the graphics adapter

PCI slots; used for various add-in cards

ISA slot; used for older add-ins only

Figure 6-7: The PCI slots can be used for various types of add-in cards.

QUICKFACTS: FINDING DEVICE DRIVERS

Getting new hardware to work usually involves finding the correct device driver. The best sources for device drivers are:

- The **manufacturer** of the device is generally the best source, but as hardware gets older, manufacturers stop writing new drivers. If the manufacturer provided a driver on a CD or floppy disk with the hardware, try that driver; if not, go to the manufacturer's web site (search for it if necessary). Most manufacturers put a link with a name such as Downloads, Drivers, Software, or Support in a prominent position on their home page to guide you to the drivers.

- **Microsoft** has the latest drivers for the most widely used devices and, as a part of Windows Update, the ability to scan your PC and see if Windows Update has any drivers to help you. Unless you have turned off Automatic Updates, Windows Update will check periodically for new drivers. To check immediately, click the **Start** button, click **All Programs**, and then click **Windows Update**. Your browser opens and displays the Windows Update web site. Click **Scan For Updates**, and see if a driver for your device is found.

- **Third-party** sources can be found using search engines, such as Google (www.google.com) or Yahoo! (www.yahoo.com), and searching for <u>device drivers</u>. You should find a number of sources. Some of these sources charge you for drivers; others are free. Make sure that the driver will work with Windows XP.

Install a Device Driver

XP must have the correct driver for each piece of hardware on your PC before it can communicate with that hardware and use it successfully. As discussed earlier in this chapter, the Found New Hardware Wizard automatically searches for a suitable driver for each new hardware item it detects.

SUPPLY A DEVICE DRIVER USING THE FOUND NEW HARDWARE WIZARD

When the Found New Hardware Wizard starts, proceed as follows:

1. On the Welcome To The Found New Hardware Wizard page, verify that the **Install The Software Automatically** option button is selected, load the CD or disk containing the driver (if you have one), and then click **Next**.

2. The wizard searches for a driver for the hardware. If the wizard prompts you to allow it to connect to Windows Update, do so (assuming that you have an Internet connection).

3. If the wizard finds a driver for the hardware—on your hard disk, on a removable disk you've inserted, or on the Windows Update web site—it installs the driver automatically and tells you that the hardware is ready to use. Click **Finish**.

4. If the wizard can't find a driver for the hardware, it displays the Cannot Install This Hardware page. If you have a driver for the hardware, click **Back** to return to the first page of the wizard. Select the **Install From A List Or Specific Location** option button, and click **Next**. The Please Choose Your Search And Installation Options page appears.

5. Select the **Don't Search. I Will Choose The Driver To Install** option button, and then click **Next**. The Hardware Type page appears.

6. Select the type of hardware you're installing. If you can't find a suitable device category, click the **Show All Devices** item at the top of the list. Click **Next**. The Select The Device Driver You Want To Install For This Hardware page appears.

7. In the Manufacturer list box, click the manufacturer of the device you're installing (if the manufacturer is listed). In the Model list box, select the model (if it is listed). Click **Next**. On the The Wizard Is Ready To Install Your Hardware page, click **Next**. Skip to step 10.

8. If your device isn't listed, use the options in the Install From Disk dialog box to select the disk that contains the driver. If the driver is in a folder, browse to the folder, and then click **Open**. Click **OK**. The Select The Device Driver You Want To Install For This Hardware page appears.

9. Click the driver and then click **Next**. If the Update Driver Warning dialog box appears, and you're sure you want to proceed, click **Yes**. If the Hardware Installation dialog box appears, warning you that the driver has not passed Windows Logo testing to verify its compatibility with XP, click **Continue Anyway** if you want to proceed.

10. On the Completing The Found New Hardware Wizard page, click **Finish** to close the wizard. Your new hardware should now be ready for use.

SUPPLY A DEVICE DRIVER USING THE ADD HARDWARE WIZARD

The Found New Hardware Wizard runs only if XP detects the hardware you've added. If XP doesn't detect the hardware, you can use the Add Hardware Wizard to specify the driver the hardware needs.

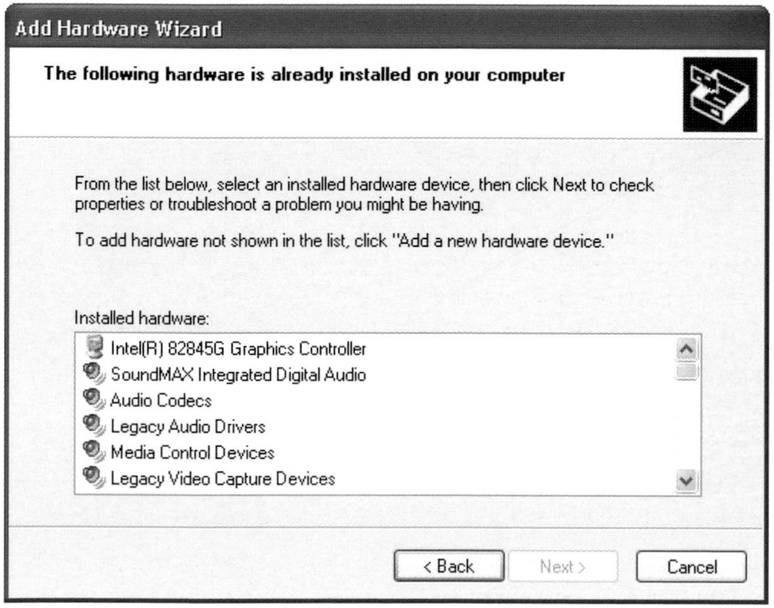

1. Click the **Start** button, and then click **Control Panel**. The Control Panel window opens.

2. In Category View, click **Printers And Other Hardware**, and then click the **Add Hardware** link in the See Also task pane. In Classic View, double-click **Add Hardware**. The Add Hardware Wizard starts. Click **Next**. The wizard then searches for new hardware that XP isn't yet using.

3. If the wizard displays the Is The Hardware Connected? page (as will usually be the case, given that the Found New Hardware Wizard wasn't able to detect the hardware), select the **Yes, I Have Already Connected The Hardware** option button, and then click **Next**. The The Following Hardware Is Already Installed On Your Computer page appears (see Figure 6-8).

4. If you can find the device in the Installed Hardware list box, select it. If not, select the last item, **Add A New Hardware Device**. Click **Next**. The The Wizard Can Help You Install Other Hardware page appears with the **Search For And Install The Hardware Automatically** option button selected.

5. Click the **Install The Hardware That I Manually Select From A List** option button, and then click **Next**. The From The List Below, Select The Type Of Hardware You Are Installing page appears.

Figure 6-8: Use the Add Hardware Wizard to install a device that XP doesn't detect automatically on your PC.

UPGRADING THE GRAPHICS ADAPTER

If your desktop PC doesn't deliver adequate graphics performance, you can upgrade your graphics adapter. (On most laptop PCs, you cannot change the graphics adapter because it is integrated into the motherboard.)

Most desktop PCs use one AGP (Aperture Graphics Port) graphics card, but also can use one or more PCI graphics cards to drive additional monitors. If you need to use multiple monitors, consider getting an AGP graphics adapter designed to drive two or more monitors. Multiple monitor–capable graphics adapters are more expensive than single-monitor versions, but they are easier to manage than multiple separate graphics adapters, which sometimes do not work in combination.

If your PC has an AGP graphics adapter installed in an AGP slot (rather than built into the motherboard), you should be able to upgrade easily. Check which variety of AGP your slot supports (AGP 2X, AGP 4X, or AGP 8X), buy a replacement graphics adapter that offers the features you need, shut down your PC and disconnect the power, remove the case, and replace the graphics adapter.

If your PC has a graphics chip built into the motherboard, you will need to disable that graphics chip in order to use a different graphics adapter. Consult your PC's documentation or manufacturer on how to do this.

6. If the type of device appears in the Common Hardware Types list box, click it. Otherwise, click **Show All Devices**, and click **Next**. The Select The Device Driver You Want To Use For This Hardware page is displayed.

7. In the Manufacturer list box, click the manufacturer of the device you're installing (if the manufacturer is listed). In the Model list box, select the model (if it is listed). Click **Next**. On the The Wizard Is Ready To Install Your Hardware page, click **Next**. Skip to step 10.

8. If the manufacturer or model isn't listed, click **Have Disk**. The Install From Disk dialog box appears. Use the options in the Install From Disk dialog box to select the disk that contains the driver. If the driver is in a folder, browse to the folder, and then click **Open**. Click **OK**. The Select The Device Driver You Want To Install For This Hardware page appears.

9. Click the driver and then click **Next**. If the Update Driver Warning dialog box appears, and you're sure you want to proceed, click **Yes**. If the Hardware Installation dialog box appears, warning you that the driver has not passed Windows Logo testing to verify its compatibility with XP, click **Continue Anyway** if you want to proceed.

10. On the Completing The Add Hardware Wizard page, click **Finish** to close the wizard. Your new hardware should now be ready for use.

Chapter 7
Securing Your PC

As you'll know if you've read a newspaper since the turn of the millennium, your PC faces a wide variety of threats. In this chapter you'll learn how to enhance your PC's physical security, prevent your PC from being used if it is stolen, install an antivirus program to defend your PC against viruses and other *malware* (malicious software), secure your PC on its local network, and secure it against attacks across the Internet.

Secure Your PC

The first (and arguably most obvious) aspect of security is securing your PC. This entails ensuring the physical security of the actual PC, setting a boot password, keeping Windows XP updated, installing and using antivirus software, avoiding potentially dangerous programs and drivers, and using an uninterruptible power supply (UPS) if you have a desktop PC.

Implement Physical Security

First, ensure your PC's physical security as much as possible. What this entails depends on your PC (a desktop or a laptop) and your circumstances.

- Most laptops have a connector for using a cable lock to connect the laptop to a less movable object. Such cable locks deter casual theft rather than determined thieves armed with bolt-cutters, but are often valuable in low- to moderate-risk situations.

- Most desktops are harder to steal discreetly than laptops because they're substantially larger and heavier and are not usually carried from place to place or used in public locations. If your desktop needs more security than your home or office provides, however, consider locking your desktop in a cabinet or custom computer safe. You'll need to deal with the awkwardness of routing all the cables into the cabinet or safe, but this is manageable.

No matter what protective measures you take, your PC's physical security may be compromised by human attack, by acts of nature, or simply by gravity. Your data will almost always be more valuable than your PC itself, so you must protect your data by backing it up regularly and frequently and by storing the backup at a different location than your PC. See "Back Up Your Data," later in this chapter.

Set a Boot Password

If your PC contains valuable data, secure it with a boot password. This is a password that you must enter when starting the PC in order to load the operating system. Consult your PC's documentation for instructions on setting a boot password.

Keep XP Updated

To protect your PC from the latest computer viruses and other threats (such as Trojan horses, worms, and buffer overflows), you must download and install the updates that Microsoft issues for Windows and its programs. XP's Automatic Updates feature is typically configured to download and install updates by default, but you should adjust the settings to suit your needs.

1. Click the **Start** button, right-click **My Computer**, and click **Properties**. The System Properties dialog box appears.

2. Click the **Automatic Updates** tab (see Figure 7-1).

3. Use the controls to specify whether to handle updates automatically, semiautomatically, or manually. Automatic updating is the best choice if your PC has a broadband Internet connection; leave the **Every Day** item selected, and choose a suitable time in the At drop-down list box. If you have a dial-up connection or if your PC is frequently disconnected from the Internet, you may prefer to update manually by clicking the link at the bottom of the Automatic Updates tab. The danger of this approach is that it is easy to skip vital updates; and because malicious software can spread worldwide within hours, it is important to install any available update as soon as possible.

4. Click **OK** to close the System Properties dialog box.

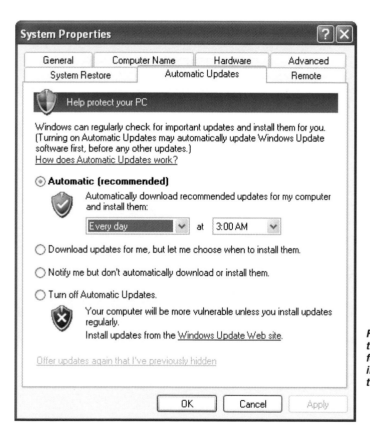

Figure 7-1: Configure the Automatic Updates feature to download and install updates at a time that suits you.

UPDATING TO SERVICE PACK 2

XP's Service Pack 2 (SP2) is a major upgrade to XP, including many vital security enhancements. SP2 is a must-have upgrade for all XP users—so if your PC doesn't yet have SP2, you should upgrade immediately.

VERIFY YOUR PC HAS SP2

To check whether your PC already has SP2:

1. Click the **Start** button, right-click **My Computer**, and click **Properties**. The System Properties dialog box appears.

2. Verify the System readout on the General tab. If the bottom line says "Service Pack 2" and lists a version number, SP2 is installed. If it says "Service Pack 1" or doesn't mention a service pack, you must install SP2.

3. Click **OK** to close the System Properties dialog box.

OBTAIN SP2

The easiest way to obtain SP2 is by clicking the **Start** button, clicking **All Programs**, and clicking **Windows Update**. An Internet Explorer window opens showing the Windows Update web site. You can either download SP2 (it's best to use a broadband connection, because SP2 is several hundred megabytes) or order an SP2 CD at a nominal shipping cost. You may also be able to obtain SP2 on CD from a computer store.

Continued...

NOTE

Each of these antivirus programs works with the XP Security Center built into XP Service Pack 2. If you choose another antivirus program, verify that it works with the Security Center so that XP knows that you have installed an antivirus program.

Install and Use an Antivirus Program

To protect your PC from viruses and other malware, you must install an antivirus program, run it all the time, and keep it updated. Viruses and malware can infect your PC even if it never connects to a network or the Internet. For example, you might load a CD that contains a virus, or someone might give you a disk that holds a Word document with a *worm* (a self-replicating piece of malware) or a game that contained a *Trojan horse* (malware hidden in an otherwise attractive program or normal document).

Figure 7-2: XP SP2's Windows Security Center lets you check for deficiencies in your PC's security and configure settings.

UPDATING TO SERVICE PACK 2

(Continued)

INSTALL SP2

After obtaining SP2, back up your PC (see "Back Up Your Data," later in this chapter), and then install SP2.

1. With XP running, close all open programs.

2. If you download SP2, the installation may start automatically. If not, double-click the file you downloaded to start the installation. If SP2 is on a CD, insert the CD in your CD drive, and follow the AutoPlay instructions to start the installation. The Windows XP Service Pack 2 Setup Wizard starts. Click **Next**.

3. Accept the license agreement if you want to proceed, and click **Next**. Allow your PC to complete the installation, and then click **Finish**. The wizard restarts your PC.

CONFIGURE SP2 SECURITY SETTINGS

When your PC restarts after installing SP2, it displays the Windows Security Center (see Figure 7-2), which shows the status of Windows Firewall, the Automatic Updates feature, and virus protection. If all is well, you'll see three green lights. If you see a red light, click the heading to expand the section (as shown in the figure), click **Recommendations**, and then follow XP's recommendations for fixing the problem.

You can open the Windows Security Center at any time by clicking the **Start** button, clicking **All Programs**, clicking **Accessories**, clicking **System Tools**, and then clicking **Security Center**. If the Windows Security Alerts icon appears in the notification area, you can open the Windows Security Center by clicking the icon. XP automatically displays the red version of this icon in the notification area to alert you to a security problem that you need to deal with.

The leading antivirus programs are:

- Norton AntiVirus (www.symantec.com)
- McAfee VirusScan (www.nai.com)
- Trend Micro PC-cillin (www.trendmicro.com)
- AVG Anti-Virus (www.grisoft.com, shown in Figure 7-3)

Each of these antivirus programs comes in several editions, depending on the number of PCs you need to protect. Grisoft offers a stripped-down, free edition of AVG Anti-Virus for PCs that aren't networked. Grisoft and some other vendors offer evaluation editions of their commercial antivirus programs to help you decide which program suits you best.

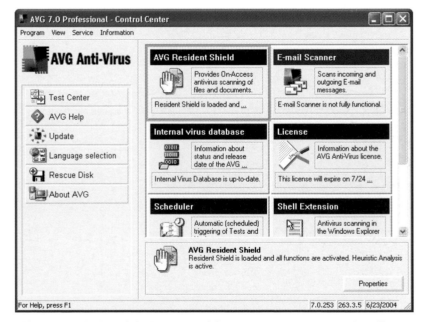

Figure 7-3: XP doesn't include an antivirus program, so you must install a third-party program to help prevent your PC from becoming infected.

7

CAUTION

Because antivirus software hooks deeply into the operating system to try to ensure that no malware takes unauthorized actions, most antivirus programs need to have your PC to themselves to function properly. Never install two or more antivirus programs on the same PC, because they will most likely conflict with each other. If you decide to switch from one antivirus program to another, uninstall the first antivirus program and reboot your PC before installing the other antivirus program.

Follow the instructions with your antivirus program to install, use, and update it. Keep the antivirus program running all the time to protect against threats. You must update your virus-definition files regularly (and frequently) to make sure that the antivirus program has the information required to identify the latest viruses and malware. Most antivirus programs prompt you by default to check for updates every week or so. For maximum protection, check for updates every day, and apply any available updates as soon as you discover them.

Avoid Unsigned Programs and Drivers

To help ensure that you can ascertain who created the programs and drivers you install, XP checks programs and drivers for *digital signatures*, encrypted identification information. When you try to install an unsigned program or driver, a security warning dialog box appears. Figure 7-4 shows two examples of security warning dialog boxes. The first is the Security Warning dialog box for a program whose publisher could not be verified (click **Run** if you're sure you want to proceed), and the second is the Hardware Installation dialog box warning that a printer driver has not passed Windows-compatibility testing (click **Continue Anyway** if you're sure the driver is safe to use).

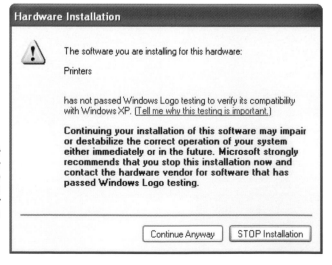

Figure 7-4: When XP warns you that it can't verify the source or XP compatibility of a program or driver, it's best not to install the program or driver; however, you will not be able to use the program or hardware that needs the driver.

CHOOSING A UPS

The more power you need it to deliver, the heavier the UPS is and the more it costs. Before buying a UPS, calculate how much power your PC needs. The easiest way to calculate the power is to use a template, such as the one at American Power Conversion Corporation's web site (www.apcc.com/template/size/apc/; this web site requires your browser to accept cookies in order to work; see Chapter 3 for more information on cookies).

Unless you will be at your PC all the time it's on, get a UPS that can shut down your PC automatically when there's a sustained power outage and you're not there. Newer UPSs connect to your PC via USB (Universal Serial Bus), while older models connect via a serial port. USB is now a better bet. Make sure that the UPS includes software for shutting down your PC automatically. (One example of such software is APC's PowerChute.)

Use an Uninterruptible Power Supply

The battery in a laptop enables it to ride out power outages for up to several hours, depending on how fully the battery is charged and how much power the laptop consumes. With a desktop PC, you can use an uninterruptible power supply, or UPS, to prevent your PC from crashing when the power goes out. Your PC's power cord plugs into the UPS, which in turn plugs into a wall outlet. The UPS contains batteries that will supply power to your PC for a short time (from 5 to 30 minutes), enough to get you through brief power interruptions or allow you to shut down your PC "gracefully" (under control) on longer outages.

A UPS helps protect your PC from electric spikes that come through the electric wires, but it's a good idea to unplug both the PC and the phone line during electrical storms in case lightning strikes nearby and sends a huge spike through the wires.

The procedure for installing a UPS depends on the model of UPS, but in general it involves these steps:

1. Plug the UPS into an electrical outlet, and charge it for the time specified in the instructions.

2. If your PC is running, shut down XP and turn off the computer.

3. Plug your CPU, monitor, and any external hard drives into the UPS.

4. Connect the UPS to your PC via a serial cable or a USB cable (the cable may be included with the UPS). A USB cable must connect directly to a port on the PC, not through a USB hub.

5. Switch on the UPS, switch on your PC, and log on to XP.

6. If the UPS came with an installation program (or if you can download an installation program from the manufacturer's web site), run the installation program. This will install the power-management software and configure XP's power options to use the UPS. Skip to step 10.

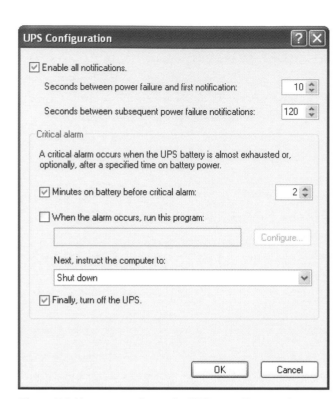

Figure 7-5: You can configure the UPS to notify you of a power failure, run a program when the battery is critically low, shut down your PC, and turn itself off.

NOTE

This book talks about setting up local user accounts, which are set up on your PC. If your PC is part of a server-based network that uses domains (administrative units), your network administrator will set up user accounts through the domain. See *Windows XP Professional: The Complete Reference* (published by McGraw-Hill Osborne Media) for details on using XP in a domain.

7. Most UPSs that connect via USB are configured automatically, but if the UPS connects via a serial cable, you must configure it. If you don't have an installation program, click the **Start** button, and click **Control Panel.** In Category View, click **Performance And Maintenance**, and then click **Power Options**. In Classic View, double-click **Power Options**. The Power Options Properties dialog box appears.

8. Click the **UPS** tab, and then click **Select**. Select the UPS in the UPS Selection dialog box, and specify the serial port to which it is connected (COM1 is the first serial port, and COM2 is the second serial port), and then click **Finish**. The UPS tab of the Power Options Properties dialog box shows the UPS you chose. Click **Configure**, use the options in the UPS Configuration dialog box (see Figure 7-5) to specify what you want to happen when there's a power outage, and then click **OK**.

9. Click **OK** to close the Properties dialog box. Click **Close** to close the **Performance And Maintenance** or **Control Panel window**.

10. Close any open programs, and simulate a power outage by unplugging the UPS from the electric socket. Check that the actions you specified occur—for example, that the UPS sounds the alarm, shuts down your PC, and then shuts itself down.

11. Plug the UPS back into the electric socket, switch it back on, and then restart your PC.

Implement User Security

After ensuring your PC's basic security by using locks, a boot password, a UPS, and an antivirus program, minimize threats to the PC from the people who use it. This means setting up a user account for each user of your PC, making him or her use a password, ensuring that your PC requires a password after being roused from a screen saver or sleep, and securing each user's files from all other users (except for files he or she wants to share).

NOTE

This section assumes that you are logged on as an administrator. The user account you create during installation is an administrator account, so you are probably already logged on as an administrator. If you're not sure whether you're an administrator or not, open the User Accounts window by clicking the **Start** button, clicking **Control Panel**, and clicking (in Category View) or double-clicking (in Classic View) **User Accounts**. See whether your account is labeled "Computer Administrator" or "Limited Account."

Figure 7-6: To help secure your PC, set up a separate user account for each user, require a password for each account, and turn off the Guest account.

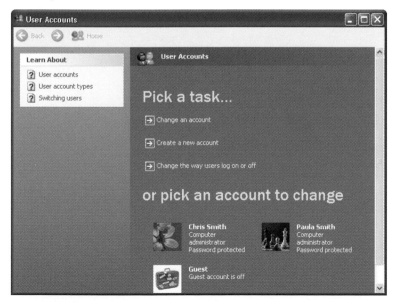

Control Users and Passwords

After the boot password, your PC's first line of security is XP's login screen. To prevent an unauthorized person from logging on to XP, you must create a user account for each person who uses your PC and assign a password to each user account. You must also turn off the Guest account.

CREATE A USER ACCOUNT AND APPLY A PASSWORD

To create a user account:

1. Click the **Start** button, and click **Control Panel**. In Category View, click **User Accounts**; in Classic View, double-click **User Accounts**. The User Accounts window opens (see Figure 7-6).

2. Click **Create A New Account**, type a name of up to 20 characters on the Name The New Account page, and then click **Next**. The Pick An Account Type page is displayed.

3. Unless the new user will administer your PC, select the **Limited** option button instead of the default Computer Administrator option button.

4. Click **Create Account**. You are returned to the main User Accounts window.

5. Click the account you just created. A window opens, showing options you can change for the account.

6. Click **Create A Password**. The Create A Password window opens.

7. Type the password twice, type a password hint if you think the user will need it (a password hint is always bad for security), and click **Create Password**. You are returned to the previous screen.

8. Click **Home** in the upper-left area to return to the main User Accounts window so that you can work further with user accounts, or click **Close** to close the window.

After creating the user account and password, tell the person the user name and password, and instruct him or her on how to change the password the first time he or she logs on to XP.

SET PASSWORDS FOR OTHER USERS

Every user of your PC must have a password for the PC to be even moderately secure. You can use steps 5 through 8 of the previous section to set passwords for existing users, but doing so causes them to lose access to key information, including any passwords they've stored for network resources or web sites. For this reason, it's better to persuade users to change their passwords themselves by using the steps in the next section.

SET YOUR OWN PASSWORD

You must also set a password for your own account to ensure that nobody else can log on to it.

1. Click the **Start** button, and click **Control Panel**. In Category View, click **User Accounts**; in Classic View, double-click **User Accounts**. The User Accounts window opens.

2. Click your account. A window opens, showing options you can change for the account.

3. Click **Create A Password**, type the password twice, and click **Create Password**. A window opens, asking if you want to make your files and folders private.

4. Click **Yes**, **Make Private**. XP changes the access permissions on the files and folders in your My Documents folder so that other users cannot access them. The Account Options window then opens.

5. From the Account Options window, you can also change the picture associated with your user account, change your account type (from administrator to limited), change your user name, or remove your password.

TURN OFF THE GUEST ACCOUNT

The Guest account is an unprotected account intended for use by people who need to use the PC only temporarily and take only limited actions with it. You should ensure that the Guest account is turned off except when someone needs to use it. To turn off the Guest account:

1. Click the **Start** button, and click Control Panel. In Category View, click User Accounts; in Classic View, double-click User Accounts. The User Accounts window opens.

2. If the Guest account entry says "Guest account is on," click **Guest**, click **Turn Off The Guest Account**, and then click **Close** to close the User Accounts window.

Password-Protect Your PC after Screen Saver or Standby

Usually, your screen saver kicks in when you leave your PC unattended (or when the phone or a colleague has claimed your attention). For security, make sure that whoever interrupts your screen saver has the authority to use your PC. If you use standby, ensure that waking your PC requires a password.

1. Right-click blank space on the desktop, and then click **Properties**. The Display Properties dialog box appears.

2. Click the **Screen Saver** tab.

3. Select the **On Resume**, **Password Protect** check box (on XP Professional) or the **On Resume**, **Display Welcome Screen** check box (on XP Home Edition).

4. Click **Power**. The Power Options Properties dialog box appears.

5. Click the **Advanced** tab, select the **Prompt For Password When Computer Resumes From Standby** check box, and click **OK**.

6. Click **OK** to close the Display Properties dialog box.

Secure Your Folders from Other Users

By default, XP allows all administrators to see the files and folders stored in your My Documents folder. For security, you should make your folders private so that other administrators can't see them. To do so, set a password as described in "Set Your Own Password," earlier in this chapter, and then click **Yes, Make Private** when asked if you want to make your files and folders private.

After making your My Documents folder private, you may never need to allow other users to access it. If you do, however, remove the privacy setting.

1. Click the **Start** button, and then click **My Computer**. A My Computer window opens.

2. Right-click the documents folder with your user name (for example, Dana Smith's Documents, if your user name is Dana Smith), and then click **Properties**. The My Documents Properties dialog box appears.

Dana Smith Properties   ? ✕

General | **Sharing** | Customize

Local sharing and security

To share this folder with other users of this computer only, drag it to the <u>Shared Documents</u> folder.

To make this folder and its subfolders private so that only you have access, select the following check box.

☑ Make this folder private

Network sharing and security

As a security measure, Windows has disabled remote access to this computer. However, you can enable remote access and safely share files by running the <u>Network Setup Wizard</u>.

If you understand the security risks but want to share files without running the wizard, click here.

Learn more about <u>sharing and security</u>.

[OK] [Cancel] [Apply]

Figure 7-7: You can turn on and off the privacy setting on your My Documents folder by using the Make This Folder Private check box.

NOTE

A *firewall* is a protective barrier between your computer and other computers to which it is connected. When turned on and configured correctly, the firewall permits only approved data to pass and blocks the passage of any data that is not approved.

---

3. Click the **Sharing** tab, and then click the **Another Folder** link at the bottom. The Properties dialog box for your user folder appears (see Figure 7-7).

4. Clear the **Make This Folder Private** check box. (To make your folders private again later, select this check box.)

5. Click **OK**.

Implement Network and Internet Security

If your PC is part of a network or if it is connected to the Internet, you must implement adequate security to make sure that no malefactor can connect to it or otherwise harm it from a remote PC. That means turning on and configuring XP's built-in firewall, sharing folders safely, turning off any unnecessary network services, and securing your web browser as much as possible.

Turn On and Configure Windows Firewall

If your PC connects to a network or the Internet, you must turn on Windows Firewall. In versions of XP without service packs and XP with Service Pack 1, the firewall is called Internet Connection Firewall (ICF) and is turned off by default, leaving your PC unsecured. When you have installed XP Service Pack 2 on your PC, the firewall is called Windows Firewall and is turned on by default. Whichever version of XP you have, you should verify that the firewall is turned on and correctly configured.

QUICKSTEPS

RESETTING A PASSWORD

To avoid losing data if you forget your password, create a password-reset disk.

CREATE A PASSWORD-RESET DISK

1. Click the **Start** button, and click **Control Panel**. In Category View, click **User Accounts**; in Classic View, double-click **User Accounts**.

2. Click your account.

3. In the Related Tasks area, click **Prevent A Forgotten Password**, and then click **Next**.

4. Verify that your PC's floppy drive is selected in the drop-down list box, and then click **Next**.

5. Insert a floppy disk into your PC's floppy drive. The disk must be formatted, but can contain other files provided that it has a few kilobytes free.

6. Type your current password, and click **Next**. After the wizard creates the disk, click **Next** and then click **Finish**.

7. Eject the disk, label it, and store it securely where nobody else can use it to access your account.

RESET YOUR PASSWORD

You'll typically need to use your password-reset disk when you find that XP's Welcome screen won't accept what you thought was your password.

1. On the Welcome screen, click the arrow to the right of the box for your password, and then click the **Use Your Password Reset Disk** link. The Password Reset Wizard starts. Click **Next**.

2. Insert the disk, verify the drive, and click **Next**.

3. Type a new password twice, type a password hint if you think you're likely to forget your new password, click **Next**, and then click **Finish**.

4. At the Welcome screen, type your new password and press **ENTER** to log on.

From now on, use the new password. Your password-reset disk remains valid, so you don't need to create a new reset disk.

TURN ON WINDOWS FIREWALL

1. Click the **Start** button, and click **Control Panel**. In Category View, click **Security Center** and then, with XP Service Pack 2, click **Windows Firewall**; in Classic View, double-click **Windows Firewall**. The Windows Firewall dialog box appears with the General tab displayed (see Figure 7-8).

2. Verify that the **On (Recommended)** option button is selected.

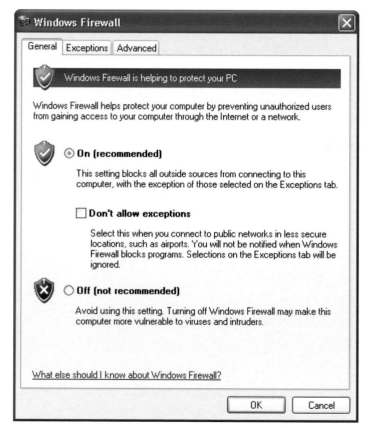

Figure 7-8: Make sure that Windows Firewall is turned on to protect your PC from network and Internet dangers. Select the Don't Allow Exceptions check box if you use your PC to connect to public networks (for example, via Wi-Fi hotspots).

3. If you need to connect to public networks via hotel networks or Wi-Fi hotspots, select the **Don't Allow Exceptions** check box to instruct Windows Firewall to block access to your PC via any of the exceptions you've set up.

4. If you need to arrange for other people to access your PC, follow the instructions in the next sections. Otherwise, click **OK** to close the Windows Firewall dialog box, and then click **Close** to close the Control Panel window.

CONFIGURE WINDOWS FIREWALL

Normally, XP configures Windows Firewall automatically. In order to allow some programs to communicate across your network and the Internet, however, you may need to configure Windows Firewall manually.

To configure Windows Firewall manually:

1. With the Windows Firewall dialog box open (as discussed in the previous section), click the **Exceptions** tab (see Figure 7-9).

2. Examine the list of exceptions. Remote Assistance, Remote Desktop, and Windows Messenger will normally need to be able to pierce the firewall, but other applications are less likely to need passage. In particular, ensure that the **File And Printer Sharing** check box is not selected. If you need to make a change to allow a particular program to run, use the **Add Program** button or the **Add Port** button to add the program or configure the port.

3. If necessary, click the **Advanced** tab, and configure settings separately for each of your network and Internet connections. This tab also contains options for creating a security log of the attempts to access your PC, configure Internet Control Message Protocol (ICMP) messages (which are used to share information about your PC with computers on the network or the Internet), or restore the default settings of Windows Firewall.

4. Click **OK** to close the Windows Firewall dialog box, and then click **Close** to close the Control Panel window.

Figure 7-9: You may sometimes need to add exceptions to prevent Windows Firewall from blocking vital programs. More often, you should scan the Exceptions tab to make sure that malicious software hasn't added exceptions that shouldn't be there.

Secure Your Internet Browsing

At this writing, Internet Explorer is the most widely used web browser in the short history of the Web. Unfortunately, many security loopholes have been discovered in Internet Explorer; and these loopholes have been used by malicious hackers trying to promote products, extract sensitive information from others' PCs, or simply inflict damage.

SECURE INTERNET EXPLORER

If you use Internet Explorer to browse the Internet, you must secure it as much as possible by using the features in Internet Explorer's Internet Options dialog box (see Chapter 3).

- Set a High security level for the Internet zone on the Security tab.

- Block as many cookies as you can without disabling the web site functionality you need by using the controls on the Privacy tab.

- Block pop-up ads from the Privacy tab.

- Use the Restricted Sites feature (on the Security tab) and the Content Advisor (on the Content tab) to keep yourself or other users from accessing sites that are known or likely to harbor malicious or undesirable content.

USE ANOTHER BROWSER

Given that Internet Explorer is the favorite target of malicious hackers, one straightforward security strategy is to use a different browser instead of Internet Explorer. Several other browsers are available, including Mozilla Firefox (www.mozilla.org; freeware; shown in Figure 7-10) and Opera (www.opera.com; $39 for the full version), which claims to be the fastest browser on earth. In time, these browsers, too, may be targeted by malefactors and security holes may be exposed, but at this writing, these browsers offer an easy way to sidestep attacks aimed at Internet Explorer.

Figure 7-10: Alternative browsers, such as Mozilla Firefox, enable you to sidestep Internet Explorer–specific threats and may offer extra features, such as the ability to open different web pages on tabs in the same window.

AVOID OR REMOVE SPYWARE

Spyware is the term for software that is installed without your permission on your PC and that executes a function that you don't want. Examples include:

- Changing your home page to a different page (such as a pornography site) and restoring the home page to that page if you change it back manually
- Adding bookmarks to Internet Explorer, to the Quick Launch toolbar, and to your desktop
- Running an application that monitors your PC usage or attempts to show you advertisements or learn your passwords or other sensitive data

The best way to avoid spyware is to prevent it from being installed.

- If a pop-up window (see the example here) prompts you to take an action, don't take it unless you trust the site you're visiting.

- If you're prompted to install an ActiveX control (a unit of program code), as in the example here (which appears across the top of the details area in the Internet Explorer window), don't install it unless you're sure the site is trustworthy.

> This site might require the following ActiveX control: 'the latest version of Flash Talk? By clicking...' from 'BetterInternet'. Click here to install...

Even if you're careful in your browsing and refuse all suspicious pop-ups and ActiveX controls, spyware may still infiltrate your PC through a security loophole. To get rid of it, or simply to ensure that your PC is clean, try Spybot Search & Destroy (www.safer-networking.org; freeware) or LavaSoft Ad-aware (www.lavasoft.de; freeware). Figure 7-11 shows Spybot Search & Destroy in action.

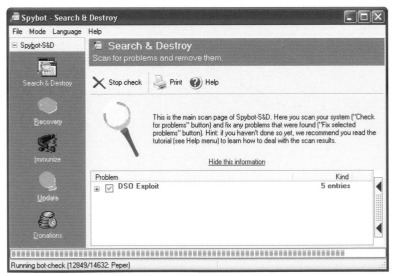

Figure 7-11: Use a tool such as Spybot Search & Destroy to remove any spyware that has been installed on your PC.

Secure Your Data

To ensure that you don't lose your valuable data if your PC fails or is stolen, you must secure your data by backing it up to a safe location. If your PC has XP Professional rather than XP Home Edition, you have the option of encrypting your files so that other people who access your computer cannot open your files and see their contents.

Back Up Your Data

Backing up your data means storing a copy of it in a safe location. XP includes a utility named Backup for backing up data.

1. Click the **Start** button, click **All Programs**, click **Accessories**, click **System Tools**, and then click **Backup**. The Backup Or Restore Wizard starts.

2. Click **Next**, verify that the **Back Up Files And Settings** option button is selected, and then click **Next** again. The What To Back Up page is displayed.

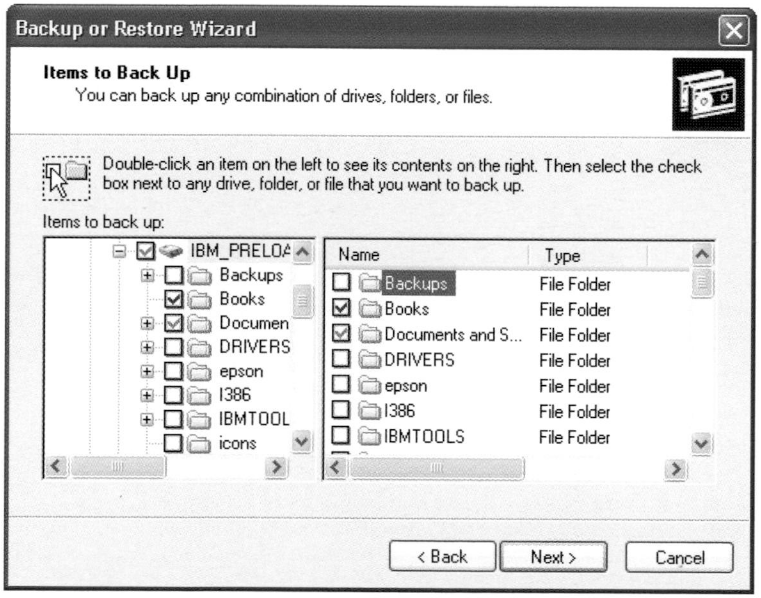

Figure 7-12: Select the check box for each file or folder you want to back up.

3. Choose what to back up: My Documents And Settings, Everyone's Documents And Settings, All Information On This Computer (on XP Professional only), or Let Me Choose What To Back Up (if backup space is limited or if you have many documents you don't need to back up, this choice is best). Click **Next**.

4. After deciding what to back up, the Items To Back Up page is displayed (see Figure 7-12). Select the folders and files to back up, and then click **Next**. The Backup Type, Destination, And Name page is displayed.

5. Select the backup type and the media to use. Type a descriptive name for the backup (for example, the date and the contents). Click **Next**. The Completing The Backup Or Restore Wizard page is displayed.

1 2 3 4 5 6 7 8 9 10

CAUTION

The All Information On This Computer backup option works only on XP Professional, not on XP Home Edition. This option enables you to create a full backup along with a system-recovery disk that you can use to restore XP after a major disaster. If you use this option, you must store the backup file on a drive other than the system drive (the drive on which XP is installed). It is best to store the backup file on a high-capacity external drive that you can detach from your computer and keep elsewhere for added security.

6. Click **Finish**. The Backup Progress dialog box appears and displays the status of the backup (see Figure 7-13).
7. When the backup is complete, click **Close** to close the wizard.

Encrypt Your Data

If you have XP Professional rather than XP Home Edition, you can use its Encrypting File System (EFS) feature to encrypt your files and folders so that they cannot be read without the encryption key. The key is attached to your user account, which has a unique security identifier (SID). When you log on to XP, you can use your files as if they were not encrypted. If someone else logs on, however, he or she cannot access the files; even if he or she copies the files and takes them to another PC, all that will be displayed is gibberish. You can, however, grant other users access to your encrypted files as necessary.

EFS encrypts and decrypts files on-the-fly as you work with them. For example, if you've encrypted a workbook, you can open it directly from Excel as if it weren't encrypted: XP decrypts the data in the encrypted file and passes it to Excel, which displays the data.

APPLY ENCRYPTION

To encrypt a folder or a file:

1. Open a Windows Explorer window, and browse to the folder that contains the folder or file you want to encrypt. For example, to encrypt your My Documents folder, click the **Start** button, click **My Documents**, and then click **Up**. The Windows Explorer window displays your Desktop folder, which contains your My Documents folder.
2. Right-click the file or folder to be encrypted, and click **Properties**. The Properties dialog box appears. Click the **General** tab if it isn't already selected.

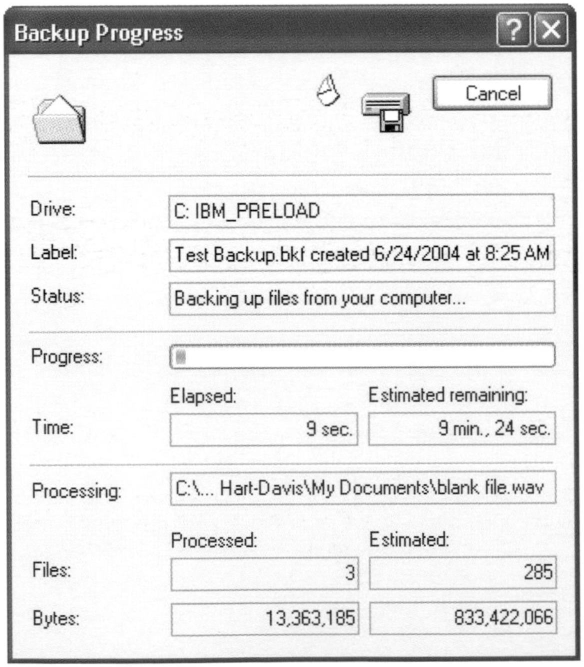

Figure 7-13: The length of time required to make a backup depends on the amount of data and the media you're using. Often, the most convenient time to start a backup is just before you take a break.

3. Click **Advanced**. The Advanced Attributes dialog box appears (see Figure 7-14).

4. Select the **Encrypt Contents To Secure Data** check box, and then click **OK**.

5. In the Properties dialog box, click **OK**. The Confirm Attribute Changes dialog box appears (see Figure 7-15) if you are encrypting a folder. Verify that the **Apply Changes To This Folder**, **Subfolder And Files** option button is selected, and then click **OK**. You'll see the Applying Attributes dialog box as XP encrypts the folder or file you specified.

6. Click **Close** to close the Windows Explorer window.

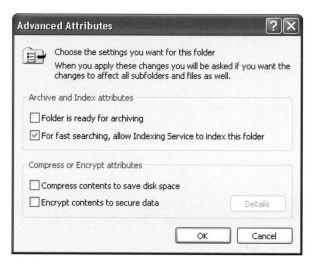

Figure 7-14: XP Professional lets you encrypt files or folders to protect them from other people who manage to access them against your wishes.

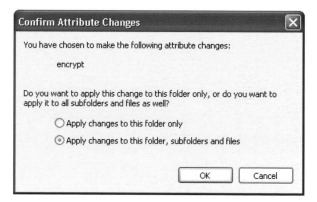

Figure 7-15: In the Confirm Attribute Changes dialog box, you will almost always want to select the Apply Changes To This Folder, Subfolders And Files option button.

REMOVE ENCRYPTION

To remove encryption from a file or folder, follow the steps in the previous section, but clear the **Encrypt Contents To Secure Data** check box in the Advanced Attributes dialog box for the file or folder. XP displays the Confirm Attribute Changes dialog box so that you can specify whether to apply the change only to the folder or to its subfolders and files as well.

WORK WITH ENCRYPTED FILES AND FOLDERS

XP handles EFS encryption and decryption transparently, letting you work with encrypted files in Windows Explorer or in applications just as you would work with unencrypted files. When you create a file in an encrypted folder, XP encrypts it; when you create a file in a folder that's not encrypted, XP doesn't encrypt it. When you back up encrypted files and folders to a backup application that supports EFS (for example, Windows XP's Backup Utility), the files and folders in the backup remain encrypted.

Encryption gets more complex when you move or copy files.

- If you copy or move an unencrypted file or folder into an encrypted folder, XP automatically encrypts the file or folder without displaying any notification.
- If you copy or move an encrypted file or folder from an encrypted folder to a folder that's not encrypted and is located on a volume formatted with NTFS, XP preserves the encryption on the file or folder.
- If you copy or move an encrypted file or folder from an encrypted folder to a folder that's not encrypted and is located on a volume formatted with a file system other than NTFS (for example, FAT32, FAT16, or FAT12), XP lets you choose whether to lose the encryption or cancel the copy or move operation.
- If you try to compress an encrypted file or folder, XP warns you that the file or folder needs to be decrypted first.

NOTE

By default, encrypted files and folders appear in a different color in Windows Explorer windows. This display is controlled by the Show Encrypted Or Compressed NTFS Files In Color check box on the View tab of the Folder Options dialog box. Encrypted files and folders are displayed in the default color in common Windows dialog boxes (for example, the common Open dialog box).

In order to recover files you've encrypted if you lose your encryption key (for example, if you need to reinstall XP to fix a configuration problem), you must create recovery certificates and set up another user account as your recovery agent. This procedure is complex, but you must perform it to make sure you don't lose access to your files.

CAUTION

EFS uses powerful encryption that can provide strong protection for your files—protection so strong that you will never be able to decrypt the files again if you lose your encryption key and have not implemented a recovery plan.

1. Click the **Start** button, click **All Programs**, click **Accessories**, and then click **Command Prompt**. A Command Prompt window opens.

2. Type cipher /r: and the path and file name where you want to create the recovery agent certificates, and then press **ENTER**. For example, type cipher /r:C:\Temp\Certs to create the recovery agent certificates in files named Certs in the Temp folder on your C: drive.

3. When prompted, type a password (you won't be able to see what you typed), press **ENTER**, type the password again to confirm it, and press **ENTER** again. The Cipher command creates one certificate file in the CER format and another in the PFX format. (CER and PFX are file formats for certificate files.)

4. Type exit and press **ENTER** to close the Command Prompt window. Click the **Start** button, click **My Computer**, locate the CER and PFX files, and copy the certificate files to removable media (such as a USB key or a floppy disk) or a secure online folder. Delete the original files from your PC.

5. Click the **Start** button, and click **Log Off** to log off from your user account.

6. Log on to the user account that you want to make your recovery agent.

7. Click the **Start** button, and click **Run**. The Run dialog box appears. Type certmgr.msc and press **ENTER**. The Certificates window opens (see Figure 7-16).

Figure 7-16: The Certificates window is a tool for managing all kinds of digital certificates, including recovery agent certificates for decrypting files.

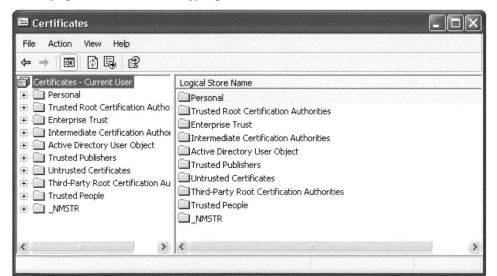

8. In the left pane, right-click the **Personal** item, click **All Tasks**, and then click **Import**. The Certificate Import Wizard starts. Click **Next**. The File To Import page is displayed.

9. Click **Browse**, select **Personal Information Exchange (*.pdx, *.p12)** in the Files Of Type drop-down list box. Open the **Look In** drop-down list, and locate the drive and folder that contains the certificate you created, select the certificate, and click **Open**. The certificate name appears in the wizard. Click **Next**. The Password page is displayed.

10. Type the password for the certificate, select the **Mark This Key As Exportable** check box, and click **Next**. The Certificate Store page is displayed.

11. Select the **Automatically Select The Certificate Store Based On The Type Of Certificate** option button, and click **Next**.

12. On the Completing The Certificate Import Wizard page, click **Finish**. In the message box telling you that the import was successful, click **OK**. Click the **Close** button (or click the **File** menu, and then click **Exit**) to close the Certificates window.

13. Click the **Start** button, and click **Run**. The Run dialog box appears. Type secpol.msc and click **OK**. The Local Security Settings window opens.

Figure 7-17: Use the Local Security Settings window to add a data recovery agent to another user account so that you can decrypt your encrypted files if disaster strikes.

14. Click **Security Settings** in the left pane, and then double-click **Public Key Policies** in the right pane. Right-click **Encrypting File System** in the right pane, click **All Tasks**, and click **Add Data Recovery Agent** (see Figure 7-17). The Add Recovery Agent Wizard starts. Click **Next**. The Select Recovery Agents page is displayed.

15. Click **Browse Folders**, use the **Open** dialog box to select the CER certificate file you created, click **Open**, and then click **Next**. On the Completing The Add Recovery Agent Wizard page, click **Finish**. Click **Close** to close the Local Security Settings window.

UNDERSTANDING THE LIMITATIONS OF EFS

Before using EFS it is important to understand it and its limitations.

- EFS works only on drives formatted with the NTFS file system (the default file system used by XP), not on volumes formatted with the FAT32 file system. On NTFS drives, you can encrypt either individual files or entire folders.

- You can't encrypt your system files, such as the files in your Windows folder. (In any case, you should encrypt only your data files.)

- You can't apply both compression and encryption to a file. In order to encrypt a compressed file, XP decompresses it first. When you try to compress an encrypted file, XP warns you that the file needs to be decrypted first. You can cancel the compression operation at this point.

- To safeguard your files if you lose your encryption key, you must designate another user account as the recovery agent that can recover your files. You must be able to log on to this other account in order to set up the recovery agent. If your PC connects to a corporate network running Windows, your network administrator will probably set up a recovery agent for you. If you use EFS on a standalone PC, you must set up the recovery agent yourself.

REMOVE THE RECOVERY AGENT'S KEY

Once you've added the recovery agent's certificate, XP includes the recovery agent's encryption key in any files you encrypt. You must then remove the recovery agent's key from your PC to prevent an attacker from being able to use the key to decrypt your encrypted files.

1. Still working in your recovery agent's user account, click the **Start** button, and click **Run**. Type certmgr.msc and press **ENTER**. The Certificates window opens.

2. Click **Certificates – Current User** in the left pane, double-click **Personal** in the right pane, and double-click **Certificates**. Right-click the certificate with your name, click **All Tasks**, and then click **Export**. The Certificate Export Wizard starts. Click **Next**. The Export Private Key page is displayed.

3. Select the **Yes**, **Export The Private Key** option button, and click **Next**. The Export File Format page is displayed.

4. Verify that the **Personal Information Exchange – PKCS #12 (.PFX)** option button is selected. Select the **Enable Strong Protection** check box and the **Delete The Private Key If The Export Is Successful** check box, and then click **Next**. The Password page is displayed.

5. Type a password, confirm it, and click **Next**. The File To Export page is displayed.

6. Click **Browse**. The Save As dialog box appears. Select the folder, type the file name for the certificate file, and click **Save**. In the wizard, click **Next**. On the Completing The Certificate Export Wizard page, click **Finish**. In the message box telling you that the export was successful, click **OK**.

7. Click **Close** to close the Certificates window.

8. Click the **Start** button, click **Log Off**, and then click **Log Off** on the Log Off Windows screen to log off from your recovery agent's user account. If you want to continue working, log on to your user account.

9. Store the recovery agent's certificate on removable media somewhere safe away from your computer. If you lose the recovery agent's certificate as well as your certificate, you won't be able to decrypt your encrypted files.

> **NOTE**
>
> The easiest way for another user to create an EFS certificate is for that person to encrypt a file or folder under his or her account. Doing so causes XP to create an EFS certificate automatically.

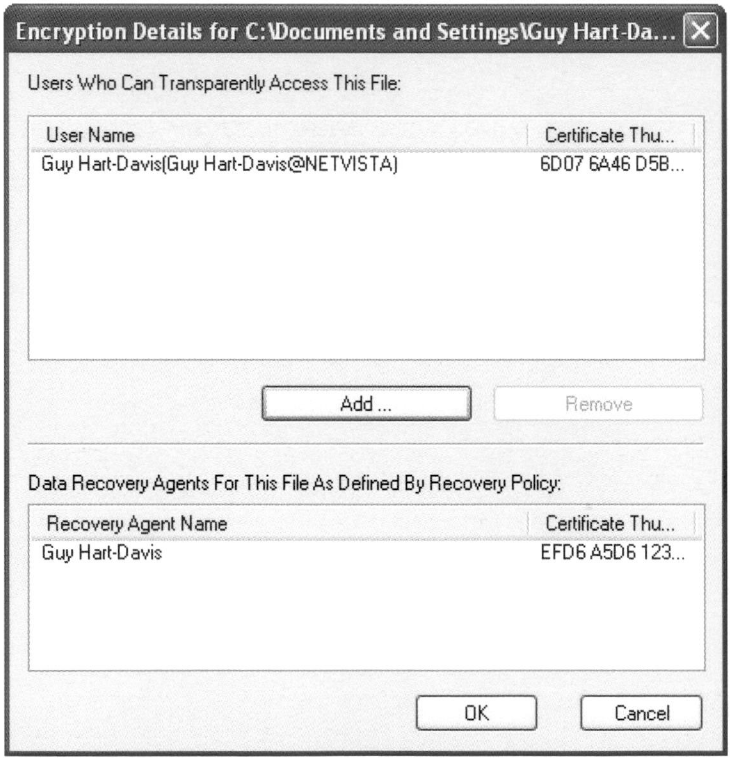

Figure 7-18: The Encryption Details dialog box lets you allow other users to access your encrypted files.

RECOVER ENCRYPTED FILES

If you lose your encryption key, you must use your recovery agent to recover your encrypted files.

1. Log on to the account you designated as your recovery agent.
2. Use the procedure in steps 7 through 12 under "Set Up a Recovery Agent" to import your recovery agent certificate. Close the **Certificates** window. You will then be able to decrypt the encrypted files.

LET OTHERS USE YOUR ENCRYPTED FILES

Because files and folders you encrypt with EFS are encrypted using a key linked to your SID, other people can't use the files unless you specifically allow them to. Even then, each user whom you permit to use your encrypted files needs to have an EFS certificate.

To allow another user to use a file that you've encrypted:

1. Open a Windows Explorer window, and browse to the folder that contains the encrypted folder or file you want to share.
2. Right-click the file or folder, and click **Properties**. The Properties dialog box appears. Click the **General** tab.
3. Click **Advanced**. The Advanced Attributes dialog box appears.
4. Click **Details**. The Encryption Details dialog box appears (see Figure 7-18).
5. Click the **Add** button, use the **Select User** dialog box to specify the user or users to add to the Users Who Can Transparently Access This File list, and then click **OK** to close each of the dialog boxes. Click **Close** to close the Windows Explorer window.

USING OTHERS' ENCRYPTED FILES

To use files that another user has encrypted with EFS, supply that user with your EFS certificate and have this person add you to his or her Users Who Can Transparently Access This File list for the appropriate file, as described in the previous section.

Chapter 8
Setting Up a Home Network

Networking is the sharing of resources and information between two or more connected computers—at home, within an organization, or around the world. A connection to the Internet (discussed in Chapter 3) is a form of networking known as a wide area network, or WAN.

Choose the Type of Network

The first step in setting up a home network is to decide the type of network you need. This section explains the several networking technologies that are available for home networks and helps you choose the technology best suited to your needs.

Understand Wired Ethernet

The most common way of connecting PCs is to use cables and equipment that conform to one of the wired Ethernet standards, which are based on speed and

UNDERSTANDING NETWORK TYPES

Computers on a network are divided into two roles. A *server* computer provides services, such as file storage or printing, to other computers. A *client* computer uses the services that the servers provide.

The type of network discussed in this chapter is a *peer-to-peer network*, a network in which each computer functions both as a client and as a server. For example, in a small peer-to-peer network, Andrea's PC might share a printer with Bill's PC and Chris's PC, while Bill's PC might share its Internet connection, and Chris's PC might share its scanner. Sharing resources causes some extra work for a peer PC, so it may run a little more slowly than normal, but the difference is usually negligible in a small network.

The other main type of network is client/server, which features a stricter division of labor: the servers provide the services, and the clients use the services without providing any services themselves. Client/server networks are more efficient than peer-to-peer networks because the servers can be administered centrally so that the services they provide are consistently available. (By contrast, in the peer-to-peer network mentioned previously, if Bill shuts down his PC, Andrea and Chris lose their Internet connection.) Client/server networks offer other benefits, including security and backup.

If you have an extra PC, you can easily create a client/server network instead of a peer-to-peer network. The "Turning an Old PC into a Server" QuickSteps, later in this chapter, explains how to create a server and set up a client/server network.

cable type. The three most common standards are:

- **10BaseT** provides a network that operates at the regular Ethernet speed of 10 Mbps (megabits, or millions of bits, per second).

- **100BaseT**, or Fast Ethernet, provides a network that operates at 100 Mbps.

- **Gigabit Ethernet** provides a network that operates at speeds of around 400 Mbps— not the 1 Gbps (gigabit, or billion bits, per second) that its name suggests.

Gigabit Ethernet is used mostly in corporate networks that need extremely fast networks. For most home, home-office, and small-office networks, a Fast Ethernet network, or even a regular Ethernet network, is fast enough.

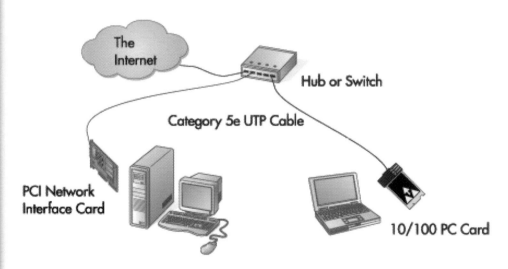

Figure 8-1: A wired Ethernet network consists of a network connection on your PC, a hub or switch into which other PCs are connected, and a cable connecting the two.

WEIGHING THE PROS AND CONS OF WIRED ETHERNET

The advantages of wired Ethernet are:

- It gives fast and reliable connections over distances of up to 100 meters per cable.

- The hardware is inexpensive. It usually costs less than $30 to network a PC via wired Ethernet.

- It offers good security. Unless someone can physically connect to the wires of your network or access your network across your Internet connection, he or she will not be able to break in without using fairly serious surveillance equipment.

The disadvantages of wired Ethernet are:

- You must run the cables from one PC to another. Typically, this means drilling holes from room to room or leaving digital tripwires lying around.

- Each PC must be connected to the network via a cable. This works well for desktop PCs but makes it awkward to move a laptop PC around.

NOTE

In the Ethernet standards names 10BaseT and 100BaseT, the "10" or "100" indicates the operating speed in Mbps; the "Base" stands for "baseband," a type of transmission; and the "T" indicates the type of cable required (twisted-pair cable).

A wired Ethernet or Fast Ethernet network, shown in Figure 8-1, has three major components:

- The **network connection** on your PC connects it to the network.
- A **hub**, **switch**, or **router** joins several PCs together to form the network.
  - A **hub**, the simplest and cheapest device, links the PCs using the network equivalent of a telephone party line.
  - A **switch** is a little more expensive than a hub, but all PCs are on the equivalent of a private telephone line. This arrangement allows switches to deliver better network performance than hubs.
  - A **router** joins two different networks—for example, joining a LAN to the Internet. A router often is combined with a hub or a switch, either in a single device or in separate devices, to join several PCs to each other and to the Internet.
- An **unshielded twisted pair (UTP)** cable with a simple RJ-45 connector (like a telephone connector, only bigger) joins the network connection to the hub, switch, or router. The most widely used types of UTP cable are Category 5 (Cat 5) or enhanced Category 5 (Cat 5e).

Ethernet networks are easy to set up (see "Set Up a Wired Ethernet Network," later in this chapter), have become pervasive throughout organizations, and typically cost less than $30 per PC on the network. Depending on the PC, a network connection may be built into the system board (or motherboard) or installed separately.

Understand Wireless Ethernet

Wireless LANs (WLANs) replace the cable used in a wired network with small radio *transceivers* (combined transmitters and receivers) at the PC and at the hub or switch. Several wireless standards are used at this writing with further standards being developed to provide faster data transmission and greater security.

The most common standard is 802.11b, which is widely referred to as *Wi-Fi* (wireless fidelity), and provides data transfer of up to 11 Mbps with tolerable security. A newer standard, 801.11g, is quickly gaining popularity because it is five times faster than Wi-Fi (up to 54 Mbps), is compatible with 802.11b, and is not that much more expensive. Another standard, 802.11a, also offers 54-Mbps speed, but because it's not compatible with 802.11b or 802.11g, it's best avoided.

A WLAN typically has two components (see Figure 8-2):

- An **access point** is connected to the wired Ethernet network via a hub, a switch, or a router. It uses one or more transceivers to communicate wirelessly with cards installed in or attached to PCs using the WLAN.

- An **adapter** is installed in or plugs into your PC and has a transceiver built in to communicate wirelessly to an access point within its range. For laptop PCs, built-in adapters are increasingly common. For desktop PCs, adapters are typically either installed in the PC as a PCI card or attached to the PC via USB (Universal Serial Bus).

If the access point is connected to a hub or switch on a wired network, the wireless PCs within the range of the access point operate on the network in exactly the same way as they would operate with a cable connection, only a little slower.

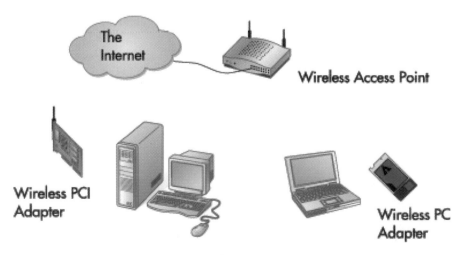

Figure 8-2: A wireless network consists of a card in your PC and an access point connected to a wired network, the Internet, or both.

WEIGHING THE PROS AND CONS OF WIRELESS NETWORKS

The advantages of wireless networks are:

- **No cables** Having no cables saves expense, effort, and the awkwardness of laying and maintaining cables.

- **Speed and flexibility** Wireless networks are great for temporary networks or for premises you can't change (for example, a rented apartment or office).

- **Simplicity** Adding users to and removing them from the network is extremely easy. Similarly, visitors can easily connect to the network if you grant them permission.

- **Movement and roaming** Users can move easily from office to office or roam within an area—for example, carrying their laptops to a meeting.

The disadvantages of wireless networks are:

- **Expense** Wireless network equipment is more expensive than wired network equipment, typically costing at least $50 per PC, but this price is coming down.

- **Speed** Wireless networks are substantially slower than wired networks. The maximum speed of 802.11g networks is theoretically 54 Mbps, compared to 100 Mbps for Fast Ethernet, but the data rate drops when multiple users use the wireless network.

- **Security** Because wireless network adapters and access points are essentially radios, wireless networking is inherently insecure. To make a wireless network adequately secure for moderately sensitive data, you must take several security measures, starting with encryption and passwords and progressing to more serious measures. Even so, a malefactor can attack your wireless network from a distance—even from several miles away, if he or she uses a high-gain antenna. By contrast, if you have a wired network, a malefactor must usually have direct access to the physical network to attack it.

Understand Other Networking Technologies

If you're planning a home network, you should also know about the following networking options:

- **FireWire connections** enable you to create a small network of PCs equipped with FireWire ports. The advantages are high speed (up to 800 Mbps) and easy setup. The disadvantages are that the PCs must be close to each other, as the maximum cable length is 4.5 meters (about 15 feet), and preferably few in number. Most PCs don't have FireWire built in, so you'll need to add it. Given that many current and recent PCs have either wired Ethernet or wireless Ethernet built in, you're not likely to want to use FireWire unless your PCs happen to have it already.

- **Powerline networks** enable your PCs to communicate across your home's electrical wiring using special adapters. The advantages are easy setup and not needing to run wires or drill holes. The disadvantages are higher cost than Ethernet networks, slower network speeds, and security concerns if your electric wiring is shared with neighbors.

- **Phone line networks** enable your PCs to communicate across your home's phone lines. The advantages are easy setup (provided you have phone jacks in suitable places) and not needing to run wires or drill holes. The disadvantages are higher costs and lower speeds than Ethernet networks.

- **USB networks** enable you to quickly connect two to four PCs together via their USB ports and a special cable. The advantages are easy setup and not needing to run wires or drill holes. The disadvantages are higher costs, lower speeds, and all PCs needing to be within a short cable's distance of the USB networking device.

- **Direct cable connections** enable you to connect two PCs running Windows via their parallel ports or serial ports. The advantage is that you can transfer data from one PC to another without needing a better networking technology. The disadvantages are that the speed is so low and the connection so awkward that this technology is best left for cases when no better networking technology is available.

- **Bluetooth connections** enable you to create cable-free networks between PCs within the same small area. The advantage is that you can set up a network without any infrastructure so that you can transfer files. The disadvantages are that Bluetooth is slow and short-range, so you probably won't want to use it for networking unless all the other networking options are unavailable. Bluetooth is primarily intended for transferring data among personal devices, such as mobile phones and PDAs, or between a personal device and a PC.

SELECTING WIRED ETHERNET HARDWARE

To set up a wired Ethernet network, you'll need:

- A network connection in each PC
- A hub or switch to form the link point in the network
- A cable to connect each PC to the hub or switch

Many brands of network hardware are available. Having an unreliable network wastes time and effort, so buying bargain-basement network hardware tends to be a bad idea. To ensure that your network is reliable and that you can get support when you need it, stick with name-brand products from companies that are likely to be around for a while. Respected brands include 3Com, D-Link, Linksys (now a division of networking giant Cisco Systems), and Netgear.

SELECT A NETWORK ADAPTER

Many PCs come with a network connection built in, and if you buy a new PC to run Windows XP, you'll almost certainly have the option of having a network connection installed. If you're not sure whether your PC has a network connection, look on the back of the PC (or the side of some laptop PCs) for a connector that looks like an oversized phone connector marked with the symbol <...>.

If your PC doesn't have a network connection, you can add a network adapter via a PCI card (for a desktop PC), via a PC Card (for a laptop PC), or via USB (for either a desktop PC or a laptop PC).

Continued...

Set Up and Use the Network

When you installed XP, a basic set of networking services was installed and configured using the choices you made, some default settings, and the details of the hardware that XP found on your system. If XP found a network connection (also called a *network card* or *network adapter*), networking may already be set up on your PC and you may not need to perform any configuration.

Set Up the Network

This section walks you through creating a network using the three means you're most likely to use: wired Ethernet, wireless using an access point, and wireless without an access point. It then shows you how to check that your network configuration is working and how to make key changes to it.

If your PC doesn't have a network connection, you must physically connect or install the network adapter and install and configure it in XP. XP installs and configures many network adapters automatically, but if you have an unusual network adapter, you may need to configure it manually.

INSTALL A NETWORK ADAPTER

Install the network adapter in your PC or connect it to your PC.

- For a PCI network adapter, shut down the PC, disconnect the power supply, open the PC case (as discussed in Chapter 6), insert the adapter in a free PCI slot, close the case, reconnect the power, and restart the PC.
- For a PC Card network adapter, insert the PC Card in a free slot while XP is running.
- For a USB network adapter, connect the USB cable to a USB port on your PC (or on a USB hub connected to your PC) while XP is running.

When XP detects the network adapter, it displays a pop-up window above the notification area (as shown here) and then starts the Found New Hardware Wizard. Follow the steps of the wizard, and provide the driver if XP cannot find a suitable driver on its own.

SELECTING WIRED ETHERNET HARDWARE *(Continued)*

SELECT A SWITCH

To connect your wired Ethernet network, you need a switch. Switches run from under $50 for an 8-port switch to under $150 for a 24-port switch. You need a port for each user, but you can plug one switch into another switch to increase the number of ports on your network. If you plan to do this, choose switches that are designed to stack one on top of the other for neatness and for speed (their interconnecting bus is faster than a wire connection).

SELECT CABLING

For 10/100 Ethernet cabling, you need Category 5 (Cat 5) or Category 5 enhanced (Cat 5e) cabling; for Gigabit Ethernet, you need at least Cat 5e, which is the best choice for 10/100 cabling if you think you might need faster speeds in the future. Cat 5e costs only marginally more than Cat 5.

Cat 5 and Cat 5e cable come in various colors and in lengths of up to 100 feet with the connectors molded on. Alternatively, you can buy a spool of cable (typically 1,000 feet) and a crimping tool, cut the cables to the lengths you need, and crimp connectors on yourself.

If XP displays a pop-up window at the end of the Found New Hardware process saying that your new hardware is installed and ready to use, as shown here, your network adapter should be correctly configured.

To verify that your network adapter is correctly configured:

1. Click the **Start** button, and click **Control Panel**.
2. In Category View, click **Network And Internet Connections**, and then click **Network Connections**; in Classic View, double-click **Network Connections**. The Network Connections window opens. If the window contains an icon labeled Local Area Connection, the network adapter is properly installed.

SET UP A WIRED ETHERNET NETWORK

To create a wired Ethernet network, you need a Cat 5 or Cat 5e cable for each computer that will be connected and a hub or switch with enough ports for all computers or other devices that you will connect. Switches deliver faster network throughput than hubs and cost only a little more, so unless you already have a hub or you're squeezing every cent, a switch is a better choice.

You can connect two PCs directly without a hub or switch using a *crossover* cable, a special cable that reverses the wires in the cable from their standard arrangement. You can buy a crossover cable from most computer stores.

Connect the PCs

To connect your PCs:

1. If the PCs are running, shut them down.
2. Plug one end of an Ethernet cable into your switch and the other end into the network adapter on your PC (see "Install a Network Adapter" earlier in this chapter).
3. Repeat the process for each of the other PCs that will be part of the network.
4. Turn on the power for the switch.

Run the Network Setup Wizard

After connecting your PCs, run the Network Setup Wizard to set up the network.

1. Turn on each of the PCs, and log on to XP.

2. If one of your PCs will share its Internet connection with the other PCs, set up that PC first. Before you start the Network Setup Wizard, establish the Internet connection (for example, connect to your ISP via dial-up). If your Internet connection is broadband that is connected directly to the network (for example, via a residential gateway), it doesn't matter which PC you set up first.

3. Click the **Start** button, click **All Programs**, click **Accessories**, click **Communications**, and then click **Network Setup Wizard**. The Network Setup Wizard starts. Click **Next**, read the checklist on the Before You Continue page, and then click **Next** again. The Select A Connection Method page appears (see Figure 8-3).

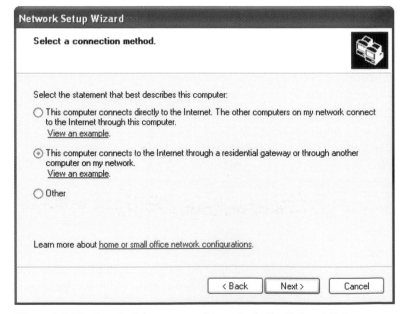

Figure 8-3: The key decision you need to make in the Network Setup Wizard is specifying how your PC connects to the Internet.

QUICKSTEPS

SELECTING WIRELESS HARDWARE

Hardware for a wireless network includes a wireless adapter and a wireless access point.

SELECT A WIRELESS SPEED

If you're buying hardware for a new wireless network, buy 802.11g equipment to get the fastest data rate available—54 Mbps. The faster rate is especially important if you're building a multiuser network, as each PC has to share the capacity with all the other PCs on the network at any given time.

Even if the PC for which you're buying a wireless network card will connect to an existing 802.11b network, buy an 802.11g card rather than an 802.11b card so that you can upgrade the network in the future.

If you'll need only to connect to public Wi-Fi networks, such as those in airports and coffee shops, you can get away with the 802.11b standard and its 11-Mbps data rate. Given that 802.11g equipment can connect to 802.11b networks, 802.11g is usually a better choice— but see the next section for limitations.

SELECT A WIRELESS ADAPTER

Higher-end laptop PCs come with wireless adapters built in. You can install wireless adapters in or on any other laptop or desktop PC.

- Plug a PC Card wireless adapter into a laptop computer.
- Install a PCI wireless adapter inside a desktop computer.
- Plug a USB wireless adapter into a laptop or a desktop PC.

Continued...

4. Specify how your PC connects to the Internet.

- If one of your PCs will share its Internet connection, verify that the **This Computer Connects Directly To The Internet** option button is selected, and then click **Next**.

- If the PC isn't sharing its Internet connection and it connects through a PC that does share its Internet connection or through a residential gateway (a device for sharing a broadband internet connection), select the **This Computer Connects To The Internet Through A Residential Gateway Or Through Another Computer On My Network** option button, and then click **Next**.

- If your PC connects through a switch or hub, select the **Other** option button, click **Next**, and select the **This Computer Connects To The Internet Directly Or Through A Network Hub** option button on the Other Internet Connection Methods page, and then click **Next**.

5. On the Give This Computer A Description And Name page, type a description and name for your PC. The description is to help humans identify the PC, and the name is to help computers identify it. Click **Next**. The Name Your Network page appears.

6. Type a name for your workgroup in place of the default name, MSHOME, and then click **Next**. The File And Printer Sharing page appears (see Figure 8-4).

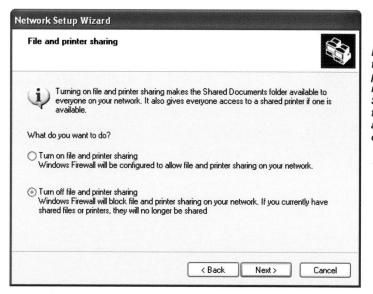

Figure 8-4: You can turn on file and printer sharing to make your PC's Shared Documents folder and printer available to all users of your network.

SELECTING WIRELESS HARDWARE *Continued*

For a desktop PC, a USB wireless adapter with a medium-length cable is usually a better choice than a PCI wireless adapter because you can not only connect and disconnect it easily, but can also position the antenna portion in the best place for connecting to the access point. By contrast, a PCI wireless adapter is harder to install but has the advantage of being mostly hidden inside the CPU box.

SELECT A WIRELESS ACCESS POINT

Wireless access points come in simple versions that plug into a wired Ethernet network and in more sophisticated versions, called "wireless broadband routers," that terminate a DSL or cable Internet connection. Wireless access points also come in different speeds.

CAUTION

When you add a device using 802.11b to an otherwise 802.11g network, the whole network usually drops down to the 802.11b speed.

7. If you need to share your PC's Shared Documents folder and printer (if any), select the **Turn On File And Printer Sharing** option button. Otherwise, select the **Turn Off File And Printer Sharing** option button. Click **Next**. The Ready To Apply Network Settings page appears.

8. Verify the settings and go back and make changes if necessary. When you are satisfied, click **Next**. Wait while the Network Setup Wizard sets up the network. The You're Almost Done page appears.

9. If you need to add PCs running older versions of Windows to the network, select the **Create A Network Setup Disk** option button on the You're Almost Done page, click **Next**, insert a floppy disk, and click **Next** again to create this disk. You then insert this disk in each of the other PCs in turn, start the wizard, and follow the automated setup procedure.

10. If you don't need to add PCs running older versions of Windows, select the **Just Finish The Wizard** option button, click **Next**, and then click **Finish**. The System Settings Change dialog box appears.

11. Click **Yes**. XP restarts your PC and finishes the network configuration.

SET UP A WIRELESS NETWORK USING AN ACCESS POINT

A wireless network is usually much easier to set up than a wired network because you don't have to run the cables among the items of network hardware. You can create a wireless network with an access point (as described in this section) or without an access point (as described in the next section).

To create a wireless network with an access point, you need a wireless adapter installed in or connected to each PC and a wireless access point. The wireless adapters and the wireless access point must be compatible with each other in one of the following ways:

- All Wi-Fi–certified 802.11g products if you want 54-Mbps speed

- A mixture of Wi-Fi–certified 802.11g products and Wi-Fi–certified 802.11b products or all Wi-Fi–certified 802.11b products if 11 Mbps is good enough

UNDERSTANDING NETWORKING PROTOCOLS

Networking protocols are sets of standards used to package and transmit data over a network. The protocol determines how the information is divided into packets for transmission, how it is addressed, and what is done to ensure it is transferred reliably.

To transmit data between your PC and other computers, XP by default uses a protocol called Transmission Control Protocol/Internet Protocol (TCP/IP), the networking protocol used on the Internet. TCP/IP is a powerful and complex protocol. XP makes TCP/IP configuration as straightforward as possible, masking most of the ugly details from your sight, but it helps if you understand a few essentials about TCP/IP.

IP ADDRESSES

TCP/IP identifies different computers (technically, it identifies different network interfaces) on a network using addresses called *IP addresses*. An IP address takes the form of four groups of three decimal numbers separated by periods—for example, 192.168.0.1. The first group (192) defines the largest unit; the second group (168) defines the unit within that unit; the third defines another unit within the second unit; and the fourth defines another unit within the third. Roughly speaking, each of the numbers can go up to 255 (although there are exceptions to this).

For identification, each IP address must be unique on the network, so each network interface is assigned a different IP address. Many PCs come with several ways to connect to another computer or network: a network connection, a modem, the serial port and parallel port,

Continued...

Set Up the Wireless Access Point

How you set up your wireless access point depends on whether it can accept automatic configuration from a USB flash drive (a small memory device the size of a pack of gum that plugs into a USB port). If so, you can use the automated procedure involving the Wireless Network Setup Wizard described in the next section. If your wireless access point has a USB port, it probably supports automatic configuration. Check the documentation to be sure.

If your wireless access point doesn't have a USB connector, you can be sure it doesn't support automatic configuration. Set up your access point by following the instructions that come with it. A typical manual setup process for an access point involves connecting your PC to it using an Ethernet cable so that you can communicate via a wired network in order to configure the wireless network. Configuration typically also includes the following:

- Specifying the name, or service set identifier (SSID), of the wireless network—often simply a descriptive text name (for example, Wireless1)—and choosing whether to broadcast it.

- Choosing whether to use encryption. If your access point offers a choice, choose Wi-Fi Protected Access (WPA) over Wired Equivalent Privacy (WEP), an older standard that includes known compromises; but even Wired Equivalent Privacy is better than no encryption at all.

- Choosing whether to restrict the network to a specified list of wireless adapters (identified by their Media Access Control number, or MAC number) or to leave it open to any wireless adapter within range. Specifying the wireless adapters that can connect is a good security measure, although it can be bypassed by a malefactor learning an approved MAC number and configuring a wireless adapter to use that number. The MAC address is usually printed on the wireless adapter. You can also learn it by double-clicking the **Wireless Network Connection** icon in the notification area to display the Wireless Network Connection Status dialog box, clicking the **Support** tab, clicking the **Details** button, and then looking at the **Physical Address** readout.

UNDERSTANDING NETWORKING PROTOCOLS *(Continued)*

and (rarely) a FireWire port. You can use two or more connections at the same time, so one PC can have two or more IP addresses at once. These IP addresses can be on the same network, but they'll typically be on different networks. For example, when your PC is connected directly to the Internet, it has one IP address on the Internet and another IP address on your local network.

The Internet functions as a single huge TCP/IP network, so each computer on the Internet has to have a unique IP address. When you connect your PC to the Internet, your ISP (Internet service provider) assigns it an IP address from the block of IP addresses allocated to the ISP. For a typical dial-up connection, the IP address is *dynamic*, meaning that it is likely to be different each time you establish the connection: the ISP allocates one of the addresses assigned to its modem pool. For a typical broadband connection, the IP address is *static*, meaning that you keep the same IP address all the time (your ISP reserves the IP address for you).

NETWORK ADDRESS TRANSLATION

To reduce the number of computers directly connected to the Internet, many networks use a process called Network Address Translation (NAT). In NAT, one computer (or a special-purpose device, such as a router) is connected to the Internet and has an IP address on the Internet. The NAT computer shares the Internet connection with the other computers on the internal network as required, funneling Internet requests and replies through its IP address.

Continued...

Install or Connect the Wireless Adapters

If you haven't already installed the wireless adapters in (or connected them to) your PCs, do so now. For example, insert a PC Card wireless adapter in a PC Card slot, or plug a USB wireless adapter into a USB port.

Run the Wireless Network Setup Wizard

Run the Wireless Network Setup Wizard to set up your wireless network. For the quickest and easiest setup, you need a USB flash drive, but you can also set up your network manually.

1. Click the **Start** button, click **All Programs**, click **Accessories**, click **Communications**, and then click **Wireless Network Setup Wizard**. The Wireless Network Setup Wizard starts. Click **Next**. The Create A Name For Your Wireless Network page appears (see Figure 8-5).

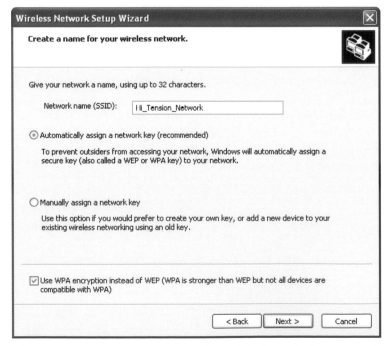

Figure 8-5: If your wireless access point and wireless adapters support WPA, use WPA instead of WEP.

UNDERSTANDING NETWORKING PROTOCOLS *(Continued)*

OBTAIN AN IP ADDRESS

IP addresses can be allocated either manually or automatically. Manual allocation is handy for some situations, but automatic allocation is the norm for most networks because it is more efficient. Most automatic allocation is performed by a DHCP (Dynamic Host Configuration Protocol) server, either at your ISP (for an Internet connection) or on your local network.

When your PC detects that no DHCP server is available, it falls back on Automatic Private IP Addressing (APIPA). APIPA assigns an IP address in the address range 169.254.0.0 through 169.254.255.255 after checking that no other computer on the network is using that IP address.

TIP

Disable SSID broadcasts if possible. This makes it harder for unauthorized people to connect to your wireless access point. A wireless network that broadcasts its SSID is described as *open*; one that doesn't is *closed*.

NOTE

Always use encryption on your wireless network. Encryption doesn't provide full security, but without it your network is open to anybody within broadcasting range of your wireless access point—up to several hundred yards in open surroundings or up to several miles if somebody aims an antenna toward your access point.

2. Type a name for the network, verify that the **Automatically Assign A Network Key** option button is selected, and select the **Use WPA Encryption Instead Of WEP** check box if your wireless equipment supports WPA. Click **Next**. The How Do You Want To Set Up Your Network? page appears.

3. If you have a USB flash drive, connect it, select the **Use A USB Flash Drive** option button, click **Next**, select the flash drive by its drive letter on the Save Settings To Your Flash Drive page, and click **Next**. Unplug the flash drive, and plug it into your wireless access point for 30 seconds to configure the access point. Unplug the flash drive from the access point, plug it into each of the other PCs or devices that will be part of the wireless network in turn, and follow the prompts. Finally, plug the flash drive back into the first PC, and then click **Next**.

4. If you don't have a USB flash drive, select the **Set Up A Network Manually** option button, click **Next**, click **Print Network Settings**, and then click **Finish**. You will need to configure the other devices for the wireless network manually, as described next.

Configure a Wireless Adapter Manually

If you don't have a USB flash drive or if your wireless access point doesn't support automatic configuration, you'll need to configure the other PCs in the wireless network manually.

1. Click the **Start** button, and click **Control Panel**. In Category View, click **Network And Internet Connections**, and then click **Network Connections**. In Classic View, double-click **Network Connections**. The Network Connections window opens.

2. Right-click the **Wireless Network Connection** icon, and click **Properties**. The Wireless Network Connection Properties dialog box appears.

TIP

The Wireless Network Setup Wizard automatically creates a secure network using WPA (if it is available) or WEP (if WPA is not available).

TIP

Set a strong password on your access point to prevent intruders from being able to manipulate it.

CAUTION

If the Wireless Network Setup Wizard warns you that your wireless network adapter doesn't support WPA, click **OK**, click **Back**, clear the **Use WPA Encryption Instead Of WEP** check box, and then click **Next**.

TIP

When you plug the USB flash drive into each of the other PCs that you want to add to the wireless network, the Wireless Network Setup Wizard should start automatically. If it doesn't, click the **Start** button, and click **My Computer**. A My Computer window opens. Right-click the icon for the flash drive, and click **AutoPlay**. The Removable Disk dialog box appears. Click **Wireless Network Setup Wizard**, and click **OK**.

3. Click the **Wireless Networks** tab (see Figure 8-6).

4. Click **Add**. The Wireless Network Properties dialog box appears (see Figure 8-7).

5. Using the printout you made from the PC on which you created the network, type the network name, clear the **The Key Is Provided For Me Automatically** check box, and enter the details in the **Network Authentication** drop-down list box, the **Data Encryption** drop-down list box, and the **Network Key** and **Confirm Network Key** text boxes. Leave the **Key Index** set to 1 unless your printout shows a different value. Verify that the **This Is A Computer-To-Computer (Ad Hoc) Network** check box is cleared.

6. Click the **Connection** tab. If you want your PC to connect automatically to this wireless network whenever your PC is within range of the access point, verify that the **Connect When This Network Is In Range** check box is selected; otherwise, clear this check box. Then click **OK**. XP enters the details of the network in the Preferred Networks box on the Wireless Networks tab of the Properties dialog box.

7. Click the **General** tab. Verify that the **Show Icon In Notification Area When Connected** check box is selected. This icon provides an easy way to quickly access your wireless network configuration.

8. Click **OK**. The Properties dialog box closes.

Figure 8-6: The Wireless Networks tab of the Properties dialog box is the central point for managing your connections to wireless networks.

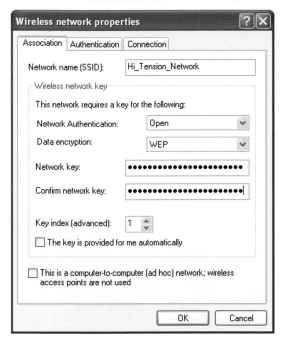

Figure 8-7: If you don't have a USB flash drive, you must manually enter the details of the wireless network connection.

Connect to an Open Wireless Network

To connect to a closed wireless network (one that doesn't broadcast its SSID), you must know the SSID and must enter it manually using the steps in "Configure a Wireless Adapter Manually." You can connect to an open wireless network by scanning for available networks.

1. Right-click the **Wireless Network Connection** icon in the notification area, and click **View Available Wireless Networks**. The Wireless Network Connection window opens (see Figure 8-8).

2. Click the network to which you want to connect, and then click **Connect**. If the network is unsecured, you are connected immediately. If the network is secured, you are prompted for the network key, as shown here; type the network key twice, and click **Connect**.

Figure 8-8: Click the Refresh Network List link in the Wireless Network Connection window to update the list of open networks in range.

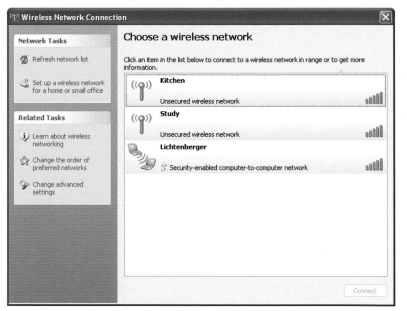

NOTE

You can't prevent an ad-hoc wireless network from broadcasting its SSID. As a result, your wireless network can be seen by any wireless device within broadcasting range, so you must apply a password to keep it secure.

NOTE

The password must be 13 ASCII (regular-text) characters for 128-bit WEP or 5 ASCII characters for 40-bit WEP.

SET UP AN AD-HOC WIRELESS NETWORK

If you don't have an access point, you can set up an *ad-hoc* or *computer-to-computer* wireless network among two or more PCs. This capability means that one PC starts broadcasting an SSID and other PCs can join the network. Ad-hoc computer networks work well for small numbers of computers, but if you plan to add more than half a dozen computers to your wireless network, an access point will give you better results.

To set up an ad-hoc wireless network:

1. Right-click the **Wireless Network Connection** icon in the notification area, click **View Available Wireless Networks**, and then click **Change Advanced Settings** in the Related Tasks task pane. The Wireless Network Connection Properties dialog box appears.

2. Click the **Wireless Networks** tab, and then click **Add**. The Wireless Network Properties dialog box appears.

3. Type the name for the new network, clear the **The Key Is Provided For Me Automatically** check box, choose the desired types of authentication and data encryption, and enter the network key. Select the **This Is A Computer-To-Computer (Ad Hoc) Network** check box.

4. Click **OK**.

You can now join other PCs to the network as described in "Connect to an Open Wireless Network," earlier in this chapter.

Access and Share Network Resources

Once you've established a connection to the network, either wired or wireless, you can access the resources on it. Typically, this means that you can use a shared Internet connection to connect to the network, access files and folders stored on shared drives on the network, and print to shared printers. Depending on the configuration of the network, you may also be able to use other resources, such as shared scanners, faxes, and other hardware. You can also share resources on your PC with users of other PCs.

NOTE

The shares (shared folders, disks, and other resources) that appear in My Network Places are the result of your PC having searched your workgroup (or domain) for shares and other resources. When you first set up networking, you won't see any shares until they have been shared by other PCs and your PC has had time to find them.

Figure 8-9: Shares are drives and folders on other PCs that you can access via the network.

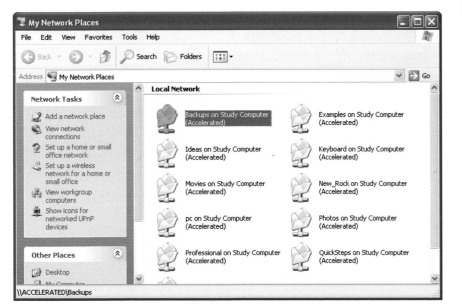

To see what's available to you on the network, you can explore it. The best way to start is to use the My Network Places view in Windows Explorer.

1. Click the **Start** button, and then click **My Network Places**. The My Network Places window opens (see Figure 8-9). In the detail pane of the My Network Places window are *shares*—folders or disks on other computers that have been shared and are available to you.

2. Double-click one of the shares. It opens to display the files and folders that you can access.

3. Click **Back** to return to the My Network Places window. Click **View Workgroup Computers** to display the computers in your workgroup. (If your PC is part of a domain rather than part of a workgroup, the option will be named View Domain Computers and will display the computers available in your PC's domain.)

4. Double-click one of the computers in the workgroup or domain to display the shares, printers, and other resources on that computer.

5. Click **Back** and then click **Close** to close the My Network Places window.

PERMANENTLY CONNECT TO A NETWORK SHARE

If you use a specific network share frequently, you may want your PC to connect to it permanently so that you can use it as if it were a drive on your PC. You do this by mapping a network drive to the share. When you create such a mapping, XP reconnects to the share and represents it as a drive letter each time you log on until you disconnect the mapping from the share.

1. Click the **Start** button, and click **My Network Places**. Click **Folders** on the toolbar.

2. In the Folders pane, click **Entire Network**, click **Microsoft Windows Network**, click your workgroup or domain, and click the PC that contains the share to which you want to map a drive. The share appears in the detail pane.

USING NETWORK ADDRESSES

Network addressing uses the *Uniform Naming Convention*, or *UNC*, to identify files, folders, and other resources on any computer on the network.

IDENTIFY A NETWORK SHARE

A network share, which is a folder or disk on a computer on the network, is identified by \\computername\ pathname\folder or disk name. For example, a share named "2005 Budgets" in the Budgeting folder on the computer named "Server1" would have the UNC address of \\Server1\Budgeting\2005 Budgets. In most cases, you can also write \\Server1\2005 Budgets.

IDENTIFY A NETWORK PRINTER

Identifying a network printer is similar to identifying a share. The printer's name takes the form \\computername\printername. For example, a printer named "HP4500" on Server1 would have the UNC \\Server1\HP4500.

3. Right-click the share in the detail pane, and click **Map Network Drive**. The Map Network Drive dialog box appears (see Figure 8-10) with the share name already entered in the Folder text box.

4. If necessary, change the drive to use for the share. XP suggests the next unused letter working backward from the end of the alphabet.

5. If you want to reconnect to the share every time you log on to your PC, verify that the **Reconnect At Logon** check box is selected.

6. Click **Finish**. The share opens in a separate window. Click the **Close** button to close that window.

7. Click **Close** to close the My Network Places window.

DISCONNECT A MAPPED DRIVE

When you no longer want XP to map a drive to a network share, you disconnect the share.

1. Click the **Start** button, and click **My Computer**. A My Computer window opens.

2. Right-click the mapped drive, and click **Disconnect**. The mapping disappears from the My Computer window.

Figure 8-10: Mapping a network drive gives you a permanent connection to that share.

CONNECT OUTSIDE YOUR WORKGROUP OR DOMAIN

My Network Places shows you only computers or shares in your workgroup or domain. To connect to another computer or share outside your workgroup or domain, you must use a different procedure.

1. Click the **Start** button, and click **My Network Places**. The My Network Places window opens.

2. Click **Add A Network Place** in the Network Tasks task pane. The Add Network Place Wizard starts.

3. Click **Next**. Click **Choose Another Network Location**, and click **Next**.

4. Type the network address of the other computer or share (see the QuickFacts "Using Network Addresses"), and click **Next**.

5. If prompted for a user name and password, type them, and click **OK**. Type the name for the network place, and click **Next**. Click **Finish**.

6. The wizard opens a Windows Explorer window showing the contents of the network place. Work with these items, or click **Close** to close the window.

SHARE YOUR FOLDERS AND PRINTERS

When you run the Network Setup Wizard to connect your PC to a wired Ethernet network, you are offered the opportunity to share your PC's Shared Documents folder and any printers connected to your PC (see "Run the Network Setup Wizard," earlier in this chapter). If you choose to share these items, the Network Setup Wizard configures Windows Firewall to allow other computers on the network to access the Shared Documents folder and your printer.

To turn file and printer sharing on and off, run the Network Setup Wizard again, and make the appropriate choice on the File And Printer Sharing page.

After you have turned on file and printer sharing using the Network Setup Wizard, you can control which folders and printers are shared manually.

CAUTION

If you run the Network Setup Wizard again, you must enter the correct workgroup name on the Name Your Network page; otherwise the wizard uses the default name of MSHOME, which will put your PC in the wrong workgroup.

Share a Folder Manually

1. Open a Windows Explorer window, and browse to the folder that contains the folder you want to share. For example, click the **Start** button, click **My Computer**, and then double-click the drive that contains the folder.

2. Right-click the folder, and click **Sharing And Security**. The Properties dialog box appears with the Sharing tab at the front (see Figure 8-11).

3. Select the **Share This Folder On The Network** check box, and change the name in the Share Name text box, if needed.

4. Select the **Allow Network Users To Change My Files** check box if you want other users to be able to change and delete existing files or create new files in this folder.

 epson

5. Click **OK** to apply the sharing. Windows Explorer displays a hand under the folder to indicate that it is shared.

Program Files

Share a Printer Manually

1. Click the **Start** button, and click **Control Panel**. In Category View, click **Printers And Other Hardware**, and then click **Printers and Faxes**; in Classic View, double-click **Printers And Faxes**. The Printers And Faxes window opens.

2. Right-click the printer, and click **Sharing**. The Properties dialog box for the printer appears with the Sharing tab displayed.

3. Select the **Share This Printer** option button, change the name in the Share Name text box as necessary, and then click **OK**.

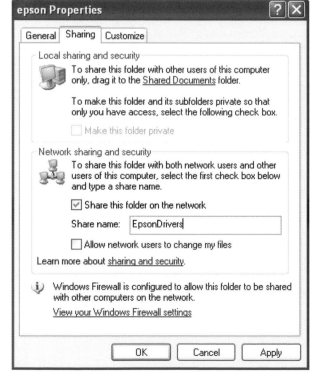

Figure 8-11: For security, share as few folders as possible on the network. Even when you share a folder, you do not usually need to allow other users to change the files in the folder.

Troubleshoot Home Network Problems

With new networking hardware and XP, you usually can set up a network easily using default settings and a minimum of effort—but not always. This section shows you techniques for resolving the problems that are most likely to crop up when you're setting up a home network. These techniques include installing a network adapter manually, configuring TCP/IP, and checking that a network connection is working.

Install a Network Adapter Manually

If the Found New Hardware Wizard is unable to identify your network adapter and install a driver for it, you'll need to install the network adapter manually.

1. Click the **Start** button, and click **Control Panel**. In Category View, click **Network And Internet Connections**, and then click **Network Connections**; in Classic View, double-click **Network Connections**. The Network Connections window opens. If the window contains an icon labeled Local Area Connection, as shown here, the network adapter is properly installed, and you can go on to the next section, "Configure TCP/IP for the Network Adapter."

2. If the Network Connections window doesn't contain a Local Area Connection icon, you must install the network adapter using the Add Hardware Wizard. Ensure that you have a suitable driver for the network adapter and Windows XP before proceeding. If necessary, use another PC to download the driver from the manufacturer's web site, and copy it to a removable disk or burn it to a CD.

3. From the Network Connections window, in Category View, click **Back**, click **Printers And Other Hardware** in the detail pane, and then click **Add Hardware** in the See Also task pane. (In Classic View, click **Back** and then double-click **Add Hardware**.) The Add Hardware Wizard starts.

8

TURNING AN OLD PC INTO A SERVER

If you have an extra PC, you can easily create a client/ server network instead of a peer-to-peer network. The advantage is that by centralizing all the services on the server, you remove the burden of providing services from the client PCs, which you can then use at their full speed. You also don't need to worry about services becoming unavailable to other users when you turn off the peer that's sharing them: as long as the server stays up and running, the services remain available.

Creating a server can also be a good way of getting more use out of a PC that's too old or underpowered to use for demanding applications. By replacing the old PC's hard disk with one large enough to contain all the files you need to have served, you can move it into a role in which its lack of processor speed won't be a hindrance.

Whether you buy (or build) a new computer or repurpose an existing computer will determine your choices for your server. Key components for the server include:

- **Operating system** The server can run XP, Windows 2000, or Windows NT Workstation if you have a copy that you can spare; if you don't, you might consider using a less expensive (or even free) operating system, such as one of the many distributions of Linux.

- **Processor** The server can run on a modest processor—even an antiquated one by today's standards, such as a 500-MHz or faster processor.

- **RAM** The server needs only enough RAM to run the operating system unless you need to run applications on it. For example, 256 MB of RAM is adequate for a server running XP or Linux.

- **Disk space** The server must have enough disk space to store all the songs you want to have available—and perhaps store video files, too, in the

Continued...

4. Click **Next**. When the wizard asks you if the hardware is connected, select the **Yes, I Have Already Connected The Hardware** option button, and then click **Next**. A list of installed hardware appears. You may or may not see your network adapter on the list, as shown in Figure 8-12. If your network adapter is listed and doesn't have a problem icon (an exclamation point), XP thinks that the adapter is installed and running properly. If you double-click the adapter, XP displays a message saying that the device is working properly. If you see your adapter and you don't see a problem icon, click **Finish** to close the Add Hardware Wizard. The problem probably lies in the adapter's configuration.

5. If you don't see your network adapter, scroll down to the bottom of the Installed Hardware list, click **Add A New Hardware Device**, and click **Next**. Select the **Install The Hardware That I Manually Select From A List** option button, and click **Next**. Skip to step 7.

Figure 8-12: Check for your network adapter in the list of installed hardware in the Add Hardware Wizard.

TURNING AN OLD PC INTO A SERVER *(Continued)*

near future. A desktop PC is likely to be a better bet than a laptop PC because you can add internal drives to it. Alternatively, you might use one or more external USB or FireWire drives to provide plenty of space.

- **Network connection**   The server must be connected to your network, either via a network cable or via a wireless connection. A wireless connection is adequate for serving a few computers, but in most cases, a wired connection (Fast Ethernet or Gigabit Ethernet) is a much better choice, particularly if you store audio or video files on the server.

- **Monitor**   If the server will simply be running somewhere convenient (rather than being used for other computing tasks, such as running applications), all you need is an old monitor capable of displaying the bootup and login screens for the operating system. After that, you can turn the monitor off until you need to restart or configure the server.

- **Keyboard and mouse**   Like the monitor, the keyboard and mouse can be basic devices because you'll need to use them only for booting and configuring the server.

- **CD-ROM drive**   Your server needs a CD-ROM drive only while you're installing its operating system.

- **Sound card**   Your server needs a sound card only if you'll use it for playing music.

- **Reliability**   Make sure that the server has plenty of cooling capability (for example, enough fans), and configure its power settings so that it doesn't go to sleep or hibernate.

- **Location**   If you choose to leave your server running all the time, locate it somewhere safe where it won't be switched off accidentally. Because the running server will probably make some noise, you may be tempted to hide it away in a closet. If you do, make sure there's enough ventilation so that it doesn't overheat.

6. If your network adapter appears in the list with a problem icon (as in Figure 8-12), double-click the network adapter. You will most likely see a Device Status message telling you that a driver was not installed. Click **Finish** to close the Add Hardware Wizard. Depending on the hardware and the missing driver, either the Upgrade Device Driver Wizard or the Hardware Update Wizard starts.

   - In the Upgrade Device Driver Wizard, click **Next**. Select the **Display A List Of Known Drivers** option button, click **Next**, and then go to the next step.

   - In the Hardware Update Wizard (and if you have an Internet connection), allow the wizard to connect to Windows Update to search for a driver. Otherwise, click **No, Not This Time**, and then click **Next**. Select the **Install From A List Or Specific Location** option button, and click **Next**. Use the controls on the Please Choose Your Search And Installation Options page to specify where XP will find the driver, click **Next**, and follow the procedure of finding and installing the driver.

7. Whether or not your network adapter was listed, double-click **Network Adapters** in the Common Hardware Types list. A list of network adapters appears. Insert the disk containing the driver, and click **Have Disk**. Enter the drive letter of the disk containing the driver, or click **Browse** and select it. Then click **OK**. Select the entry for your network adapter, and click **Next**. When the wizard tells you that the device will be installed, click **Next** again.

8. If XP displays a message stating that the driver you are about to install does not have a digital signature, you will need to decide whether to proceed with the installation (and possibly compromise the stability or security of your PC) or abort the installation (and be unable to use this network adapter). If you decide to proceed, click **Yes** to install the driver and any supporting software it needs.

9. Click **Finish**. The Local Area Connection icon should now appear in the Network Connections window. If it does not, double-check that you are using the correct driver for your network adapter. If you are and the network adapter is still not functional, you will probably need to try another network adapter.

Configure TCP/IP for the Network Adapter

The network adapter in your PC not only needs a driver to tell XP how to communicate with it, it also needs networking software to tell it how to communicate with the networks to which your PC connects. When you successfully install a network adapter, XP automatically installs four components of networking software:

- **Client For Microsoft Networks** enables your PC to connect to Microsoft networks.
- **File And Printer Sharing For Microsoft Networks** enables your PC to share its files and printers with other PCs and use the files and printers that other PCs are sharing.
- **QoS Packet Scheduler** prioritizes network traffic, giving time-dependent data priority over data that isn't time-dependent. (QoS is the abbreviation for Quality Of Service.)
- **Internet Protocol (TCP/IP)** tells your computer how to connect to networks using the ubiquitous TCP/IP protocol suite.

Depending on how your PC connects to the network, you may need to configure TCP/IP. You will not need to configure Client For Microsoft Networks, File And Printer Sharing For Microsoft Networks, or QoS Packet Scheduler.

To configure TCP/IP:

1. Click the **Start** button, and click **Control Panel**. In Category View, click **Network And Internet Connections**, and then click **Network Connections**; in Classic View, double-click **Network Connections**. The Network Connections window opens.

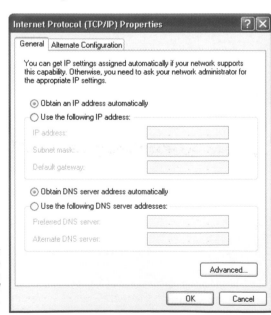

Figure 8-13: For most networks, you should use dynamic IP addresses so that your PC obtains an IP address automatically, but sometimes you will need to enter a fixed IP address.

2. Right-click the connection you want to configure, and click **Properties**. The Properties dialog box for the connection appears with the General tab at the front.

3. Double-click **Internet Protocol (TCP/IP)** in the This Connection Uses The Following Items list box. The Internet Protocol (TCP/IP) Properties dialog box appears (see Figure 8-13).

4. If your PC will obtain its IP address from a computer or device sharing an Internet connection (for example, a DSL router), select the **Obtain An IP Address Automatically** option button and the **Obtain DNS Server Address Automatically** option button. If your ISP or an administrator has given you a static IP address and a DNS (Domain Name Service) server address, select the **Use The Following IP Address** option button and the **Use The Following DNS Server Addresses** option button; and type the IP address, subnet mask, default gateway, and DNS server addresses in the text boxes.

5. Click **OK** to close the Internet Protocol (TCP/IP) Properties dialog box, and click **OK** to close the Properties dialog box for the network connection. If prompted to restart your PC, do so.

Troubleshoot a Network Connection

To verify that the network adapter is working and test a network connection:

1. Click the **Start** button, and click **Control Panel**. In Category View, click **Network And Internet Connections**, and then click **Network Connections**; in Classic View, double-click **Network Connections**. The Network Connections window opens.

2. Double-click **Local Area Connection** to open the Local Area Connection Status dialog box (see Figure 8-14). You should see activity on both the Sent and Received sides. If you do see activity, all is well and you can stop troubleshooting; if you don't see activity on both sides, continue to follow these steps. In either case, close both the **Local Area Connection Status** dialog box and the **Network Connections** window.

3. Click the **Start** button, click **All Programs**, click **Accessories**, and then click **Command Prompt**. A Command Prompt window opens.

TIP

The IP address 127.0.0.1 is a special address set aside to refer to the computer on which it is entered. This address is called the *loopback* address. By pinging the loopback (by specifying either ping loopback or ping 127.0.0.1), you can check that your network connection is working.

Figure 8-14: Use the Status dialog box for a connection to check quickly that it is both sending and receiving data.

GETTING A BLOCK OF IP ADDRESSES

The block of IP addresses you use with Internet Protocol depends on whether the computers to be assigned the addresses will be private or public.

GET PRIVATE IP ADDRESSES

If the computers will be operating only on an internal network, where they are separated from the public network by a router or bridge, they are *private* and need be unique only on the internal network. Four blocks of IP addresses have been set aside and can be used by any organization for its private, internal needs without coordination with any other organization, but these blocks should not be used for directly connecting to the Internet. These private-use blocks of IP addresses are:

- 10.0.0.0 through 10.255.255.255 (typically used for large networks)
- 169.254.0.0 through 169.254.255.255 (used for the Automatic Private IP Addressing protocol, or APIPA)
- 172.16.0.0 through 172.31.255.255 (typically used for medium-sized networks)
- 192.168.0.0 through 192.168.255.255 (widely used for small networks, used by XP's Internet Connection Sharing feature, and frequently automatically assigned by DSL routers for the local area network)

GET PUBLIC IP ADDRESSES

Computers that are connected directly to the Internet are *public* and thus need a globally unique IP number. If you want a block of public IP addresses, you must request it from one of several organizations, your choice of which will depend on the size of the block that you want. At the local level, a moderate-sized block of IP addresses can be assigned by your local ISP. For a larger block, a regional ISP may be able to handle the request.

Continued...

4. Type <u>ping loopback</u> and press **ENTER**. You should see replies from the network adapter, as shown here. If you don't, there is a problem with the network setup or the network adapter. The loopback address is a special address that refers to the computer on which it is entered. The loopback address is assigned the IP addresss 127.0.0.1.

```
Command Prompt                                    _ □ ×

C:\>ping loopback

Pinging NETVISTA [127.0.0.1] with 32 bytes of data:

Reply from 127.0.0.1: bytes=32 time<1ms TTL=128
Reply from 127.0.0.1: bytes=32 time<1ms TTL=128
Reply from 127.0.0.1: bytes=32 time<1ms TTL=128
Reply from 127.0.0.1: bytes=32 time<1ms TTL=128

Ping statistics for 127.0.0.1:
    Packets: Sent = 4, Received = 4, Lost = 0 (0% loss),
Approximate round trip times in milli-seconds:
    Minimum = 0ms, Maximum = 0ms, Average = 0ms

C:\>_
```

5. Type <u>ipconfig</u> and press **ENTER**. You will see a readout of your network configuration, including the IP address, the subnet mask, and the default gateway (most likely your connection to the Internet), as shown here.

```
Command Prompt                                    _ □ ×

C:\>ipconfig

Windows IP Configuration


Ethernet adapter Local Area Connection:

        Connection-specific DNS Suffix  . :
        IP Address. . . . . . . . . . . . : 192.168.0.151
        Subnet Mask . . . . . . . . . . . : 255.255.255.0
        Default Gateway . . . . . . . . . : 192.168.0.1

C:\>_
```

6. Type ping and the address of the default gateway (for example, ping 192.168.0.1). If you get four replies from the gateway, your network connection is working. If you don't, you will need to change your TCP/IP configuration to enable the PCs to communicate. The most likely problem is that the PCs' IP addresses are not in the same subnet (network segment), which prevents them from "seeing" each other. You should also check your network hardware for problems, such as disconnected cables or a switched-off access point.

```
Command Prompt

C:\>ping 192.168.0.1

Pinging 192.168.0.1 with 32 bytes of data:

Reply from 192.168.0.1: bytes=32 time<1ms TTL=128
Reply from 192.168.0.1: bytes=32 time<1ms TTL=128
Reply from 192.168.0.1: bytes=32 time<1ms TTL=128
Reply from 192.168.0.1: bytes=32 time<1ms TTL=128

Ping statistics for 192.168.0.1:
    Packets: Sent = 4, Received = 4, Lost = 0 (0% loss),
Approximate round trip times in milli-seconds:
    Minimum = 0ms, Maximum = 0ms, Average = 0ms

C:\>
```

7. Click **Close** to close the Command Prompt window.

8. If you do find a problem, review the earlier sections on setting up network hardware and configuring TCP/IP to isolate and fix the problem.

Chapter 9

Getting Maximum Use out of Your Laptop PC

Laptop PCs are great because you can easily take them with you almost anywhere you go. They have disadvantages, however: you pay a higher price than desktop PCs (as discussed in Chapter 1), you sacrifice some flexibility in configuration (see Chapter 6), and you must guard more vigilantly against theft (see Chapter 7). All in all, though, most current laptop PCs offer impressive power and terrific convenience for their size.

To get the most out of your laptop PC, you'll need to put more work into configuring and managing it than you would for most desktop PCs. The main areas to focus on are power settings, network configurations, synchronizing files, using docking and DualView, and how you will use your laptop PC on the road.

Manage Laptop PC Power Usage

Unlike desktop computers, laptop PCs have two sources of power: batteries and
and current from electrical outlets, converted by the laptop's power adapter.
This means that you have several extra tasks with a laptop PC to manage how
you use these two power sources and conserve limited battery power.

Maximize Your Battery Life

If you use your laptop computer extensively on the road, your first concern
is likely to be maximizing your battery life so that you can get plenty of work
(or play) done without having to plug in your computer. The main ways of
maximizing battery life are:

*Figure 9-1: Your laptop PC may include a graphical
configuration utility that enables you to turn off features
you're not using to reduce power consumption.*

- **Decrease the screen brightness** Your laptop PC's
  screen probably consumes the greatest proportion of battery power, so you can increase battery life by decreasing
  the screen brightness. Most laptop PCs have function
  keys for decreasing screen brightness. Some laptop PCs
  have hardware controls (for example, a slider).

- **Turn off unnecessary components** Many laptop PCs
  let you disable components that you're not using in order
  to reduce power consumption. For example, when on the
  road, you might turn off your laptop PC's serial, parallel,
  and infrared ports if you don't need them. Consult your
  laptop PC's manual for details on what you can turn off
  and how to do so. In some laptop PCs, you must change;
  others provide graphical configuration utilities, such as
  that shown in Figure 9-1.

- **Get a high-capacity battery** Some manufacturers make
  high-capacity batteries for certain laptop PC models.
  These almost always protrude beyond the standard battery compartment, usually doubling as a stand to elevate
  the back of the laptop PC, which improves the typing position and the airflow to the underside.

CHOOSING LAPTOP PC BATTERIES

Lithium ion (Li-ion) batteries usually give longer battery life than do nickel metal hydride (NiMH) batteries, but they are more expensive. Most makes of laptop PC can take only one type of battery, so the only time you can choose between battery technologies is when buying a laptop PC.

Laptop PC batteries typically lose capacity after two or three years. To continue using your laptop PC on the road, you may need to replace the battery. Because capacity declines after the battery is manufactured regardless of use, you should buy the replacement battery only when you need it, not at the time you buy your laptop PC. You should also check the replacement battery's date of manufacture, if possible, to make sure you're not buying an old battery.

● **Use an extra battery (or two)** Some laptop PCs enable you to insert an extra battery in place of the optical drive or another component. If not, carry an extra battery separately. When the first battery runs out, shut down your laptop PC, replace the battery, and then start your PC again.

● **Get an external battery** If your laptop PC can't take a high-capacity battery or an extra battery, consider getting an external battery for extra power. External batteries typically weigh several pounds and are around the size of a compact laptop PC, so they're an awkward solution—but they can deliver up to six or eight hours of extra battery life.

● **Get an auto adapter or air adapter** To charge your laptop PC from your car battery, get an auto adapter; to charge your laptop PC in a plane, get an air adapter. Many different models are available, from custom models designed for specific laptop PCs to standard power inverters that deliver AC current that can power any device.

● **Get a second power adapter** If you commute with your laptop PC, get a second power adapter so that you can keep one at home and one at work, decreasing your laptop PC's travel weight and the chance of forgetting to take the adapter with you.

● **Get a portable solar panel** If you need to use your laptop PC away from other sources of energy, consider a portable solar panel designed for powering a laptop PC. These are popular with computer-toting hikers as well as with those whose jobs require the use of a computer away from standard power sources. See sites such as It Connections, Ltd (www.portablesolar.com) for examples.

● **Configure aggressive power management settings** Reduce your laptop PC's power consumption by using aggressive power management settings. See "Configure Power Settings," later in this chapter.

● **Keep your battery fully charged** Modern battery technologies don't need to be fully discharged before being recharged to avoid the "memory effect" that reduced the charge capacity of older batteries, so it's best to keep your laptop PC plugged in whenever you have a power source available. That way, the battery will remain as fully charged as possible.

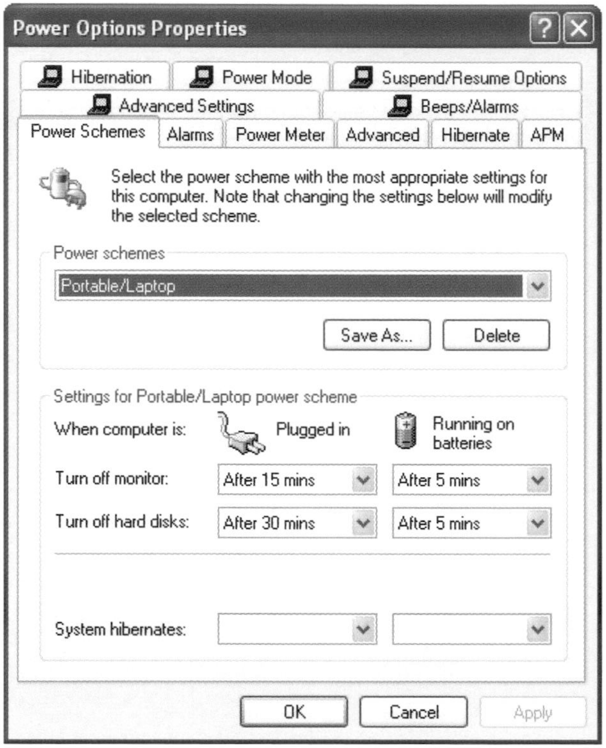

Configure Power Settings

You should configure power management settings on your laptop PC so that it runs at full speed when the power adapter is delivering power but reduces its power consumption to a sensible minimum when running off the battery.

To configure power settings, display the Power Options Properties dialog box in either of these ways:

- Click the **Start** button, and click **Control Panel**. In Category View, click **Performance And Maintenance**, and then click **Power Options**. (In Classic View, double-click **Power Options**.)

  –Or–

- Right-click open space on the desktop, and click **Properties**. The Display Properties dialog box appears. Click the **Screen Saver** tab, and click **Power** in the Monitor Power area.

The Power Options Properties dialog box appears. The number of tabs it contains depends on the capabilities that XP detects in your laptop PC and whether your PC manufacturer has installed any custom power management options. Figure 9-2 shows a highly customized version of the Power Options Properties dialog box. Each tab with a laptop PC icon is a custom tab; those tabs without laptop PC icons are standard tabs.

Figure 9-2: The number of tabs in the Power Options Properties dialog box depends on your laptop PC's capabilities and whether any custom power management software is installed.

Set Up Power Schemes

To define the overall power settings XP uses, you configure a power scheme.

1. In the Power Options dialog box (see "Configure Power Settings"), click the **Power Schemes** tab (shown in Figure 9-2).

2. Open the **Power Schemes** drop-down list, and click **Portable/Laptop** if it's not selected already.

3. Use the **Turn Off Monitor**, **Turn Off Hard Disks**, **System Standby**, and **System Hibernates** drop-down lists in the Plugged In column to specify how long to keep each component running when the laptop PC is plugged in.

NOTE

Depending on your laptop PC, only the System Standby drop-down list or the System Hibernates drop-down list may appear on the Power Schemes tab.

NOTE

Standby mode allows you to suspend and resume your work at a moment's notice and is great for short interruptions to your work. Standby mode shuts down your hard drive and display but keeps data in RAM, which takes a little power. If the power runs out, you lose the data in the RAM.

TIP

You can save a custom power scheme by clicking **Save As** so that you can quickly apply the settings again from the Power Schemes drop-down list. For example, you might create different power schemes for dual-battery and single-battery configurations.

4. Use the drop-down lists in the Running On Batteries column to specify how long to keep each component running when the laptop PC is on battery power. To increase battery life, make these settings as short as comfortable, especially the Turn Off Monitor setting.

Set Battery Alarms and Alarm Actions

Some laptop PCs automatically hibernate when the battery reaches a critically low level. You can also set alarms and alarm actions in XP for when the battery runs low.

1. In the Power Options dialog box (see "Configure Power Settings"), click the **Alarms** tab (see Figure 9-3; note the different selection of tabs—this is a different laptop PC than in the previous figure).

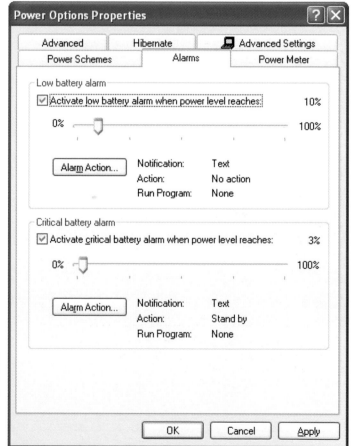

Figure 9-3: Configure alarms and alarm actions to control what happens when your battery power reaches low and critical levels.

2. Configure a low-battery alarm to warn you when you're reaching the end of your battery power.

3. Select the **Activate Low Battery Alarm When Power Level Reaches** check box, and drag the slider to the percentage at which you want to be warned. Click the top **Alarm Action** button, and use the options in the Low Battery Alarm Actions dialog box to specify what XP should do: display a message to warn you; sound an alarm; or take an action, such as making the PC stand by or shut down. This dialog box is the same as the Critical Battery Alarm Actions dialog box (shown in Figure 9-4), it just has a different name. Click **OK** to close the dialog box.

4. Configure a critical battery alarm to stand by or shut down your laptop PC if you don't respond to the low-battery warning.

5. Select the **Activate Critical Battery Alarm When Power Level Reaches** check box, and drag the slider to a suitable percentage (this must be less than that for the low-battery alarm). Click the bottom **Alarm Action** button, and use the options in the Critical Battery Alarm Actions dialog box (see Figure 9-4) to specify what XP should do. Typically, you'll want to select the **When The Alarm Goes Off, The Computer Will** check box, and choose either **Stand By** or **Shut Down** in the drop-down list. Select the **Force Stand By Or Shutdown Even If A Program Stops Responding** check box to ensure that a program error can't prevent the action from being taken. Click **OK** to close the dialog box.

Figure 9-4: Configure the critical battery alarm to shut down your laptop PC or put it into standby mode.

Configure Power and Sleep Button Settings

You can configure how XP interprets the power controls on your laptop PC.

1. In the Power Options dialog box (see "Configure Power Settings"), click the **Advanced** tab (see Figure 9-5).

2. In the Options area, choose whether to show the power icon in the taskbar (in the notification area) and whether to have XP prompt you for your password when you resume from standby mode (a good idea for security).

3. In the Power Buttons area, use the three drop-down lists to specify which action XP should take when you close your laptop PC's lid, press the power button, or press the sleep button. For example, you might make your laptop PC go into standby mode when you close the lid.

Figure 9-5: Tell XP how to respond when you push the power button, push the sleep button, and close the lid of your laptop PC.

Set Up Hibernation Mode

Standby mode requires power, so it continues to use the battery and is best used for only short periods. If you need to leave your laptop PC for a longer time (say, several days) without shutting it down, use hibernation mode instead. In hibernation mode, XP saves the data held in RAM to the hibernation file on your hard drive so that it can shut down the computer completely.

To set up hibernation mode:

1. In the Power Options dialog box (see "Configure Power Settings"), click the **Hibernate** tab (see Figure 9-6).

2. Look at the **Disk Space For Hibernation** readout, which shows how much disk space you have free and how much space hibernation mode requires, to ensure that hibernation mode won't run you out of disk space.

3. Select the **Enable Hibernation** check box.

After you finish configuring the power options, click **OK** to close the Power Options Properties dialog box.

You can then hibernate by:

- Pressing the appropriate power button or closing the lid.

  –Or–

- Clicking the **Start** button, clicking **Turn Off Computer**, holding down SHIFT to change the Stand By button to a Hibernate button, and clicking **Hibernate**.

To awaken your laptop PC from hibernation mode, press the power button.

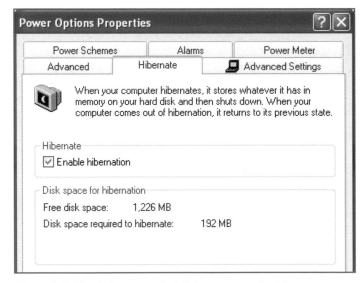

Figure 9-6: Check the amount of disk space required for hibernation mode and the amount of free space on your laptop PC's hard drive.

Check Your Laptop PC's Battery Status

To check the status of your laptop PC's battery:

- If you choose to display a power icon in the notification area on the right of the taskbar, hover the mouse pointer over it.

  –Or–

- Click the **Power Meter** tab in the Power Options Properties dialog box. If your laptop PC has two batteries, you can choose whether to view their details separately or together.

Power Options Properties

Tabs: Advanced Settings | Beeps/Alarms | Hibernation | Power Mode | Suspend/Resume Options | Power Schemes | Alarms | Power Meter | Advanced | Hibernate | APM

☑ Show details for each battery.

Power status

Current power source: AC power
Total battery power remaining: 100%

#1
100%

Click an individual battery icon for more information.

[OK]   [Cancel]   [Apply]

Synchronize Your Laptop PC with Your Desktop PC

If you use both a laptop PC and a desktop PC, you'll often need to network the two and share files between them. You can do so in four ways:

- **Move or copy the files manually** Use the techniques discussed in Chapter 2 to move or copy the files from one computer to another. This works well for the occasional file, but quickly becomes awkward with large numbers of files.

- **Keep all the files on the laptop** PC By keeping the files on the laptop PC and accessing them from the desktop PC when necessary, you can have all your files with you when you take your laptop PC on the road.

- **Use XP's Briefcase feature** XP Home Edition and XP Professional both include the Briefcase, a modest feature for synchronizing batches of files. See "Use the Briefcase Feature" later in this chapter.

- **Use XP Professional's Offline Files feature** XP Professional's Offline Files feature lets you automatically store copies of files located on a network on your laptop PC so that you can work with them when the network isn't available. XP Home Edition doesn't have this feature. See "Use Offline Files in XP Professional," later in this chapter.

Use the Briefcase Feature

The Briefcase feature enables you to create a special Briefcase folder for keeping files synchronized on two computers.

1. Create a Briefcase on your laptop PC.
2. Copy the files from your desktop PC to your laptop PC.
3. Work on the files on the laptop PC.
4. Synchronize the files in the Briefcase with the files on your desktop PC when you return.

To create and work with a Briefcase:

1. Connect your computers. For example, connect your laptop PC to your home network.
2. Right-click open space on the desktop, click **New**, and then click **Briefcase**. XP creates a Briefcase named New Briefcase.
3. Click the new Briefcase, pause, and click it again to display the edit box. Type a descriptive name, and press **ENTER**.

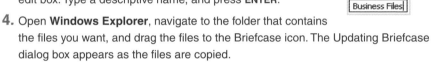

4. Open **Windows Explorer**, navigate to the folder that contains the files you want, and drag the files to the Briefcase icon. The Updating Briefcase dialog box appears as the files are copied.
5. Disconnect your laptop PC, and work with the files in the Briefcase as usual. You can delete files from and create new files in the Briefcase.

6. Reconnect your laptop PC to your desktop PC.

---

7. Right-click the Briefcase, and click **Update All**. A dialog box appears, showing the files that need updating (see Figure 9-7).

8. Check the list of updates. To change an action, right-click the file, and click your preferred action in the shortcut menu.

9. Click **Update** to update your files with the changed versions.

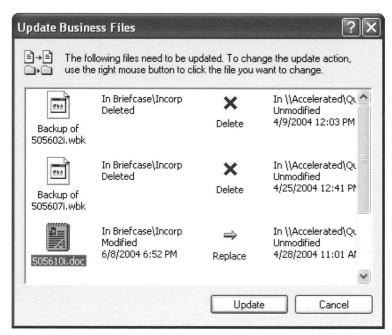

Figure 9-7: Check the updates that XP intends to make to the Briefcase files and to the original files.

Use Offline Files in XP Professional

If your laptop PC has XP Professional rather than XP Home Edition, you can use the Offline Files feature for synchronizing files instead of the Briefcase feature. Offline Files is more powerful than the Briefcase feature, but it's somewhat more complicated to use. You must also switch off the Fast User Switching feature if it's switched on, because Offline Files doesn't work when Fast User Switching is on.

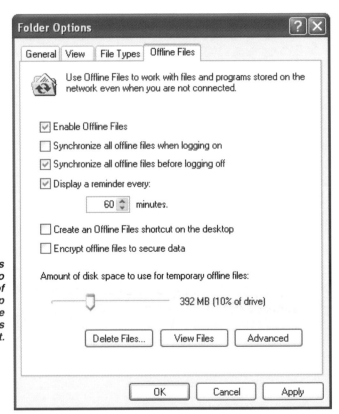

Figure 9-8: The Offline Files feature enables you to automatically make copies of network files on your laptop PC and then synchronize the copies with the network files when you reconnect.

ENABLE AND CONFIGURE OFFLINE FILES

Before you can use Offline Files, you must enable and configure the Offline Files feature.

1. If Fast User Switching is enabled, turn it off. Click the **Start** button, click **Control Panel**, and, in Category View, click **User Accounts**. (In Classic View, double-click **User Accounts**.) In the Pick A Task list, click **Change The Way Users Log On Or Off**. Clear the **Use Fast User Switching** check box, and click **Apply Options**. Click **Close** to close the User Accounts window. Click **Close** to close the Control Panel window.

2. Click the **Start** button, and click **My Computer** to open a My Computer window.

3. Click the **Tools** menu, click **Folder Options**, and then click the **Offline Files** tab (see Figure 9-8).

4. Select the **Enable Offline Files** check box. XP enables all the other options on the tab.

5. Choose how to synchronize offline files.

- Select the **Synchronize All Offline Files When Logging On** check box to perform a quick synchronization of offline files each time you log on. For technical reasons, this is a quick synchronization rather than a full synchronization of offline files and is best not used.

  –Or–

- Select the **Synchronize All Offline Files Before Logging Off** check box to perform a full synchronization of offline files each time you log off. This is a full synchronization and may take anywhere from a few seconds to many minutes to complete.

  –Or–

- Clear both these check boxes if you prefer to synchronize files manually.

6. To receive a reminder that you're working with offline files rather than network files, select the **Display A Reminder Every *NN* Minutes** check box, and adjust the number accordingly. This reminder can be useful when you're connected to the network and haven't synchronized; when you're aware you're not connected, however, you might find it irritating.

7. Select the **Create An Offline Files Shortcut On The Desktop** check box if you want XP to create such a shortcut.

8. Select the **Encrypt Offline Files To Secure Data** check box if you want to encrypt your offline files for security. This is a good idea for protecting important files in case your laptop PC is lost or stolen.

9. Drag the **Amount Of Disk Space To Use For Temporary Offline Files** slider to specify the maximum amount of your laptop PC's hard drive that Offline Files can take up. How much space you need depends on how many files you must take with you.

10. Click **OK** to apply your choices and close the Folder Options dialog box.

MAKE FILES AVAILABLE FOR OFFLINE USE

After enabling Offline Files, specify which files you want to make available.

1. Open **Windows Explorer**, and navigate to the folder that contains the files you want.

2. Select one or more files or folders.

3. Click the **File** menu, and click **Make Available Offline**.

NOTE

The first time you use the Make Available Offline command, XP Professional runs the Offline Files Wizard. If you've chosen options as described in "Enable and Configure Offline Files" earlier in this chapter, click **Next**, click **Next** again, and then click **Finish** to close the wizard. (If not, work through the options the wizard offers.)

4. If the objects you're making available offline include a folder that contains subfolders, the Confirm Offline Subfolders dialog box appears (shown here). Usually, you'll want to leave the **Yes, Make This Folder And All Its Subfolders Available Offline** option button selected to make the subfolders available offline. Click **OK**.

5. XP Professional synchronizes the files, displaying the Synchronizing dialog box as it does so.

When synchronization is complete, XP Professional closes the Synchronizing dialog box and displays an Offline Folders icon, consisting of two curving blue arrows, on each offline item.

Photos

587202_figures.zip
629 KB

alarm.tif
Microsoft Office Document Im...
625 KB

WORK WITH OFFLINE FILES

After setting up Offline Files and specifying the files and folders to make available offline, you can disconnect your laptop PC from the network and work with the files. The files still appear to be in their network locations even though you are working with copies saved on your laptop PC's hard drive.

QUICKFACTS

UNDERSTANDING SYNCHRONIZATION

XP Professional synchronizes your offline files with the network files as follows:

- If the network file is unchanged and the offline file is changed, the offline file replaces the network file.
- If the network file is changed and the offline file is unchanged, the network file replaces the offline file.
- If both the network file and offline file are changed, XP prompts you to decide which one to keep.
- If the network file has been deleted and the offline file is unchanged, XP deletes the offline file.
- If the network file has been deleted, but the offline file is changed, XP prompts you to decide whether to delete the offline file or save it to the network.
- If the offline file has been deleted and the network file is unchanged, XP deletes the network file.
- If the offline file has been deleted, but the network file has changed, XP doesn't delete the network file.
- If there are new offline files, XP creates copies of them on the network.
- If there are new network files, XP creates offline copies of them.

SYNCHRONIZE YOUR OFFLINE FILES

After you reconnect to your network, synchronize your offline files. XP Professional supports automatic synchronization at logon and logoff, when your laptop PC is idle, and according to a synchronization schedule, but usually it's best to synchronize files manually as soon as you return.

To synchronize files manually:

1. Connect your laptop PC to your network.

2. Click the **Start** button, and click **My Computer** to open a My Computer window.

3. Click the **Tools** menu, and click **Synchronize**. The Items To Synchronize dialog box appears (see Figure 9-9).

Figure 9-9: Manual synchronization is the fastest and easiest way to keep your offline files up to date.

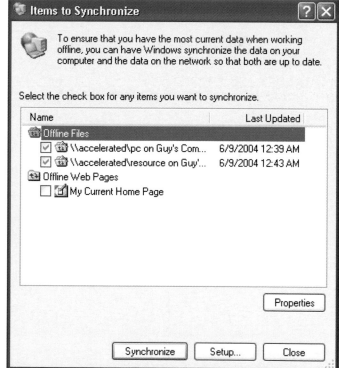

4. Select the check box for each set of offline files you want to synchronize. Usually, you'll want to synchronize all offline files, but you may not want to synchronize your offline web pages unless you need to be able to browse parts of the web while you're not connected to the Internet.

5. Click **Synchronize**. XP Professional synchronizes the files. If it requires you to make any decisions, XP Professional displays the Resolve File Conflicts dialog box (see Figure 9-10). Select the appropriate option button. Select the **Do This For All Conflicts** check box if you want to take the same action on all conflicted files, and click **OK**.

6. Click **Close** to close the My Computer window.

Figure 9-10: If both the offline file and the network file have changed, you will need to resolve the conflict.

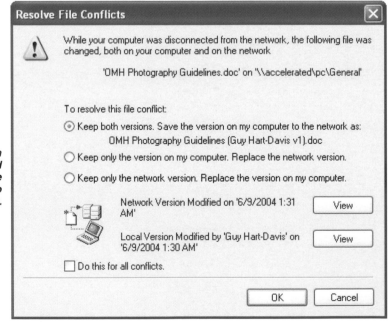

USE DUALVIEW

Many laptop PCs can use an XP feature called DualView that allows you to use your laptop PC's monitor and an external monitor at the same time, with a different part of the desktop displayed on each. DualView can greatly increase your laptop PC's usability by providing more screen space for your work (or play).

1. Check your laptop PC's documentation to see if it supports DualView.

2. Connect an external monitor to your laptop PC's external video connector, and switch it on. If you've turned off the external video connector to save power, turn it back on.

3. When XP detects the extra monitor, it installs the drivers for it. If XP doesn't have suitable drivers, it prompts you to provide them.

4. Right-click open space on the desktop, and click **Properties**. The Display Properties dialog box appears. (XP may display the Display Properties dialog box automatically.)

5. Click the **Settings** tab, click the icon for the external monitor, and make sure the **Extend My Windows Desktop Onto This Monitor** check box is selected. Click **Apply**.

6. Drag the icons for the monitors to positions that correspond to the physical arrangement of the laptop PC and the external monitor. For example, if you've placed the external monitor to the left of the laptop PC, drag the icon for the external monitor to the left of the laptop PC's icon. The way you position the icons tells XP how to arrange your desktop across the monitors.

7. Click **OK**.

Use Your Laptop PC at Home

If your laptop PC is your main (or only) PC, make sure it's as comfortable as possible for working with. Comfort and ergonomics should have played a major role in your choice of laptop PC, but you can increase both in several ways when using your PC in its main location.

- **External keyboard** Plug in an external keyboard to use instead of the built-in keyboard. Even if you don't buy a special ergonomic keyboard, you'll probably benefit from having the numeric keypad and from being able to adjust the position of the keyboard relative to the laptop PC.

- **External mouse** Plug in your favorite type of pointing device to use instead of, or in addition to, your laptop PC's touchpad or pointing stick. If your laptop PC has only one PS/2 connector (the round connector used for keyboards and mice), and you need to connect both a PS/2 keyboard and PS/2 mouse, get a splitter cable to provide two PS/2 connectors.

- **External monitor** You can use an external monitor instead of—or in many laptop PCs, in addition to—your laptop PC's monitor. If you have a large monitor, you may find it easier to use than your laptop PC's monitor. Otherwise, by adding even a modest-sized external monitor, you can substantially increase the size of your desktop and the amount of information you can see at once. See the QuickSteps "Use DualView."

- **Laptop PC stand** Consider getting a custom laptop PC stand to improve your laptop PC's work angle and increase ventilation to its underside. Alternatively, prop up the back of the laptop PC on a book or a stack of CD jewel cases.

- **Docking station** If you need to connect a full suite of hardware to your laptop PC each time you bring it home, consider a docking station. A docking station is a component with connectors for keeping all the docked components (keyboard, mouse, monitor, printer, and so on) connected. You can then attach, or dock, your laptop PC to the docking station with a single connection. Docking stations are convenient, but tend to be expensive because they're custom components for particular laptop PCs. You can find third-party "universal" docking stations (ones that work with many models of laptop PCs) from manufacturers such as Kensington Technology Group (www.kensington.com) and Belkin Corporation (www.belkin.com).

NOTE

XP creates a default hardware profile, called Profile 1, when you install it. XP then automatically uses that hardware profile each time you start your computer until you create another profile.

Figure 9-11: If you dock your laptop computer, create a new hardware profile for docked use.

Use Hardware Profiles

If you connect your laptop PC to several extra components each time you bring it home, you should create separate hardware profiles for docked and undocked use so that XP knows which hardware is supposed to be there.

CREATE A HARDWARE PROFILE

To create a hardware profile for the docked configuration of your laptop PC:

1. Turn on your laptop PC, and allow XP to load. Log on as usual.

2. Press ▓+**BREAK** to display the System Properties dialog box.

3. Click the **Hardware** tab, and then click **Hardware Profiles**. The Hardware Profiles dialog box appears (see Figure 9-11).

4. With the default profile, **Profile 1 (Current)**, selected, click **Rename**, type a descriptive name (such as <u>Undocked</u>) in the Rename Profile dialog box, and click **OK**.

5. With the newly renamed profile selected, click **Copy**, type a descriptive name for the new profile (such as <u>Docked</u>) in the Copy Profile dialog box, and click **OK**.

6. With the new profile selected, click **Properties** to display the profile's Properties dialog box (see Figure 9-12).

7. Select the **This Is A Portable Computer** check box, the **The Computer Is Docked** option button, and the **Always Include This Profile As An Option When Windows Starts** check box. Click **OK**.

8. In the Hardware Profiles dialog box, select the **Select The First Profile Listed If I Don't Select A Profile In** option button. Adjust the number of seconds to give yourself time to select a profile when you start your laptop PC.

9. Click **OK** to close the Hardware Profiles dialog box.

10. Click **OK** to close the System Properties dialog box.

Docked Properties

General

Docked

Dock ID: Unavailable

Serial Number: Unavailable

☑ This is a portable computer

○ The docking state is unknown
◉ The computer is docked
○ The computer is undocked

Hardware profiles selection

☑ Always include this profile as an option when Windows starts

OK   Cancel

Figure 9-12: Specify the details of the profile in the profile's Properties dialog box.

SWITCH TO ANOTHER HARDWARE PROFILE

To switch to another hardware profile:

1. If your laptop PC is running, restart XP (click the **Start** button, click **Turn Off Computer**, and then click **Restart**). If your laptop PC isn't running, start it.

2. When XP displays the Hardware Profile/Configuration Recovery Menu (see Figure 9-13), use the **DOWN ARROW** and **UP ARROW** keys to select the profile, and then press **ENTER**.

3. Log in as usual.

SET UP THE PROFILE

After switching to a profile, set it up with all the device drivers it needs.

1. Dock your laptop PC, or connect all the hardware devices you want to include in the profile.

2. Install any device drivers that are required for the hardware. These device drivers will be installed into the current profile, not into the other profile.

Figure 9-13: Select the profile from the Hardware Profile/ Configuration Recovery Menu.

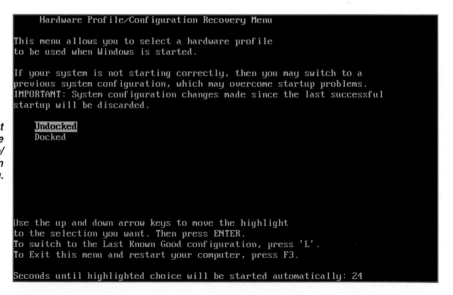

```
       Hardware Profile/Configuration Recovery Menu

This menu allows you to select a hardware profile
to be used when Windows is started.

If your system is not starting correctly, then you may switch to a
previous system configuration, which may overcome startup problems.
IMPORTANT: System configuration changes made since the last successful
startup will be discarded.

      Undocked
      Docked




Use the up and down arrow keys to move the highlight
to the selection you want. Then press ENTER.
To switch to the Last Known Good configuration, press 'L'.
To Exit this menu and restart your computer, press F3.

Seconds until highlighted choice will be started automatically: 24
```

Use Your Laptop PC on the Road

When you need to take your laptop PC on the road:

1. Charge the main battery and any spare batteries.
2. Copy or synchronize all the files you need to the laptop PC.
3. Disconnect the laptop PC from whatever docking arrangement you've created.
4. Pack your laptop PC, power adapter, spare batteries, modem cable, wireless network adapter, and any other items you need.
5. Leave.

This section discusses two specific features that you may need to use while on the road: multiple configurations for dial-up networking and wireless networks.

Switch among Dial-Up Locations

If you use a dial-up Internet connection when you're on the road, you should create a separate network location for each place from which you connect rather than constantly change the phone number and other details of your main dial-up connection.

To create a new location:

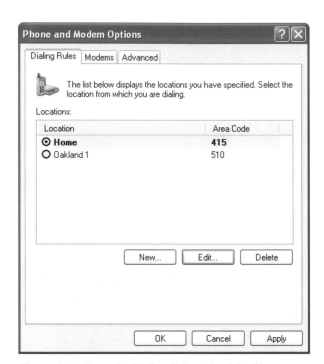

Figure 9-14: From the Dialing Rules tab of the Phone And Modem Options dialog box, you can create new locations and switch among existing locations.

1. Click the **Start** button, and click **Control Panel**. In Category View, click **Printers And Other Hardware**, and then click **Phone And Modem Options**. (In Classic View, double-click **Phone And Modem Options**.) The Phone And Modem Options dialog box appears (see Figure 9-14).
2. Click **New** on the Dialing Rules tab to open the New Location dialog box (see Figure 9-15).
3. Type a descriptive name in the Location Name text box.
4. Specify the country and area code for the location.
5. Set up any dialing rules for the connection: the number to dial for an outside line for local or long-distance calls, the carrier code to use for long-distance and international calls, whether to disable call waiting (and which code to use), and whether to use tone or pulse dialing.

NOTE

To switch to another location, display the **Phone And Modem Options** dialog box, select the location in the Location list, and click **OK**.

Figure 9-15: Use the three tabs of the New Location dialog box to specify the details of the networking location.

6. If necessary, use the options on the Area Code Rules tab to create rules for dialing in particular area codes, and use the options on the Calling Card tab to set up a credit card or calling card to use for making calls.

7. Click **OK** to close the New Location dialog box. XP adds the location to the list in the Phone And Modem Options dialog box.

8. If you want to use the new location immediately, select it in the Locationlist.

9. Click **OK** to close the Phone And Modem Options dialog box.

10. Click **Close** to close the Printers And Other Hardware window.

Use Public Wireless Networks

XP's ability to switch quickly among dial-up locations simplifies the chore of connecting via modem while you're on the road, but dial-up connections remain slow and awkward. If your laptop PC has built-in Wi-Fi, or if you're prepared to buy a Wi-Fi adapter, you can often make a much faster connection by using a public wireless network, or Wi-Fi hotspot.

At this writing, many hotels, airports, and coffee shops offer wireless Internet access, some for free and the others for a modest fee. These hotspots are good for ad-hoc Internet access, but in most cases you'll do better to plan your access locations ahead of time by using a hotspot aggregator service, such as Boingo Wireless (www.boingo.com), T-Mobile (www.t-mobile.com), or GoRemote (www.goremote.com). Check the latest service plans from competing aggregators; use their online tools to find out whether they have hotspots where you need them; and establish which one will work best for your needs.

Beyond these formal public wireless networks, most cities contain many

NOTE

Another option for connecting to the Internet at higher speeds when you're on the road is the in-room Internet access that many hotels now offer. Include a lightweight Ethernet cable in your computer bag so that you can take advantage of these services without having to rent or buy a cable. Most of these services require you to reboot your PC so that it refreshes its network connections and requests an IP address from the service's DHCP server.

CAUTION

Whether you can legally access an open wireless network that you discover is disputed. The laws that cover such situations were written for different technologies, so they don't fit together and (in some cases) directly contradict each other. For example, accessing a Wi-Fi network without authorization can be viewed as the same kind of offense as hacking into a major computer installation across the wires. Simply running an open wireless network that others can access is arguably the same as pirating cable or satellite service.

wireless networks that have been left open by their owners, some intentionally (so that other people can use them as needed), but most through ignorance or incompetence. Tools such as NetStumbler (www.netstumbler.com) can help you quickly locate open networks within range of your wireless-enabled device. Sites such as Warchalking (www.warchalking.org) provide information about open networks, means of discovering them, and the meaning of the symbols marked on walls or sidewalks to denote the presence of a wireless network, its name (or SSID), and its status.

Chapter 10

Troubleshooting Hardware

PCs are notorious for giving their users trouble, and you may be one of the unlucky users who find that this reputation is wholly justified. This chapter shows you how to troubleshoot the hardware and software problems you're most likely to encounter: problems starting your PC, problems with XP running unstably, and problems that require you to get help from someone you know.

This chapter isn't exhaustive—large tomes have been written about troubleshooting PCs (if you're looking for a comprehensible and graphical treatment of this topic, see *PC Upgrading and Troubleshooting QuickSteps*, also published by McGraw-Hill/Osborne)—but it will enable you to solve key problems and let you know when you must call in your local guru or get professional help.

CREATING A BOOT FLOPPY OR CD

A boot floppy is a floppy disk that contains copies of three key system files: NTLDR, NTDETECT.COM, and BOOT.INI. If your PC doesn't have a floppy drive, you can create a boot CD instead, provided you have CD-burning software that can make the CD bootable (so that the PC can start from it).

To format a floppy disk and create a boot floppy:

1. Insert the floppy disk into the floppy drive, click the **Start** button, click **My Computer**, right-click **3½ Floppy (A:)**, and click **Format**. The Format dialog box appears.

2. Click **Start** in the Format 3½ Floppy dialog box. If you want to format that disk, click **OK** when warned that formatting will erase all data on the disk. When you see the message "Format Complete," click **OK** again and close the **Format** dialog box.

3. In the My Computer window, double-click your startup drive (usually C:) to display its contents.

4. If you see the These Files Are Hidden screen, click **Show The Contents Of This Folder**.

5. Click the **Tools** menu, and then click **Folder Options**. The Folder Options dialog box appears. Click the **View** tab.

6. In the Advanced Settings box, select the **Show Hidden Files And Folders** option button, and then clear the **Hide Protected Operating System Files** check box. A Warning dialog box appears. Click **Yes**. In the Folder Options dialog box, click **OK**. The hidden and system files, including BOOT, NTDETECT, and NTLDR, appear in the Local Disk (C:) window (see Figure 10-1). (If you don't see these files, you're looking at the wrong drive. Click **Up** and then double-click the correct drive.)

Continued…

Troubleshoot Problems Starting Your PC

Problems that occur when you start your PC can be tricky to deal with because you can't use most of XP's problem-solving tools. For safety, you should create an XP boot floppy or boot CD that will enable you to start your PC if vital system files get corrupted.

Deal with Startup Errors

This section discusses how to deal with the startup errors that you're most likely to see and that you stand a good chance of dealing with on your own. For other startup errors, you will probably want to consult a PC technician.

Figure 10-1: Creating a boot floppy allows you to start your computer in several circumstances when it wouldn't otherwise start.

NOTE

You may need to configure your PC so that it starts from the floppy drive. See the "Configuring Your PC's Boot Drives" QuickSteps in this chapter.

"NON-SYSTEM DISK OR DISK ERROR" MESSAGE

The message "Non-system disk or disk error" usually means that you have left a floppy disk in the floppy drive and your PC is trying to start from it. Remove the disk and press **CTRL+ALT+DELETE** to restart your PC.

If there's no floppy disk in the floppy drive, your PC probably has a disk error. Try restarting it a couple of times. If you get the same error, seek professional assistance.

"NTLDR IS MISSING" MESSAGE

The message "NTLDR is missing. Press Ctrl+Alt+Del to restart" typically means that the NTLDR (NT Loader) system file has been corrupted or deleted. To recover from this error:

1. Insert your XP boot floppy in your PC's floppy drive.

2. Press **CTRL+ALT+DELETE** to restart your PC using the copy of NTLDR on the floppy disk.

3. If your PC starts correctly, log on to XP, and then copy the working NTLDR file from the floppy disk to the root folder on your PC's boot drive (for example, C:), replacing the version that has been corrupted or deleted.

4. Remove the floppy disk, and boot the PC as normal.

If this procedure does not enable your PC to boot, seek professional assistance.

"NTDETECT FAILED" AND BLACK SCREEN

If your PC briefly displays the message "NTDETECT failed" during startup and then immediately reboots, the NTDETECT.COM system file has been corrupted or deleted.

1. Insert your XP boot floppy in your PC's floppy drive.

2. Press **CTRL+ALT+DELETE** to restart your PC using the copy of NTDETECT.COM on the floppy disk.

3. If your PC starts correctly, log on to XP, and then copy the working NTDETECT.COM file from the floppy disk to the root folder on your PC's boot drive (for example, C:), replacing the version that has been corrupted or deleted.

4. Remove the floppy disk, and boot the PC as normal.

⏰UICKSTEPS

CONFIGURING YOUR PC'S BOOT DRIVES

Most PCs can *boot*, or start, from the hard drive, from an optical drive, or from a floppy drive (if the PC has one). You may sometimes need to change the list of drives from which your PC tries to boot and the order in which it tries those drives. For example, if you often work with floppy disks and tend to leave them in the drive, configure your PC so that it doesn't try to start from the floppy drive; and if you need to boot from a boot floppy, configure your PC so that it tries the floppy drive first.

1. Start or restart your PC.
2. Press **DELETE** or **F2** during startup (following the on-screen prompt). The BIOS screen appears.
3. Choose the option for changing boot settings. These vary depending on the BIOS in your PC.
4. Choose the order in which you want the drives to be used.
5. Exit the BIOS settings, and choose the option for saving your changes. Your PC then restarts automatically using the drives and order you specified.

"WINDOWS WAS NOT SHUT DOWN PROPERLY"

If XP starts by announcing that "Windows was not shut down properly" and suggesting that you start in Safe Mode, it's usually best to attempt to start XP normally. Press **DOWN ARROW** to move the selection to the **Start Windows Normally** option, and then press **ENTER**. If XP then runs normally, all is probably well. If XP fails to start properly and hangs (stops responding) before the Welcome screen appears:

1. Press **CTRL+ALT+DELETE** to restart your PC. You'll see the same screen again. This time, verify that the **Safe Mode** item is selected, and then press **ENTER**. The Please Select The Operating System To Start screen appears.

2. Verify that **XP** is selected (as it will be if it is the only operating system installed on your PC), and then press **ENTER**. XP starts in Safe Mode.

3. At the Welcome screen, click your user name. If prompted for your password, type it, and press **ENTER**. The Desktop dialog box appears, warning you that you are working in Safe Mode.

4. Click **Yes** or press **ENTER**. Safe Mode appears (see Figure 10-2), using the 640 × 480 screen resolution and only 16 colors for compatibility with your video hardware (in case this is what is making XP unstable).

Figure 10-2: Safe Mode simplifies XP by eliminating as many device drivers and services as possible so that you can troubleshoot problems without your PC crashing.

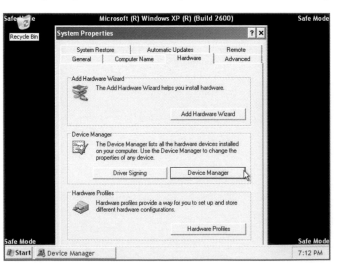

NOTE

Your mouse may or may not work in Safe Mode. In case it doesn't, many of the instructions in this chapter describe how to use the keyboard for what needs to be done. If your mouse is working, use it as normal.

CAUTION

Unless XP is severely unstable and you are trying to troubleshoot it, you normally do not want to change the settings in System Configuration Utility.

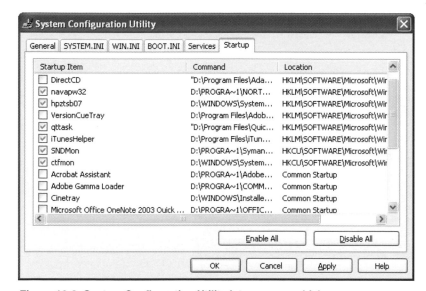

Figure 10-3: System Configuration Utility lets you see which programs XP is starting automatically and prevent specific programs from being started.

5. Troubleshoot the program or hardware that you think is causing the problem. See the next section, "Solve Problems When XP Is Running," for the tools you'll probably want to use.

6. After you finish working in Safe Mode, restart XP normally.

Solve Problems When XP Is Running

Problems that occur when XP is running (as opposed to when XP won't start) include a particular program or a hardware device making XP unstable, you deleting or losing files that you need, and you needing to restore XP to an earlier configuration to make it run stably again.

Prevent Programs from Starting Automatically

If XP starts successfully and you can log in as usual but XP then becomes unstable before you open any programs or take any actions, the culprit may be a service (a system process) or a program that XP is starting automatically. You can control which services and programs start automatically using System Configuration Utility.

1. Click the **Start** button, and then click **Run**. The Run dialog box appears.

2. Type <u>msconfig</u> and then press **ENTER**. System Configuration Utility opens.

3. Click the **Startup** tab (see Figure 10-3). This tab lists all the programs that XP starts automatically.

4. Clear the check boxes for the programs you don't want to start the next time XP starts, and then click **OK** to close System Configuration Utility. XP displays the System Configuration dialog box, telling you that you must restart your PC.

5. Click **Restart** to restart your PC.

6. Click **OK** when you are told that the System Configuration Utility has made changes to the way XP starts. The System Configuration Utility dialog box appears once more. Click **Close**. If you don't want to see the message or have System Configuration Utility open automatically when XP restarts, select the **Don't Show This Message Or Launch The System Configuration Utility When Windows Starts** check box.

7. See if preventing those programs from running has cured the instability. If not, try clearing the check boxes for other programs.

Figure 10-4: Use Device Manager to uninstall a hardware device that you think is making XP unstable.

Remove a Problem Device

If a hardware device seems to be making XP unstable, remove the device. A device might be the culprit if the problems you're experiencing start just after you install the device, XP displays error messages related to the device, or attempting to use the device causes XP to become unstable.

1. Click the **Start** button, right-click **My Computer**, and click **Properties**. The System Properties dialog box appears. Click the **Hardware** tab, and then click **Device Manager**. Device Manager opens (see Figure 10-4).

2. Right-click the offending device, and click **Uninstall**. XP removes the device's driver and stops using the device.

3. Shut down Windows, turn off your PC, and then physically remove the device from your PC. You should then be able to restart your PC without a problem.

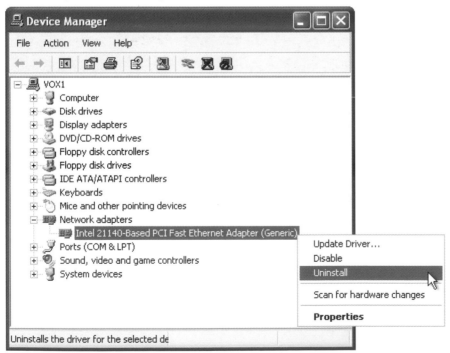

Update a Driver for a Problem Device

If a device isn't working properly, you may be able to fix it by updating its driver.

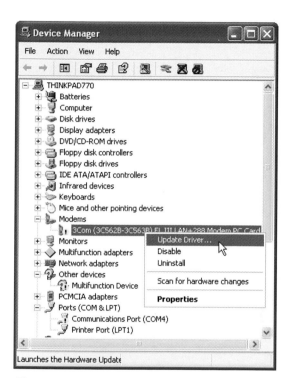

Figure 10-5: Device Manager displays an exclamation point next to any device that's not working properly.

1. Click the **Start** button, right-click **My Computer**, and click **Properties**. The System Properties dialog box appears. Click the **Hardware** tab, and then click **Device Manager**. Device Manager opens (see Figure 10-5).

2. Right-click the problem device, and click **Update Driver**. The Hardware Update Wizard starts. If the wizard prompts you to allow it to connect to Windows Update to search for software, select the **Yes, This Time Only** option button or the **Yes, Now And Every Time I Connect A Device** option button (as appropriate to your connection and your preferences) if you have an Internet connection. Click **Next**.

3. To check Windows Update for a new driver, leave the **Install The Software Automatically** option button selected, and click **Next**. The wizard searches and, if it finds a suitable driver, installs it. On the final page of the wizard, click **Finish**. If you see the Cannot Continue The Hardware Update Wizard page and you have a driver you want to try, click **Back**; otherwise, click **Finish** to leave the device with its existing, unsatisfactory driver, and go to step 8.

4. If you've downloaded a driver from the manufacturer's web site (or from a driver site), select the **Install From A List Or Specific Location** option button, and click **Next**. The Please Choose Your Search And Installation Options page is displayed (see Figure 10-6).

Figure 10-6: If the Hardware Update Wizard cannot find a suitable driver for a problem device, you can try to supply a driver manually.

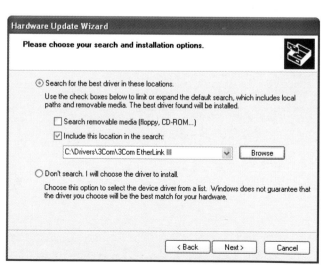

5. You can choose between having XP search particular folders you specify for a suitable driver and specifying the driver manually. In most cases, it's easiest to try searching with XP first and resort to specifying the driver manually if XP cannot find it. Select the **Search Removable Media** check box if the driver is on a floppy disk, CD, or USB (Universal Serial Bus) drive. If the driver is in a specific folder on your hard disk or on a network drive, select the **Include This Location In The Search** check box, click **Browse**, select the folder, and click **OK**.

6. Click **Next**. Again, the wizard searches and, if it finds a suitable driver, installs it. On the final page of the wizard, click **Finish**. If you see the Cannot Continue The Hardware Update Wizard page and you want to locate the driver manually, click **Back**; otherwise, click **Finish** to leave the device with its current driver, and go to step 8.

7. Select the **Don't Search. I Will Choose The Driver To Install** option button, and click **Next**. The Install page for this type of hardware is displayed. Click **Have Disk**. The Install From Disk dialog box appears. Click **Browse**, use the **Locate Folder** dialog box to select the folder that contains the driver, and click **Open**. In the Install From Disk dialog box, click **OK**. In the Hardware Update Wizard, click **Next**. The wizard installs the driver and displays its final page. Click **Finish** to close the wizard.

8. Click **Close** to close Device Manager, and then click **OK** to close the System Properties dialog box.

Restore Files from Backup

If you've backed up your valuable files, as discussed in Chapter 7, you can restore them from backup if you delete them accidentally or if your PC suffers data loss.

1. Click the **Start** button, click **All Programs**, click **Accessories**, click **System Tools**, and then click **Backup**. The Backup Or Restore Wizard starts. Click **Next**. The Backup Or Restore page is displayed.

2. Select the **Restore Files And Settings** option button, and then click **Next**. The What To Restore page is displayed (see Figure 10-7).

3. In the Items To Restore list box, double-click the file from which you want to restore items. Expand its contents as far as necessary by opening the required folders, and then select the check boxes in either the left list box or the right list box for the items you want to restore.

NOTE

If you are unable to locate a satisfactory driver for a device and you think the device is making XP unstable, uninstall the device as discussed in "Remove a Problem Device," earlier in this chapter.

Figure 10-7: You can restore anything from a single file to the entire contents of a backup.

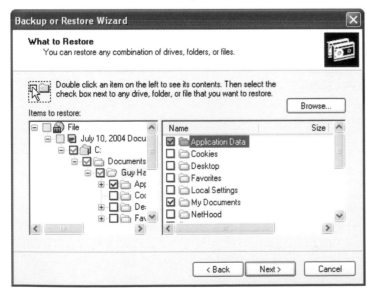

4. Click **Next**. The Completing The Backup Or Restore Wizard page is displayed. Click **Finish**. The wizard restores the files and folders you specified, displaying the Restore Progress dialog box as it does so.

5. When the restore operation is complete, click **Close**.

Restore a Full Backup

If your PC has Windows XP Professional (rather than XP Home Edition) and you've created an Automated System Recovery (ASR) set using the All Information On This Computer option in Backup, restore it as follows:

1. Insert the XP Professional CD in your CD drive.

2. Insert the ASR floppy disk in your floppy drive.

3. If your ASR backup is a removable medium, load the medium or have it ready to load. For example, if you recorded your ASR backup to CD, have the CD ready to load but leave the XP Professional CD in the drive.

4. Restart your PC. When your PC prompts you to start from the CD, press **SPACEBAR**. The XP Professional setup routine starts.

5. When Windows Setup prompts you to press F2 to start ASR, press **F2**.

6. If Windows Setup prompts you to supply your ASR backup file, do so. Otherwise, let ASR restore your computer. Toward the end of the restoration process, Backup starts and displays the Restore Progress dialog box to show you its progress.

7. At the end of the restoration, Backup should restart your PC automatically. If prompted, press **F3** to restart your PC manually.

Restore XP to an Earlier Configuration

System Restore is a semiautomatic recovery tool that keeps track of the changes made to your PC's configuration, including the software you install and the settings you choose. If a hardware change, a software installation, or a driver update causes the system not to run properly, you can use System Restore to return XP to how it was prior to that. System Restore works by creating *restore points* or *system checkpoints*, snapshots of your XP configuration, to which you can return if necessary.

CAUTION

System Restore protects your system files, program files, and the shortcuts and links on your Start menu. System Restore doesn't protect your data files or any backups you've made of them. To protect your data files, you must back them up using a utility such as Backup Utility (see Chapter 7).

10

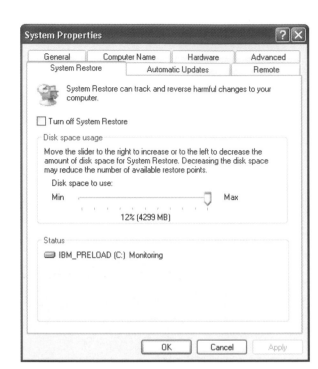

Figure 10-8: You can set up System Restore to monitor
only your system drive or all the drives on your PC.

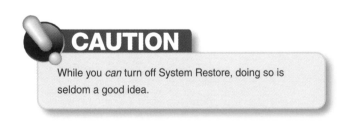

CAUTION

While you *can* turn off System Restore, doing so is
seldom a good idea.

CONFIGURE SYSTEM RESTORE

System Restore is automatically turned on in XP unless your PC has almost no
hard disk space left (less than 200 MB on the drive on which XP is installed).
You can turn System Restore off, and you can configure the amount of space it
takes up.

1. Press ⊞+**BREAK** (or click the **Start** button, right-click **My Computer**, and click **Properties**). The System Properties dialog box appears.

2. Click the **System Restore** tab (see Figure 10-8).

3. Verify that the **Turn Off System Restore** check box is cleared.

4. If your PC has only one hard drive (as is the case on a typical new PC with XP
installed), drag the **Disk Space To Use** slider to change the amount of space available to System Restore. (System Restore uses only as much of the allocated space
as it needs.) If your PC has multiple hard drives, click the drive you want to configure,
and then click **Settings**. On the system drive (generally drive C:), you can adjust only
the usage of disk space. On a second or subsequent drive, you can either adjust the
amount of space available to System Restore or prevent System Restore from using
that drive.

5. If your PC has multiple hard drives, click **OK** when you have finished adjusting the settings for a given drive. When you have adjusted the settings for all the drives you want
to configure, click **OK**.

RESTORE XP TO A RESTORE POINT

1. Close any program you're running, saving changes as necessary.

2. Click the **Start** button, click **All Programs**, click **Accessories**, click **System Tools**,
and click **System Restore**. The System Restore window opens.

QUICKSTEPS

CREATING RESTORE POINTS

System Restore automatically creates restore points the first time you use XP and thereafter at roughly 24-hour intervals (the intervals vary if your PC happens to be switched off when System Restore is due to create a restore point). System Restore automatically creates restore points when you install most programs and many drivers in case the installation destabilizes your PC and you want to revert to your previous configuration. You can also create restore points manually when you feel the urge to perform some configuration of questionable wisdom.

1. Click the **Start** button, click **All Programs**, click **Accessories**, click **System Tools**, and then click **System Restore**. The System Restore window opens.

2. Select the **Create A Restore Point** option button, and click **Next**. The Create A Restore Point window opens.

3. Type the description for the restore point (make clear what the restore point represents, but don't add the date and time because System Restore will add these automatically), and then click **Create**. System Restore creates the restore point. The Restore Point Created window opens.

4. Click **Close**.

3. Verify that the **Restore My Computer To An Earlier Time** option button is selected, and click **Next**. The Select A Restore Point window opens (see Figure 10-9).

4. Click one of the bold dates on the calendar on the left. You can navigate from month to month by clicking the < and > buttons. In the list for the date, select the restore point you want, and then click **Next**. The Confirm Restore Point Selection window opens.

5. Verify the details and click **Next** to perform the restoration.

6. After your PC restarts, check to ensure that XP is running properly. If it isn't, use System Restore to restore XP either to its previous state (undoing the restoration) or to an earlier restore point, depending on what the problem is.

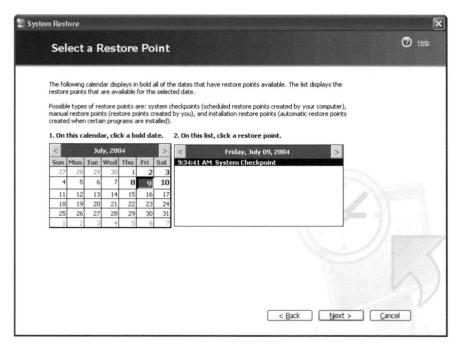

Figure 10-9: You can use System Restore to restore your PC's XP configuration to how it was at any of the restore points stored on your PC.

RUN SYSTEM RESTORE FROM SAFE MODE

If XP is too unstable to run System Restore normally, you can start System Restore in Safe Mode to return XP to an earlier state.

1. Shut down XP, turn off your PC, and wait for at least two minutes to allow all of the components to discharge fully.

2. Turn your PC on. After the memory check, press and hold down **F8**. The Windows Advanced Options Menu is displayed (see Figure 10-10).

3. Use the **ARROW** keys to move the highlight to the Safe Mode item, and then press **ENTER**. The Please Select The Operating System To Start screen appears. Verify that **XP** is selected (as it will be if it is the only operating system installed on your PC), and then press **ENTER**. XP starts in Safe Mode.

4. At the Welcome screen, click your user name. If prompted for your password, type it and press **ENTER**. The Desktop dialog box appears, warning you that you are working in Safe Mode. Click **Yes** or press **ENTER**. Safe Mode appears.

5. Press ⊞ to open the Start menu, use the **ARROW** keys to select **All Programs**, press **ENTER**, select **Accessories**, press **ENTER**, select **System Tools**, press **ENTER**, select **System Restore**, and press **ENTER**. The System Restore window opens with the **Restore My Computer To An Earlier Time** option button selected by default.

6. Press **ALT+N**. The Select A Restore Point window opens.

7. Press **TAB** several times until a dotted border appears around the dates, and then use the **ARROW** keys to select the restore date you want to use. Press **TAB** to move the focus to the list of restore points, and use the **ARROW** keys to select the restore point you want to use. Press **ENTER**. Then press **ALT+N**. The Confirm Restore Point Selection window opens.

8. Double-check your choice, and then press **ALT+N**. The restore process starts. Windows then restarts. The System Restore window opens, telling you that the restore process was successful. Click **OK**.

Figure 10-10: If XP is too unstable to run System Restore successfully, try starting XP in Safe Mode using the Windows Advanced Options menu.

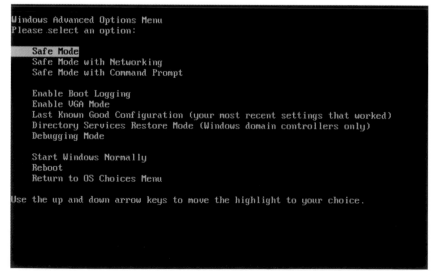

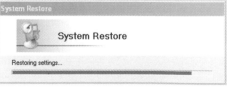

Receive and Give Help

If XP is running stably but you have a problem you can't fix, you may want to ask someone knowledgeable for help via XP's Remote Assistance feature. When the shoe is on the other foot, you can provide help to someone else who requests it.

Remote Assistance enables you to invite someone to connect to your PC from a remote PC so that this person can see what's happening, provide advice (via text or audio chat) on fixing problems, or even control your PC remotely to fix problems. The other person must be using either XP or Windows 2003 Server. You can use Remote Assistance in three ways:

- **Via Windows Messenger**   If both you and the other person have Windows Messenger accounts and are set up as contacts, you can ask the other person for help when both of you are online. This is the fastest and easiest method of using Remote Assistance and is the method discussed in detail here.

- **Via e-mail**   You can e-mail a Remote Assistance invitation to the other person that enables him or her to connect directly to your PC—provided that you're still online with the same IP address when the other person tries to contact you. (If your IP address has changed, the other person won't be able to connect via Remote Assistance.)

- **Via a file**   You can save a Remote Assistance invitation to a floppy disk or to a network file. This method of Remote Assistance is too awkward and slow for most users, however, and is not discussed further in this section.

Set Up Remote Assistance

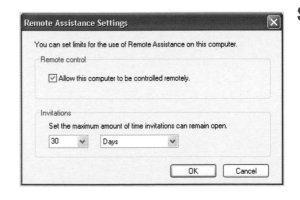

Before you can use Remote Assistance, you must set it up through the System Properties dialog box.

1. Press ⊞ +BREAK (or click the **Start** button, right-click **My Computer**, and click **Properties**). The System Properties dialog box appears.

2. Click the **Remote** tab, make sure the **All Remote Assistance Invitations To Be Sent From This Computer** check box is selected, and then click **Advanced**. The Remote Assistance Settings dialog box appears.

CAUTION

Allow your PC to be controlled remotely only if you absolutely trust the other person and his or her computer skills. If you decide to use this option, XP still prompts you to decide on each separate request from the other person to take control of your PC.

TIP

Chapter 3 discusses how to configure and use Windows Messenger.

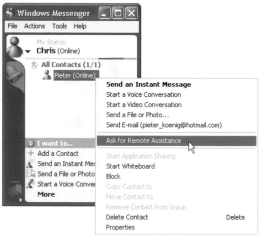

3. If you want the other person to be able to help you actively rather than just providing suggestions via chat, select the **Allow This Computer To Be Controlled Remotely** check box.

4. Change the time period specified by the two Set The Maximum Amount Of Time Invitations Can Remain Open drop-down list boxes.

- If you'll issue invitations via Windows Messenger, set a short period—for example, 30 minutes.

- If you'll issue invitations via e-mail, allow several hours or even one or two days, depending on how quickly you expect the other person to respond.

5. Click **OK** twice to close the two open dialog boxes.

Request Remote Assistance

Windows Messenger is the fastest and easiest way to request Remote Assistance because you can see instantly whether your contact is online.

To request Remote Assistance using Windows Messenger:

1. Click the **Start** button, click **All Programs**, and then click **Windows Messenger**. Windows Messenger opens. If Windows Messenger doesn't automatically sign you in, sign in manually.

2. Right-click the contact whom you want to ask for help, and click **Ask For Remote Assistance**.

3. If the contact accepts the invitation, the Conversation window tells you so and then a Remote Assistance confirmation dialog box appears. Verify that it's the right person, and then click **Yes**. The Remote Assistance window opens (see Figure 10-11).

4. To communicate with the other person, type a message in the Message Entry box, and press **ENTER** or click **Send**. Your messages and the person's replies appear in the Chat History window. If you both have sound equipment and reasonably fast Internet connections, you can speak to each other by clicking **Start Talking.**

5. If you have permitted remote control, the other person can request control of your PC. You'll see a dialog box such as the one shown here. Click **OK** if you trust the other person. You can press **ESC** (or click **Stop Control**) at any time to cut off the other person's control.

6. To end a session, send a message to that effect, click **Disconnect**, and close the **Remote Assistance** window.

Figure 10-11: Remote Assistance is a fast and effective way to get help from a more experienced Windows user.

When you receive a Remote Assistance invitation via e-mail, double-click the attached file, which is called rcBuddy.MsRcIncident. Verify that the invitation has not yet expired, type the password that the other person has given you, and click **Yes**. XP then establishes the connection.

Provide Remote Assistance

If you're asked via Windows Messenger to provide Remote Assistance, proceed as follows:

1. Click the **Accept** link (or press **ALT+T**). Remote Assistance prompts the other person to confirm that he or she wants you to connect.

2. If the other person confirms the connection, a Remote Assistance window opens on your screen (see Figure 10-12).

3. Provide advice, or take control to demonstrate what's needed.

- Type a message in the Message Entry box, and press **ENTER** or click **Send** to transmit it.

- You can toggle the screen between actual size and scaled to fit on your screen by clicking **Scale To Window** or **Actual Size**. (Which size is more convenient will depend on the size of the other person's screen, the size of your screen, and what you're trying to do.)

- Click **Take Control** to request control of the remote PC. Work on the remote PC without pressing **ESC** (the key to release control). To release control, click **Release Control** or press **ESC**.

- Click **Send File** if you need to send a file to the other PC to fix a problem. For example, you might need to download a driver and make it available to the other PC.

4. To end the Remote Assistance session, type a message and then click **Close**.

Figure 10-12: When you're providing Remote Assistance, you see the other person's screen. If you take control, you can show the other person how to perform the actions needed to remedy the problem.

Index

A

access points, 160, 162, 166-170
accounts. *See* user accounts
Address bar, 60
Address Book, 71, 83, 89
administrator accounts, 141, 143
Adobe
    Photoshop, 107
    Photoshop Elements, 107
AGP (aperture graphics port), 129, 132
antivirus programs, 133, 136-138
Appearance settings, 33, 35
audio
    cables, 128
    configuring, 113-114
    connecting to a source, 117-118
    listening to on the Internet, 64-67
    recording, 116, 117-119
    setting the volume for, 114
Automatic Updates, 135, 137
AutoPlay, 47

B

backgrounds
    for the desktop, 31
    in themes, 33
    using pictures as, 31
Backup, 83
    restoring from, 214-215
    using, 149-150
batteries, laptop PC,
    checking the status of, 183
    getting the most out of, 186-187
    setting the response to low, 189-190
BIOS, 18, 124
bitmap, 108
boot disk, 208-209
boot drive, 210

Briefcase, 193-195
broadband, 53, 57
browsers
    alternative secure, 147
    navigating with, 62
    See also Internet Explorer

C

Calculator, 83, 89
camcorders, DV
    connecting to PCs, 97
    importing video from, 112
cameras, digital
    connecting to PCs, 96
    factors for choosing, 96
    importing pictures from, 108-109
Cat 5/Cat 5e cable, 159, 163
CDs, 14
    burning, 47, 50-51
    buying, 49
    copying, 116
    copy protections on, 116-117
    drives for. *See* optical drives
    erasing, 52
    listening to, 115
    saving files to create, 49
central processing unit (CPU), 3
Character Map, 87
child folder. *See* subfolder
client/server networks, 158
color
    quality, 30-31
    schemes, 35
command button, 27, 28
command prompt, 82, 83
compatibility
    hardware, 122, 160, 166

memory, 123
    software, 93, 138
contacts
    for Windows Messenger, 74, 76-77
    in Address Book, 71
controls, 27, 28
cookies, 65-66
copying
    CDs, 47, 50-51, 116
    from the Internet, 63-64
copyright issues, 64, 116-117
Corel
    Paradox, 89
    Presentations, 88
    Quattro Pro, 88
    Word Perfect, 85
CPU, 2, 3, 13, 15
crossover cable, 163

D

data
    backing up, 149-150
    encrypting, 150-152
Deneba Canvas, ACD, 107
desktop, the, 24
    changing items in the, 8-9, 31
    navigating the, 15
    working with the, 24
desktop computers, 2-4
    choosing processors for, 5
    equipment security for, 134
    weighing against laptops, 11-12
    See also PCs
Details pane, 37-38
Details view, 43
device drivers, 122
    ensuring safe, 138

for printers, 93
    installing, 130-132
    removing, 212
    sources for, 130
    updating, 213-214
Device Manager, 212
dialog boxes, 24, 27-28
dial-up connections, 54-56, 204-206
digital cameras. *See* cameras
digital signatures, 138
directories. *See* folders
Disk Cleanup, 41
docking station, 201-202, 203
donationware, 86
drivers. *See* device drivers
drives
    checking available space on, 40
    freeing up space on, 41
    identifying local, 38
    identifying network, 39
    renaming, 40
    See also hard drives, optical drives
drop-down list box, 27, 28
DSL (digital subscriber line), 53-55, 57-58
DualView, 201
DVDs
    burning, 52
    drives for. *See* optical drives
    installing a decoder for, 111
    setting the region for, 120
    watching with Media Player, 120

E

e-mail,
  creating and sending, 68-69
  formatting, 71-73
  managing attachments to, 73-74
  obtaining Remote Assistance via, 219,
    221, 222
  receiving, 69-70
  responding to, 70
  setting up accounts, 67-68
  sorting, 70
Encrypting File System (EFS), 150-151,
  155
encryption
  applying, 150-151
  creating recovery agents for, 153-154
  removing, 152
  exporting recovery keys for, 155
  using on a wireless network, 161,
    167, 169
error messages
  Non-system disk or disk error, 209
  NTDETECT failed, 209
  NTLDR is missing, 209
  Windows was not shut down
    properly, 210-211
Ethernet
  components, 159
  standards, 157-158
  See also wired Ethernet, wireless
    networking

F

FAT32, 40, 197
files, 41
  as attachments, 73-74, 79-80
  compressing on a hard drive, 127
  copying, 46-47
  deleting, 44-45
  encrypting, 150-151, 197
  finding, 45
  managing encrypted, 152
  recovering encrypted, 156
  renaming, 43
  selecting, 43
  sharing encrypted, 156
  shortcuts to, 48
  synchronizing with Briefcase, 194-195
  synchronizing with Offline Files,
    196-200
  zipped, 48-49
Filmstrip view, 43
firewalls, 144, *See also* Windows
  Firewall
FireWire, 10, 13
  adding in PCI slots, 112
  using with new hardware, 122, 125,
    128
  See also PCI slots, installing cards in
floppy drives, 5
folders, 41
  copying, 46-47
  creating, 42
  deleting, 44-45
  finding, 45
  renaming, 43
  selecting, 43
  sharing on a network, 175-176
  shortcuts to, 48
  structure of on XP, 42

types of, 36-37
views for, 42-43
zipped, 48-49
Folders pane, 38
freeware, 86

G

gif, 109
Google, 60
graphics
  cards, 6, 9, 132
  formats, 108-109
  programs for editing, 107
  See also pictures
Grisoft, 137
group box, 28

H

hard disks. *See* hard drives
hard drives, 3, 4, 10
  choosing, 6
  formatting, 127
  initializing new, 126
  partitioning, 18, 126
  upgrading, 125
hardware, 3
  drivers for. *See* device drivers
  profiles for laptops, 202-203
Help button, 27, 28
hibernate mode, 19, 21, 189-190, 192
home page, 62
hot-pluggable devices, 122
hub, 158-159, 160, 162

I

ICMP messages, 146
icons
  choosing the size of, 34
  desktop, 8-9, 33
  hiding inactive, 35
  navigating with, 33
Icons view, 43
installing. *See* upgrading
instant messaging, 74-80, *See also*
  Windows Messenger
Internet, the 2
  audio/video on, 64-67
  browsing, 61-62
  connecting to, 53-58
  copying items from, 63-64
  ensuring security on, 144-148
  radio on, 116
  searching, 59-60
Internet Explorer,
  changing your home page on, 62
  Favorites, 61, 63
  History, 62-63, 64
  Links bar, 61-62
  Search Companion, 59
  securing, 147
IP address, 167-169, 180-183
ipconfig, 180, 182
ISP (Internet service provider), 54

J

Java Desktop System, 13
jpeg, 108

International Contact Information

AUSTRALIA
McGraw-Hill Book Company Australia Pty. Ltd.
TEL +61-2-9900-1800
FAX +61-2-9878-8881
http://www.mcgraw-hill.com.au
books-it_sydney@mcgraw-hill.com

CANADA
McGraw-Hill Ryerson Ltd.
TEL +905-430-5000
FAX +905-430-5020
http://www.mcgraw-hill.ca

GREECE, MIDDLE EAST, & AFRICA
(Excluding South Africa)
McGraw-Hill Hellas
TEL +30-210-6560-990
TEL +30-210-6560-993
TEL +30-210-6560-994
FAX +30-210-6545-525

MEXICO *(Also serving Latin America)*
McGraw-Hill Interamericana Editores S.A. de C.V.
TEL +525-1500-5108
FAX +525-117-1589
http://www.mcgraw-hill.com.mx
carlos_ruiz@mcgraw-hill.com

SINGAPORE *(Serving Asia)*
McGraw-Hill Book Company
TEL +65-6863-1580
FAX +65-6862-3354
http://www.mcgraw-hill.com.sg
mghasia@mcgraw-hill.com

SOUTH AFRICA
McGraw-Hill South Africa
TEL +27-11-622-7512
FAX +27-11-622-9045
robyn_swanepoel@mcgraw-hill.com

SPAIN
McGraw-Hill/Interamericana de España, S.A.U.
TEL +34-91-180-3000
FAX +34-91-372-8513
http://www.mcgraw-hill.es
professional@mcgraw-hill.es

UNITED KINGDOM, NORTHERN,
EASTERN, & CENTRAL EUROPE
McGraw-Hill Education Europe
TEL +44-1-628-502500
FAX +44-1-628-770224
http://www.mcgraw-hill.co.uk
emea_queries@mcgraw-hill.com

ALL OTHER INQUIRIES Contact:
McGraw-Hill/Osborne
TEL +1-510-420-7700
FAX +1-510-420-7703
http://www.osborne.com
omg_international@mcgraw-hill.com